Praise for *Gl*

"Finally, an enlightening book that recognizes the need for a new multi-disciplinary approach to navigating the vast sea of complexity that surrounds us. Philippe Rosinski has the intellectual courage to leave the path of simplicity and embrace the paradox management to help us to develop new skills and to train future leaders of a global world."

—Adolfo Martini, Learning for Development Director, Europe, L'Oréal

"A comprehensive mapping of concepts, tools, and practical information to address leaders' multifaceted challenges. I highly recommend this book, which will help everyone in creating a better unity for oneself, and for thriving on our present world's complexity."

—Vincent Lenhardt, president of Transformance Pro and senior advisor for the Boston Consulting Group

"This book is one of the best I've ever read—timely, relevant, and on-message. *Global Coaching* is a significant contribution to the coaching profession."

—Katherine Tulpa, CEO, Association for Coaching

"*Global Coaching* illustrates how coaching has evolved to give leaders a new foundation for comprehensive self-care as they learn to become more conscious and collaborative. This book is a comprehensive guide for coaching those who will lead us into a new world of work!"

—Darelyn "DJ" Mitsch, president, the Pyramid Resource Group, author of *Team Advantage*, and past president of the International Coach Federation

"Philippe Rosinski has moved the art and science of coaching to a new level."

—Peter Leyland, CEO, Penlon Ltd.

"A provocative, exciting, and wise book! Rosinski's work draws on a well-presented range of material, from psychology to medicine, economics to physics, philosophy to mysticism, and beyond—and challenges us to open up to new ways of thinking. He presents well-written business coaching cases and examines how embracing multiple perspectives will enhance our coaching and enable our clients to become more effective."

—Prof. Carol Kauffman, Harvard Medical School; director, Institute of Coaching; editor-in-chief of *Coaching: An International Journal of Theory, Research & Practice*

GLOBAL
COACHING

An Integrated Approach for Long-Lasting Results

PHILIPPE ROSINSKI

nb

NICHOLAS BREALEY
PUBLISHING

BOSTON • LONDON

First published by Nicholas Brealey Publishing in 2010.

20 Park Plaza, Suite 1115A
Boston, MA 02116, USA
Tel: + 617-523-3801
Fax: + 617-523-3708
www.interculturalpress.com

3-5 Spafield Street, Clerkenwell
London, EC1R 4QB, UK
Tel: +44-(0)-207-239-0360
Fax: +44-(0)-207-239-0370
www.nicholasbrealey.com

www.nicholasbrealey.com
www.globalcoaching.pro

Myers-Briggs Type Indicator® and MBTI® are trademarks or registered trademarks of the Myers-Briggs Type Indicator Trust.

Unless otherwise noted, all English translations of French quotations within this book are the work of the author.

Fundamental Interpersonal Relations Orientation–Behavior™ and FIRO-B® are trademarks or registered trademarks of CPP, Inc.

Printed in Finland

14 13 12 11 10   1 2 3 4 5

ISBN: 978-1-904838-22-7

Library of Congress Cataloging-in-Publication Data
Rosinski, Philippe.
  Global coaching : an integrated approach for long- lasting results / Philippe Rosinski.
      p. cm.
  Includes bibliographical references and index.
  ISBN 978-1-904838-22-7
  1. Executive coaching.   2. Personal coaching.   I. Title.
  HD30.4.R628 2010
  658.4'07124—dc22
                                                           2010012901

To my daughter Arielle,
with love

Contents

Acknowledgments

I would like to express my gratitude to several people who have contributed to this book. I cannot do justice here to all those who have made a positive difference in my life, inspiring in various ways the writing of *Global Coaching*.

I am thankful to my clients, individual coachees, teams, and, in some cases, multiple actors within the same organization. I value their confidence and partnership. I appreciate their commitment to human performance and fulfillment, and to innovations geared toward sustainable and purposeful results. Many of their real life challenges have informed the development of global coaching to help address complex situations. However, to preserve confidentiality, I have not mentioned their specific names and sensitive information.

Among those who directly contributed to the book, my special thanks go to Dr. Katrina Burrus for her excellent case study in Chapter 1, to Peter Horton for letting me share his incredible story of GM's electric car in Chapter 2, to Professor Jacques Duchateau and to my personal trainer Chris Richartz for their generous explanations, articles, reading recommendations, and expert comments regarding the fitness section in Chapter 3. I also want to thank Sherie Olmstead for sharing additional research findings and Luc Vandeputte for his help. I appreciate my MBA students' creative efforts about art and coaching across cultures, which have led to the final examples in Chapter 7. I thank Michel Chalude for his suggestion of an interesting link with process communication in Chapter 10.

I am grateful to Sir John Whitmore, who beautifully captured the spirit of *Global Coaching* in his foreword, and to the other leading authorities who honored me by enthusiastically endorsing this book. I feel we are becoming fellow companion travelers on the path of global coaching.

I also want to pay tribute to my partner Dina Zavrski-Makaric and other friends and colleagues who eagerly promote *Coaching Across Cultures* and now *Global Coaching* across the globe through our various international seminars and projects. I truly value their enthusiasm and collaboration. I thank our participants and my readers whose keenness has created unexpected opportunities.

Of course, I also would like to acknowledge my publisher. Nicholas Brealey has believed in the relevance of my first book from the beginning and his firm has readily taken on board again this new book. This time, editorial director Erika Heilman competently led the project. I am grateful for her commitment to produce the best book possible, and for her constructive suggestions and support along the way. I also want to thank managing editor Jennifer Olsen for her useful guidance and dedication, as well as Kendra DeMoura and Renee Nicholls for their contributions.

Finally, my thanks go to my family, particularly my wife, Anne, and our daughter, Arielle, whose love and support have made it easier and more enjoyable for me to devote significant time and energy to the research, preparation, writing, and revision of *Global Coaching's* manuscript and proofs.

Foreword

G lobal Coaching is indeed the complete book of coaching. It is essential for all who wish to dabble in, study, practice, or even immerse themselves in the art of coaching. I hope it will also be read by many who are not coaches, but who wish to understand and enjoy more of the riches that life has to offer.

Coaching is a term used to describe an effective methodology for facilitating ourselves and others to grow and develop into the more complete human beings that we are capable of being—if only we believe it. Global Coaching may well help us to shed some of our self-limiting beliefs in favor of these inspiring, motivating ones.

The term global, as Philippe Rosinski uses it here, takes us far beyond the boundaries implied by Philippe's very well-received previous book, Coaching Across Cultures (2003). In fact, the term here has no boundaries, for in parts, Global Coaching takes us beyond the physical earth and into the ethereal universe. As he does this, Philippe uses specific styles for each section of the book that emphasize his and its versatility. Global Coaching is constructed around six perspectives, and Philippe approaches each one with the optimum language and style for its subject matter (for example, by alternately using case studies in the "Management" section; academic models, tables, and diagrams in the "Psychology" section; and poetic language in the "Spirituality" section). In all six sections, Philippe demonstrates broad knowledge and deep understanding, supporting his assertions with many references from academia and literature—or, should I say, other wisdom.

Many coaches believe that coaches should always be on the coachee's agenda and that they should not bring their knowledge or values into sessions.

Philippe does not retreat into this belief. In fact, he does the opposite: he invites the reader to look, in some depth, at each of the main issues facing society—and indeed humanity—and take full account of them during the coaching process. This encourages further progress in the maturing of the coaching profession, which has already been underway during recent years.

Philippe accompanies the reader on a logical and helpful journey through the deeper meaning of coaching and its potential far-reaching impacts in our fast-changing, uncertain world. I have no doubt that a wide variety of readers will enjoy and benefit from this significant book—as will coachees.

John Whitmore
Performance Consultants International

Introduction

GLOBAL AND SOCIETAL CHALLENGES

Reducing pollution, reversing the destruction of ecosystems, combating poverty, preserving health, favoring access to healthcare, promoting education, curbing nuclear proliferation, building peace: these are some of the tremendous challenges we face.

One human out of six is hungry. One billion people don't have access to drinkable water. Thirteen million hectares of forest disappear every year. Animal species disappear one thousand times faster than their natural rhythm of extinction.[1] The list of global crises goes on. The financial crisis of 2008, with its brutal stock market downfall and ensuing world economic recession, also made it painfully clear that when U.S. banks build castles in the sand[2] the impact is felt worldwide. We have lost sight of the fact that everything is connected. International calamity could originate elsewhere next time.

Meanwhile, many of us are caught in a rat race of hard work that promotes futile, if not harmful, production for the sake of financial success. With the money earned from that work, we indulge in superfluous consumption that contributes to our planet's destruction and does not really make us happy.

We all have an important role to play in precluding damage and in making the world a better place for everyone, including the future generations. However, to do our part, we will need to transform ourselves.

The crises provide us with an unasked for opportunity to rise to these unprecedented challenges. Global coaching can bring an invaluable contribution in this indispensable process.

WHAT IS GLOBAL COACHING?

Global coaching is a holistic approach that calls upon multiple interconnected perspectives to facilitate the unleashing of human potential toward meaningful pursuits. In this book, the perspectives we examine cover a wide range, from the physical to the spiritual. Global coaches strive to leverage these various perspectives both for defining success in a broad and sustainable fashion (the *what* question) and for effectively enabling this success (the *how* question).

Global coaching stems from the observation that many challenges people face, particularly the hardest ones, are multifaceted. Everything is connected. Traditional coaching simply doesn't address this complexity.

Global coaching allows us to tap into the power, responsibility, and right we all have to forge a better life for ourselves and for others, and to find more joy and meaning in everything we do.

ADDRESSING PERSONAL CHALLENGES

In addition to the global and societal challenges I noted earlier, each of us faces personal challenges. Everyone, coaches and coachees alike, can benefit from improving physical fitness, energy, and resilience; developing organization and leadership skills that lead to tangible, sustainable results; honing emotional intelligence, assertiveness, and the ability to forge constructive relationships and manage conflict; learning to achieve goals while serving others; finding ways to leverage diversity for enhanced creativity; developing ways to deal with adversity; and exploring how to live a meaningful life.

We may not need to master all these competencies. However, coaching often happens in times of transition, or when new challenges require us to tap into our unexplored potential. You may need to become more assertive to deal with a new, demanding boss. Maybe you have been promoted to an executive position in which you're required to lead a culturally diverse workforce. You may wonder how to best manage your various stakeholders and how to steer your company on a sustainable development path. You may want to achieve a better work–life balance, being happy both in your career and in your family and social life. Or maybe you've started to wonder "What is the meaning of this work or career?" and are beginning a journey toward a more purposeful life (either within your current occupation or through radical changes). These could be your own challenges or those of people you coach.

Global coaching helps us face challenges in our daily lives, helps organizations and societies achieve sustainable goals, and promotes long-term benefits for our planet. Global coaching highlights how closely these goals are intertwined.

The opportunities to unleash human potential to achieve meaningful, important objectives are probably unlimited. Through global coaching, individuals increase their sense of power and discover new ways to address their challenges. They become more responsible, taking ownership and making contributions rather than blaming others. These benefits have larger implications as well, enabling individuals to more effectively contribute in our collective goals. Through global coaching, we can all play our part, modest though it may be, in fostering progress in our organizations, in our societies, and in the world at large.

Global coaching is a revolutionary approach that transcends the limited impact of traditional coaching. We live in a complex, dynamic, and interconnected world. Traditional coaching takes a binary, static, and fragmented approach. Global coaching promotes unity in place of fragmentation, at both the individual and the collective levels.

WHO CAN BENEFIT FROM GLOBAL COACHING?

Global coaching can benefit everyone. It can equip us to make a difference—in ourselves and others.

- As citizens, our voices matter and need to be heard. As I will argue, governments should be encouraged to make brave decisions in the collective interest. We need sound regulations to protect consumers from harmful food and products; to ensure adequate education, health care, and living conditions for everyone; and to preserve the planet. While corporations must play their part, we cannot expect them to substitute for government action; their financial interest is not necessarily aligned with meeting genuine public needs. We should also encourage nations to move beyond selfish national interests to reinforce worldwide governance. Global challenges will be addressed most effectively at a global level. This does not mean we must become more uniform, however. We need to forge unity in diversity.[3]

- As professionals, managers, and leaders in our organizations, we can help make sure our companies pursue constructive and meaningful ends, in the service of multiple stakeholders and with a goal of sustainable development. We can help ensure that personal fulfillment goes hand in hand with performance. Leadership excellence should become the norm.

- As human beings, we can become happier by learning to appreciate what we already have, by opening up to natural beauty and artistic creations, by not engaging in debilitating consumerism. Our simple actions can make a difference in the larger world as well: saving energy at home, repairing objects rather than throwing them away, using environmentally friendly transportation, eating less meat, purchasing local products. We gain fulfillment by learning to savor life in a more natural fashion.

Everything is connected. Global coaching helps us become actors in shaping a virtuous circle of progress in place of the vicious circle of destruction. Global coaching offers a process for promoting unity in diversity, sustainable progress, and meaningful success.

We prefer to saddle politicians, senior executives, and multinational corporations with the responsibility for making change, exonerating ourselves of our own duty. But politicians hesitate to make the right, difficult choices without support from public opinion. After all, they usually want to be reelected. Likewise, corporations are under pressure to make profit by meeting market demands. We may wish that visionary corporate leaders would build more environmentally friendly cars and make more healthful foods, but we as consumers must encourage them—by refusing to settle for less.

Global coaching is not aimed solely at professional coaches. It is for all professionals, managers, and leaders whose role (among others) is to unleash individuals' potential to achieve important, meaningful objectives. This applies in the corporate world as well as the public sector. Global coaching should permeate society. Ideally, it should be a lifelong developmental journey that starts with the education of children. Physicians, lawyers, and other professionals could benefit from embracing global coaching, and their clients would be better served as a result.

I have coached executives for almost 20 years. Increasingly, I train and coach professionals and managers to become global coaches, particularly in the advanced international coaching across cultures seminars[4] I deliver with colleagues in our worldwide Rosinski & Company network, and in MBA and postgraduate courses. I am a professor at the Kenichi Ohmae Graduate School of Business in Japan, teaching in the MBA program in globalization.

Increasingly, people recognize the power and necessity of global coaching. Positive ripple effects occur when even one person applies this approach:

more fulfilling relationships at work, improved performance, confidence and serenity in place of insecurity and stress (which in turn benefits clients, family, and social life), augmented creativity through leveraging alternative cultural perspectives.

Coaching began with practitioners rather than in academia; only later did universities begin to integrate it into their curricula and research. Coaching has a long way to go before it fully penetrates society, and it will be longer still before a global approach is adopted. I hope this book will contribute to promoting this new shift.

EMBRACING THE COMPLEXITY PARADIGM

This requires nothing short of a paradigm shift. As I will argue, the traditional Newtonian–Cartesian model of reality is insufficient to tackle the complexities we face today. That is not to say that this paradigm of simplicity should be discarded. Rather, it should be incorporated into a new paradigm of complexity. In this book, you will discover how this paradigm can help you coach more effectively. I will introduce the holographic model to describe this new reality and discuss the far-reaching implications for coaching and coaches. We will examine through some examples how such coaching has and can be deployed in practice.

For now, let me already say that the holographic model includes several interwoven notions:

- All things are dynamically interconnected.
- All things make up an undivided whole.
- Unity and infinity are linked.
- Every part is in the whole and the whole is in every part.
- Order can be either manifest (explicit, unfolded) or hidden (implicit, enfolded). There is a constant and flowing exchange between the two orders/levels of existence.
- The way the coach interacts with the coachee and the ensemble determines which aspects unfold and which remain hidden.
- Our dynamic and active enfoldings and unfoldings (holomovement) create, moment by moment, our universe.
- Multiple perspectives favor resonance: "similar to the way a laser of a certain frequency causes an image made with a laser of the same frequency to emerge from a multiple image hologram" (Talbot, 1991, 73).

Incidentally, the holographic model explains a wide range of surprising phenomena: non-locality (physics), the vastness and distribution of memory in the brain (biology), and Jung's synchronicity, archetypes, and collective unconscious (to mention just a few).

It will become apparent that the holographic model is a useful descriptor of our complex reality. Holographic coaching (equivalent to global coaching), with its holistic and multiple perspective outlook, constitutes a more complete, creative, potent, and meaningful form of coaching.

SIX ESSENTIAL PERSPECTIVES

Practically speaking, global coaching implies broadening our view to encompass multiple perspectives. I have found that the following interconnected perspectives can foster global and sustainable progress: physical, managerial, psychological, political, cultural, and spiritual.

The managerial and psychological perspectives are the two pillars of traditional coaching. Yet each perspective contains multiple perspectives. Some coaches rely on a few psychological models and could benefit from including alternative approaches. In this book, I will show how you can incorporate situational leadership and transactional analysis into a global coaching approach. I will also explore other useful models (notably psychoanalysis and positive psychology), highlighting their contribution to global coaching.

Traditional coaches often overlook political and cultural perspectives, even though experts increasingly recognize the need to integrate culture into coaching. I introduced these perspectives in a 1998 article, "Constructive Politics," and in my first book, *Coaching Across Cultures* (2003). I will particularly elaborate on the cultural perspective, and I will explain how the new Cultural Orientations Framework assessment tool can help with individual, team, and organizational development (particularly in the case of alliances, mergers, and acquisitions).

Traditional coaches also tend to ignore the physical and spiritual perspectives. They put little to no emphasis on a proactive approach to health and fitness. They may set vague goals for their coachees, such as "exercising more," without considering the coachee's individual needs or building a precise plan for covering the various fitness components: endurance, strength, power, flexibility, and balance. Malnutrition in poor countries seems to go hand in hand with what the French call "malbouffe" (bad eating) in affluent societies. You will discover a systematic approach to promoting health and fitness and find out about the multiple benefits, which go way beyond the physical realm.

Spirituality, although still often confused with religiosity, is increasingly integrated into life coaching but rarely into business coaching. Some people promote the idea that spirituality and material success cannot not be pursued in tandem. In fact, we need a spiritual perspective to give meaning and purpose to our lives and our work, to deal with hardship, and to come closer to unity, both within ourselves and in our relationships with others. Spirituality, with its promise of re-enchanting our world, is not against scientific rigor but does require scientific openness.

Together, these perspectives will help you thrive at all levels: physical, emotional, mental, and spiritual. They will equip you to help others flourish as well.

This may sound like a utopian vision. However, it is compatible with coaches' pragmatic and action-oriented approach. We strive for effectiveness rather than perfection. Moreover, what matters is that we embark on the life-long journey and progress as much as possible. We may not reach perfect coherence, complete unity. Some contradictions will not be fully surmounted. Our egos may fail to embrace all of our shadow side. What counts though, is that more of our multifaceted potential can be unleashed and geared toward positive ends. In the movie *Crash* (Haggis, 2004), police officer John Ryan (Matt Dillon) behaves obnoxiously, humiliating both Christine Thayer (Thandie Newton) and her husband. Later on, Christine Thayer, very distressed, inadvertently crashes her car in a terrible accident. Coincidentally, John Ryan crosses her path again. This time though, he does not hesitate a second to risk his own life to save Thayer. He succeeds just in time. The car goes up in flames as Ryan has barely extracted Thayer from the car. Global coaching is not about downplaying our dark side. We know the evil mankind is capable of and cannot turn away from this harsh reality. Nonetheless, global coaching is resolutely hopeful and optimistic: it is about unleashing what is best in us, about liberating our heroes within, to make a constructive difference.

Global coaching can address a wide range of challenges. For example, a manager might wish to become more confident and assertive and cope more effectively with stress. In this case, the psychological perspective might take precedence. However, the physical perspective would be useful too. The global coach could point out the connection between fitness training and stress reduction, thereby adding a resource for promoting serenity. Coaching from a managerial perspective might help with time management and personal organization, which could eliminate several stressors. Furthermore, coaching from a political perspective would allow the coachee to gain power, thereby increasing his confidence. Coaching from a cultural perspective would help the coachee examine norms, values, and assumptions that might contribute to his state. Finally, coaching from a spiritual perspective would help the coachee connect with a sense of meaning, purpose, and serenity.

A complex, multiple-perspective approach can address many challenges that resist simple and habitual solutions. A cultural perspective may best help a cross-cultural team deal constructively with its members' cultural differences; a spiritual perspective may be most effective for coaching a senior executive about the legacy she wants to leave behind. Effective global coaches can call upon diverse resources and seamlessly combine and leverage them to facilitate progress.

GOALS, LIMITATIONS, AND AN INVITATION

To summarize, this book is intended for coaches (i.e., coaching professionals and leaders using coaching) and everyone interested in unfolding human potential to help themselves and serve others. It will help you to

- develop a deeper awareness of reality, which will affect your being (openness, flow, curiosity, presence, et cetera) and doing (visible achievements), thereby enhancing and possibly transforming your coaching practice
- understand six essential coaching perspectives (many of which are typically overlooked), opening new levers of progress
- link the various perspectives in a coherent whole so you can foster unity in diversity and sustainable and meaningful success

I need to humbly underline the inevitable limitations of my enterprise. The book should open up new perspectives. You will find some illustrations in concrete coaching situations and other encouraging examples. Yet, most corporations, and society as a whole, still have to embrace this new paradigm, this post-modern reality. This is merely the beginning. More work will be needed and will hopefully be stimulated by this new book.

Finally, let me say that this book is intended to be as clear as possible. Addressing complexity does not imply being unnecessarily complicated and opting for obtuse jargon. I have attempted to avoid these pitfalls. However, let me warn you, my reader, that this book will nevertheless challenge your thinking. It does not provide a series of quick tips and simplistic methods. It requires your full attention as well as your openness to different viewpoints. You will benefit by participating actively in the reading process. I invite you to use a learning journal or another method to capture your own insights and ideas as you read. In particular, I suggest you articulate specific ways in which you can develop your coaching practice and address your own challenges. The book may also stimulate dialogues with your colleagues, leading to new realizations and innovative ventures. Global coaching is a lifelong journey. We all have many opportunities to grow and find ways to make a positive difference in our own and others' lives.

NOTES

1. Statistics from Arthus-Bertrand, 2009. His inspiring and disturbing movie *Home* was broadcast on TV worldwide on 5 June 2009, and at *www.youtube.com/homeproject*.
2. By engineering obtuse financial products based on worthless assets—mortgage payments owners could not afford to pay. See Chapter 2.
3. See Rosinski, 2003.
4. See *www.philrosinski.com* for more information.

PART I

The Global Coaching Approach

CHAPTER 1

The Multiple Perspectives Framework[1]

For as long as I can recall, I have been fascinated by multiple perspectives. As a 15-year old, I struggled to choose between the Latin-mathematics section (preparing for scientific and engineering studies) and the Latin-Greek section (preparing for the humanities). I wanted to study both! Later, after graduating from the Polytechnical Engineering School in Brussels, I studied electrical engineering at Stanford University and took all my electives in the humanities (with the exception of a windsurfing class!). I found these radically different perspectives inspiring and enriching. My fellow students usually preferred computer science, which they viewed as a more natural and practically applicable complement to electrical engineering.

Later on, this same inclination led me, as an executive coach, to introduce the concepts of global coaching and coaching from multiple perspectives. I wondered how to take advantage of new angles (notably political, cultural, and spiritual) that had not been part of traditional coaching. In my experience, such perspectives lead to more creative, powerful, and meaningful coaching.

In my view, the executive coach's mission is to facilitate the coachee's journey toward high performance and high fulfillment, toward sustainable and global success, for the benefit of the coachee herself and for others she can impact.

In practice, executive coaching often is reduced to its two traditional perspectives: psychological and managerial. Both are essential, but they usually are insufficient to unleash the coachee's full potential.

However, as coaching establishes itself as a new discipline, many "scholars" who are contributing to the "institutionalization" of coaching are adopting the view that multiple perspectives make coaching more effective and relevant. In 2006, two books illustrated this shift: both *Evidence Based Coaching Handbook* and *Excellence in Coaching* promote diverse approaches in coaching. Linda Page (2006) summarized this evolution: "There is a growing consensus that the field of coaching studies should be cross-disciplinary, multi-disciplinary, or inter-disciplinary—that is, a hyphenated field rather than one that is "owned" by any one existing academic discipline."

When it integrates multiple perspectives, coaching is a powerful vehicle for sustainable and global success (for oneself and for others). I use the term "global coaching" to refer to this broad and inclusive form of coaching. Coaching from multiple perspectives assumes an enlarged mission for the executive coach and implies readiness to engage in a lifelong journey of learning.

SIX ESSENTIAL PERSPECTIVES

I have found the perspectives in the following table particularly useful.

Multiple Perspectives for Coaching		
Perspective	**Definition/explanation**	**Two essential qualities fostered by the perspective**
Spiritual	Spirituality is an increased awareness of a connection with oneself, others, nature, and with the immanent and transcendent "divine." It is also the ability to find meaning, derive purpose, and appreciate life.	**Meaning and Unity** See comment in next section ("Cultural").
Cultural	A group's culture is the set of unique characteristics that distinguishes its members from another group. External characteristics include behaviors, artifacts, and products. Internal characteristics include norms, values, and basic assumptions.	**Diversity and Creativity** In our complex, multicultural, and turbulent environment, we must learn to embrace diversity, bridge cultural gaps, learn from cultural differences for more creativity, live meaningfully, act responsibly, overcome divisions, and strive for unity (internally and externally).

	Multiple Perspectives for Coaching *(Continued)*	
Perspective	**Definition/explanation**	**Two essential qualities fostered by the perspective**
Political	Politics is an activity that builds and maintains your power so that you can achieve your goals. Power is the ability to achieve your meaningful, important goals. Politics is a process. Power is potential, and it comes from many sources.	**Power and Service** Politics is inherent to organizational life and is essential for leadership. Politics becomes constructive when it also works in the service of others. As power gives impact and leverage, service can guide your actions.
Psychological	Psychology is the study of individual personality, behaviors, emotions, and mental processes. Psychology differs from culture in that its primary focus is the individual rather than the collective.	**Emotional and Relational** The psychological and managerial perspectives are the two pillars of traditional coaching.
Managerial	"Management is a task that consists in focusing resources on the organization's goals, and then monitoring and managing the use of these resources" (Campbell, 1991, 4).	**Productivity and Results** See comment in previous section.
Physical	The physical is anything relating to the body.	**Health and Fitness** Health and fitness are fragile foundations that can easily be taken for granted but should be actively nurtured instead. "Mens sana in corpore sano," a healthy mind in a healthy body, is a fundamental aspect of global coaching.

Reality is multifaceted, and the various perspectives are interconnected. And each general perspective contains many specific perspectives. The *Evidence Based Coaching Handbook* (2006) clearly illustrates, for example, how various schools, theories, and models within psychology can contribute to coaching. These include adult development, cognitive psychology, psychoanalysis, and positive psychology.

Coaching is an art. In any given situation, a coach must choose an approach that is most likely to generate insights and foster progress. A coach needs to juggle multiple perspectives and seamlessly link and leverage alternative viewpoints to address the coachee's challenges.

MARIE'S CASE

To make the abstract concrete, let's see how these ideas apply to a case written by my friend and colleague Dr. Katrina Burrus, Master Certified Coach.[2]

. . . .

CASE STUDY

Marie, the business developer for Asia of a prestigious, global, consumer-service company with headquarters in the UK, asks for your help. Marie's boss suggested that she work with a coach, which is unusual; her company seldom invests much in ongoing training for its people. Marie is thus surprised, and feels privileged to benefit from a coaching program. You were highly recommended to her, but live in Europe; Marie, a U.S. citizen of Anglo-Saxon descent, asks you if you can coach her in Beijing, where she has lived for the last year.

Marie tells you that she wants to use the coaching to become more effective in developing the business in the region. In a few years, she wants to have established the Asian region as one of the main business centers for her company. She also mentions that she is constantly working, and can never relax enough to simply *be*; she always has to be doing something: work, reading, or study. She wants to share more time with her husband.

With Marie's approval, you talk with her functional and regional bosses (she reports equally to both in a matrix format) to determine what they expect from a coaching program. Through these two direct supervisors, you are informed of the following:

Marie's regional boss, Joe, a British citizen living in Beijing, describes Marie as an outstanding professional with an incredible workload capacity, dealing with multiple, complex situations. "Marie," he says, "is devoted to the success of the business and obtains outstanding results. She has been sent to difficult, emerging markets in Eastern Europe to troubleshoot problems and has been able to get projects through, resolved, and in a timely manner. Socially, she is charming and pleasant, but at work she is very pushy when promoting her ideas. When she delegates, she relentlessly comes back to her direct reports to see what has been accomplished." Joe reports that this, too, is perceived as pushy.

Joe continues, "Her Asian teams, from Japan, India, and Beijing, tend to shy away from working directly with her. She has been known to shout at her direct reports publicly and humiliate other colleagues in front of their bosses. Even clients have been subject to her wrath. She needs to create a team spirit and have people happy to work with her."

Joe pauses to think and then continues, "After an argument, Marie might try to make amends with the person she has upset, but she cannot stop herself from competing to win the argument, even if it will cost her the relationship. Many of her colleagues think she has a need to compete and have the last word. What has surprised more than one of her colleagues is that Marie's self-confidence at work contrasts noticeably with her submissive attitude with her (functional) boss, Jane." Joe continues, "I have noticed that she walks briskly into the office. She looks tense. When she is annoyed with a discussion, she rolls her eyes and walks away."

Marie's functional boss, Jane, an American based in the U.S., summarizes Marie's attitude as, "She lacks confidence. Marie remains silent in meetings." She continues, "She wants to impress people and overcompensates. She tries to impress people that she is bright, and what would we do without her. When she encounters resistance with her direct reports, she becomes aggressive, hierarchical, very top-down. She has little to no empathy or social radar. She is perceived as having little sensitivity to what is required by others." Jane pauses and says thoughtfully, "She does not know how to profile herself to engage people."

Marie tells you that she is 42 years old, has been married for 12 years, and has no children. She was raised in the eastern U.S., and comes from a traditional, middle-class family. Her husband is a very successful Swiss banker who has been promoted every few years and changed countries with each promotion. Marie says that she has usually found a way to follow him while pursuing her career or studies. She also mentions that her husband admires her achievements but complains sometimes that she relies too much on him to make decisions.

When Marie gives some information on her background, you find out that she has an older brother who was the apple of their parents' eyes. All hopes were focused on his career until he decided to quit the business life to live in a retreat. She was an average student at school, but once her brother left the business world, Marie began to have outstanding results at school.

Marie talks proudly about the results she has achieved and her constant travels. She confides in you that she is driven by her own agenda and gets upset when anything gets in her way. She knows that she is perceived as pushy, and she wants to learn how to inspire rather than impose. Her company has given her the opportunity to receive coaching to work on developing her emotional intelligence, which she understands as developing her interpersonal skills. With this background information from Marie and her two bosses, your assessment of the coaching situation begins.

During workshops, I ask participants these questions after they read the case.

- What is your understanding of the situation? What key challenges and issues need to be addressed?

- How would you tackle this case? What approach would you take with Marie?

I invite you to answer these questions as well. What is your take on this situation? What would you do to help Marie?

In my experience, the vast majority of coaches—professional coaches and leaders alike—suggest psychological approaches. Interculturalists will also suggest coaching from a cultural perspective. Most coaches ignore alternative approaches, missing valuable chances to help Marie.

It makes sense to help Marie by focusing primarily on the psychological perspective and taking into account the cross-cultural dimension. However, let me briefly discuss how other perspectives could open additional possibilities and growth opportunities for Marie.

Spiritual

Marie wants to learn how to inspire. The spiritual perspective is a useful avenue here, not just to help Marie cope with her stress but to help her do her job. To inspire others, Marie needs to find a deeper sense of purpose and meaning. She has to develop a strong and calm presence. This implies becoming comfortable with herself and developing an eagerness to give and to affect people in a positive fashion.

In the Jewish mystical tradition, Kabbalah means *reception*. It suggests that an essential spiritual quality is the ability to receive light: warming up to a child's smile, rejoicing at music, or welcoming a colleague's encouragement. You have to let the light in before you can shine and reflect light toward others.

Marie can be harsh toward her co-workers, but she is also harsh toward herself. She may need to develop self-acceptance. The coach might reframe Marie's challenging situation as an opportunity to grow on her hero's journey (see Part III, "Coaching Across Cultures"). The coach could help Marie put her challenges into perspective and develop gratitude for the gifts of life she may take for granted. This attitude of appreciation will lead to inner calm and peacefulness that will help her change what can be changed and accept what cannot be changed.

Coaching from a spiritual perspective means facilitating unity. To help Marie become more united with herself, the coach needs to help her confront and embrace her shadow, her demons, and her vulnerabilities. Carl Jung (1923) described how the self emerges when the ego meets the shadow.

Marie seems all in her head. She could become more attuned to her emotions, establishing a healthy contact and adequate distance from these. Unity would imply being able to rely on a cool head and warm heart. It would equate to unfolding her feminine (loving, caring) side in conjunction with her masculine (hard and demanding) part. Likewise, Marie could become more present to her body. By becoming more united with herself in these ways, Marie could become more united with the world. To help her on that path, the coach could invite Marie to meditate on her power, right, and responsibility. When culturally appropriate, the coach might quote the Talmud here and invite her to mediate on its message: "The man who saves one man saves the world entire."

It is also written that "Every man shall say: 'It is for me that the world was created.'" And again, "Every man shall say 'the World rests on me.'"

The coach could then challenge Marie to think about the legacy she wants to leave and outline specific actions for improving the world at her level. She might want to start by replacing her current destructive communications with benevolence and respect for her colleagues.

Cultural

Marie is working in a foreign country with its own set of norms, values, and beliefs. She could benefit greatly from learning about and embracing alternative cultural ways of dealing with challenges.

Several dimensions in the Cultural Orientations Framework (see Chapter 7) seem to be at play here. I mention a few below.

Humility versus control. The coach can guide Marie to do the best she can while accepting that not everything is under her control.

Indirect and hierarchical. Partly because of the culture in which she is working, Marie may not be getting the feedback she needs. She should not take this absence of feedback as a de facto approval of her abusive behaviors. She should instead remember that bruising people is the number one derailment factor for executives, as the Center for Creative Leadership's classical research has shown.[3] Marie should realize the alienating impact of loss of face, which is particularly problematic in indirect cultures.

Being versus doing. The coach could help Marie focus on becoming more serene and developing closer interpersonal relationships. This will help her create a supportive and constructive environment conducive to high performance.

Political

The coach could help Marie devise ways to build internal alliances (see Chapter 6). She needs to recognize that her competitiveness is self-defeating. By allying with, instead of alienating, her colleagues, she could build her business in the Asian region, thereby raising her profile and influence in the organization.

Psychological

Referring to Transactional Analysis (see Chapter 5), Marie is playing psychological games, adopting various roles in the dramatic triangle, from Persecutor (OK–not OK when she shouts at her direct reports) to Victim (not OK–OK in her submissive attitude toward her boss). The coach should help Marie become assertive, adopting an OK–OK mindset.

The cultural and spiritual perspectives are related. At a deeper level, OK–OK means accepting and loving oneself and others. Accepting and even embracing alternative cultural ways will bring Marie closer to other cultures, while giving her an opportunity to grow and become more united. Others' differences give us the occasion to reflect and awaken new facets in us.

Managerial

The coach could help Marie systematically review her various projects and discover opportunities for increased productivity and results.

Physical

Marie is healthy and still fairly young (42 years old), but her body may soon rebel against the high levels of stress she is accustomed to. The global coach could help Marie acquire healthy habits and exercise to increase her well-being, reduce stress, and develop resilience. Together, Marie and her coach could set specific goals for fitness, nutrition, sleep, and having fun. Marie might also benefit from a medical checkup and personalized programs with experts such as a fitness trainer and nutritionist.

Every case is unique. Therefore, global coaching cannot be reduced to a set of techniques and fixed prescriptions. Nonetheless, Marie's case should give you a more concrete sense of how multiple perspectives can inform and enrich coaching.

Global coaching is not limited to helping individuals. In the next chapter, you will find out how it applies to teams, organizations, and societal situations.

NOTES

1 This chapter is adapted from Rosinski, "Coaching from Multiple Perspectives," 2006.

2. Katrina Burrus, PhD, MCC. *Marie's case study*. Prepared for the workshop "Leveraging multiple perspectives: Practicing on a concrete and complex case," co-facilitated with Philippe Rosinski at the International Coach Federation European Conference, Brussels, May 2006. Reproduced with permission. First published in the *International Journal of Coaching in Organizations*, 2006, 4(4).

3. See Center for Creative Leadership, 2000.

CHAPTER 2

Coaching Toward a Better World

Individuals regularly work in teams and organizations to make projects happen. These collectivities also allow people to meet their social needs. All of this occurs in the context of a society that is globally connected. Global coaches work at multiple levels, recognizing that these various levels are interrelated. Individuals can facilitate team progress (development and transformation). Teams can foster organizational change. Likewise, organizations influence teamwork, and individual growth often occurs within teams. Much has been written about individual, team, and organizational progress. Less attention has been devoted to the global context in which coaches operate and how coaches can positively affect society. In my previous book, I elaborated on executive and team coaching.[1] I also alluded to the ways in which global coaches can facilitate organizational and societal progress.

In this chapter, I will start by describing specific areas global coaches need to consider when working with leaders, teams, and organizations. I will then offer an overview of our societal state of affairs and how we might play a positive part as global coaches.

GLOBAL LEADERSHIP DEVELOPMENT[2]

Developing global leaders is a key application of global coaching. The approach typically involves a combination of consulting, training, and coaching. Consulting determines what outcomes are most desirable and feasible, given the company's context and building on its current leadership development initiatives. In this phase, the consultant also examines the various levers of progress (e.g., tailored design of a global leadership development program that may combine training and coaching, performance appraisal and reward systems, and the company's culture, vision, and strategy). Alignment and consistency breed effectiveness: ideally, the levers should reinforce each other rather than send confusing signals (e.g., a company claiming "employees are our main asset" and then mistreating its employees).

A global leadership development program could focus on the following leadership competencies. The list could easily be augmented by considering the qualities inherent in each of the six perspectives as well as their links and overall complexity. It could also be adapted for non-corporate organizations.

Empowering leadership

- *Global coaching*—adopting a coaching style enhanced with a global, multiple perspectives approach
- *Intercultural excellence*—working effectively across cultures by learning to appreciate and leverage cultural differences
- *Integrity*—being true to oneself and genuinely committed to serving others

Visionary leadership

- *Dialectic/synthetic leadership*—uniting and interconnecting ("and") rather than dividing and excluding ("or")
- *Creative leadership*—being curious and able to see reality from multiple perspectives, particularly to address leadership challenges
- *Farsighted leadership*—framing organizational goals in the broader context of improving the world

Effective communication

- *Intercultural communication*—relying on various forms of communication: explicit and implicit, direct and indirect, affective and neutral, formal and informal

In today's global, multicultural, dynamic, and competitive world, organizations have to achieve greater results with scarcer resources. They need the creativity and farsightedness to seize the new ideas and aspirations inherent in our turbulent and changing environment. Effective global leadership can address both the threats and the opportunities, thereby enabling sustainable business success. Organizations must offer global leadership development if they wish to attract, develop, and retain the talent they need to succeed.

Finally, in my view, global leadership is inseparable from a global ambition: global leaders are concerned about improving the world at large. The good news is that leaders who genuinely care about people and society are more likely to inspire people, provide meaning, and elicit best efforts. In the end, all stakeholders are better served.

GLOBAL TEAM PROGRESS

Achieving sustainable high performance with teams is no straightforward task. At best, a team may achieve synergy. The team output is superior to the sum of contributions members could have made individually. At worst, the team output is inferior to these individual contributions.

David Campbell and Glenn Hallam's research (1994) indicates that to achieve high performance, teams should consider the following factors, which in my experience constitute a very good checklist. Sustainable success implies that members are satisfied and thus inclined to devote their best efforts in the team. To succeed, the team needs adequate resources. The team needs to use those resources efficiently (doing things right) and effectively (doing the right things).

Furthermore, the team should not become complacent but keep learning and improving.

Resources	Key Elements of Success
Time and staffing	"We have enough time and people."
Information	"We get the information we need."
Material resources	"We have the right tools and space."
Organizational support	"Our organization supports us."
Skills	"We are skilled."
Commitment	"We work hard."
Efficiency	**Using Resources Well**
Mission clarity	"Our purpose is clear."
Team coordination	"We are organized and efficient."
Team unity	"We work together in harmony."
Individual goals	"I have clear goals."

Empowerment	"We are trusted and supported."
Improvement	**Learning, Growing, Staying Healthy**
Team assessment	"We seek ways to improve the team."
Innovation	"We try new and creative approaches."
Feedback	"We learn how we are doing."
Rewards	"I am rewarded for doing well."
Leadership	"We have effective leadership."
Success	**Satisfaction and Performance**
Satisfaction	"I like being on this team."
Performance	"We are performing well."

Achieving team success is already challenging with "simple" teams. It becomes even more challenging in global teams, due to two key factors: distance and diversity. This yields four types of teams, as shown in the table below.

Global teams include all categories except low distance–low diversity. However, global coaching applies even in that "simple" situation.

The challenges of distance and diversity often occur together. Still, it may be useful to also address the two issues separately.

Types of Teams

		Low DIVERSITY	**High**
DISTANCE	**High**	Geographically dispersed (virtual) and Homogenous	Geographically dispersed (virtual) and Heterogeneous
	Low	Physically together and Homogenous	Physically together and Heterogeneous

Distance

A geographically dispersed team (or virtual team) is a distributed group of people working together across distance to achieve a common purpose via technology (such as e-mail, phone, or videoconferencing). Some of these teams may be quite culturally diverse; others may be more homogeneous.

Terence Brake (2006) argues that geographically dispersed teams need to address two major challenges: isolation and confusion.

When team members lack physical proximity, they often feel isolated. Brake explains that the team has to beat isolation by building community. Members need to feel valued for who they are, not just for what they do or where they are.

In this low-context environment (see Chapter 7), with remote and possibly faceless individuals, team leader and members must make a proactive effort to build relationships and trust. As a team coach, you can question the team to elicit specific ways to achieve these goals. Typical solutions include sharing bios and photos, using videoconferences (cheap webcams and Skype offer cost-effective ways to stay in touch), and building and maintaining personal, one-on-one relationships. Keep in mind that team members may not voice problems and concerns if you don't make an effort to maintain communication.

Distance makes misunderstandings more likely. Team members may interpret goals, priorities, and tasks in different ways. Local conditions notably influence perceptions. Brake contends that teams need to beat confusion by promoting clarity. Team leaders must give members all the contextual information they need to develop shared mental models and to perform their tasks confidently. Teams should have a tasks–responsibilities matrix that clarifies what has to be done and who is responsible for doing it.

Diversity

Cultural differences can be an obstacle, sometimes triggering misunderstandings, frustrations, and even alienation. But when properly understood and managed, diversity becomes an opportunity. Leveraging cultural differences fosters creativity and effectiveness (Rosinski, 2003).

In Chapter 7, you will learn specific techniques for deciphering cultural similarities and differences, capitalizing on team assets, and overcoming obstacles. These methods will help you proactively leverage alternative cultural perspectives.

ORGANIZATIONAL PROGRESS

Global coaches can facilitate organizational development and transformation in myriad ways.

Coaches may engage directly with the organization leader (president or CEO) or the top team. They can help leaders clarify the organization's overall vision, considering both external context and organizational capabilities. They can help the top team align various levers of progress (e.g., strategy, organization, culture, competences, motivators).[3] Global coaches facilitate sustainable high performance at the top team level, so it can become exemplary and inspirational for the rest of the organization. Clear vision, unity, and healthy team dynamics at the top make it easier to drive change throughout the organization.

Incidentally, coaches' added value typically relates to process (fostering authentic engagement, unleashing human potential) rather than content (proposing a vision and prescribing strategic solutions). That doesn't mean coaches should adopt a neutral stance when it comes to *what* the company is doing. Coaches need to be clear about what they want to facilitate and, conversely what would violate their sense of meaning. They should declare this up front; all parties need to agree on a contract that meets everyone's expectations and constraints. Reaching this clarity implies that the coaches are in touch with societal imperatives (see later in this chapter) as well as their own purpose in life (spiritual perspective).

Global coaches can offer processes for engaging the entire organization on a transformational path and focus energies toward a common purpose. Vincent Lenhardt pioneered coaching in France and authored the preface of the French edition of *Coaching Across Cultures*. In his books, he describes a process to liberate organizations' "collective intelligence." The team of external coaches facilitates a "middle-out" dynamic, capitalizing on middle management's awareness of strategic imperatives as well as concrete operational realities. Middle managers contribute to constructing the company vision, which they will then more easily embrace because it is *their* vision. They also form "transversal projects teams" with members representing various functions and locations. The holographic model is at play here: in many ways the whole organization and its dynamics are manifested in these transversal projects, which in turn resonate throughout the organization. Global coaching requires seeing how the whole is manifested in the part and how the part can impact the whole. Lenhardt's approach leverages *doing* and *being* imperatives: business achievements go hand in hand with the development of collective capabilities, relationships, and goodwill. This approach relies mainly on the psychological and managerial perspectives, along with the political and spiritual. It has been described in several books, notably by Lenhardt and Bernard (2005, 147–153) and Godard and Lenhardt (2000).

Lenhardt's process can work in a global context if it is enriched with the cultural perspective, ensuring that diversity is fully appreciated and leveraged.

Organic Growth, Alliances, and Mergers and Acquisitions

Global coaches can facilitate organizational growth at all stages.

Exploration

This is the period in which executives consider options. Research suggests that organizations often act out of habit and overlook possibilities. For example, they might choose to acquire another company when an alliance would make better strategic sense. (See Dyer, Kale, and Singh, 2004.)

The coach could constructively challenge the top executive, inviting her to consider all options and highlighting psychological and cultural biases that might lead to pet, yet subpar solutions. For example, competitive cultures might favor hostile takeovers, while collaborative cultures would turn to alliances.

The coach could challenge the notion of growth. Bigger is not necessarily better. What are the real motives for pursuing growth? Do these motives serve the business and society? Examples abound of company giants on loam feet, having paid the price for their obsession with size. The near collapse of Citigroup in 2008 comes to mind.[4] Furthermore, companies need to consider Earth's limited resources. We should stop pursuing growth when it implies destroying our planet's ecosystems beyond their capacity for regeneration. We shall explore this "what" question later in this chapter.

Sometimes growth makes sense. Jeffrey Dyer et al. (2004) have outlined factors leaders should consider when choosing a growth strategy. These include the type of synergies expected. For example, nonequity alliances are usually best suited to generate *modular synergies* (i.e., "companies manage resources independently and pool only the results for greater profits," for example, when an airline and a hotel chain allow hotel guests to earn frequent flyer miles). Equity-based alliances are better for *sequential synergies* (i.e., "one company completes its tasks and passes on the results to a partner to do its bit," for example, when a biotech firm discovering new drugs partners with a pharmaceutical giant to go through the tedious FDA approvals process). Mergers and acquisitions are appropriate with *reciprocal synergies* (i.e., "working closely together and executing tasks through an iterative knowledge-sharing process," for example, when Exxon and Mobil "realized that they would have to become more efficient in almost every part of the value chain, from research and oil exploration to marketing and distribution, in order to remain competitive").

Other factors include the nature of resources. People, or "soft resources," particularly the expert professionals in demand, can more easily leave the company if they are unhappy. A hostile takeover might result in a loss of the human assets the acquiring company wanted to obtain in the first place. An equity alliance may be better. This risk does not exist with "hard resources" (plants, equipment), which lend themselves more easily to acquisitions. I refer you to the article for a more thorough examination of the various factors.

Strategies can be combined: for example, an equity alliance can serve as a gateway to an acquisition. Cisco appears as a unique example, "having successfully absorbed 36 firms in the last ten years" and entered "more than 100 alliances" in the same period. "A key reason is that Cisco has one senior vice president in charge of corporate development, who is responsible for M&A, strategic alliances, and technology incubation. By placing all three functions under the same person, Cisco is able to look internally first, and then, if there are no viable options for meeting its objectives, consider either an alliance or an acquisition." Cisco has clear criteria. For example, "when there is a high degree of uncertainty around technology, or when they aren't critical, Cisco uses alliances as stepping-stones to acquisitions." The equity relationships help Cisco "move quickly to preempt rivals and acquire firms when the time is right."

Although coaches act as facilitators rather than consultants, they should be aware of such strategic considerations so they can be effective "sparring partners" for the senior executives, asking relevant questions while challenging the soundness of supposedly rational decisions. They can underscore psychological and cultural tendencies that affect decision making.

When an organization is contemplating a merger/acquisition or an alliance, exploration is followed by a due diligence phase, which may be followed by the deal and necessary integration efforts.

Due Diligence

In this phase, the goal is to assess strategic, financial, and human aspects and ensure conditions for a successful deal and integration are met and put in place.

Scott Moeller (2006) reports on research by Towers Perrin on 1,400 mergers in 2004–2005. The research shows progress in short-term deal success, suggesting that companies may be learning lessons from past failures. Fortis did not listen to the advice "Don't try to swallow too large a company" when it acquired ABN Amro, and shareholders lost a fortune as a result. Had they been called upon, global coaches could have helped avoid such a disaster. No financial expertise was needed; they simply could have asked decision makers whether and how they were taking these research findings into account.

More rigorous due diligence may take into account factors that were previously overlooked, "such as a detailed analysis of corporate benefit programs—especially pensions—and their financial liabilities." Importantly, "by including Human Resources earlier in the M&A process, M&A teams have also grown more successful at identifying key people and cultural issues in the due diligence stage." Towers Perrin (2006) concludes that "the real area of competitive advantage will be in the art of implementation, particularly on the people side" (3–4).

Global coaches can contribute significantly to the cultural due diligence process in both M&As and alliances through a cultural audit, consisting of select interviews, administration of the Cultural Orientations Framework assessment, and analysis and presentation of findings. You will discover in Chapter 7 how this can be done in practice. Global coaches should stay within their expertise (particularly intercultural) and rather than giving definitive advice. They should frame their findings into hypotheses and questions. What follows is a coaching conversation with the client rather than a consultant's set of prescriptions.

Deal

Coaches can help negotiate a satisfying deal. They can help executives avoid falling into traps at a time when their emotions and egos can cloud sound judgment. Geoffrey Abbott brings the following traps to coaches' attention: "bidding above the target's true value," "refusing to adjust to an initial valuation even if new information about the target firm suggests the initial number is in error (i.e., anchoring)," and the "sunk cost fallacy (i.e., refusing to walk away from the deal, even if the costs are unrecoverable, because the players have invested so much time, money, effort, and reputations into making the deal happen" (Abbott, 2009, 306).

Integration

The goal is to ensure that M&As and alliances do produce the synergies, added value, and results they are meant to deliver.

This is the time when global coaches are usually called upon. The deal is done, and we have to help the companies make the most of it. Different levers (mentioned previously) will be affected. The coach can facilitate the transition to a new structure and to new work processes by involving actors and by fostering alignment with the vision and strategy.

Global coaches will be particularly helpful in bridging the gaps between organizational cultures and fostering a new culture consistent with the vision and strategy. The case in Chapter 7 illustrates how the Cultural Orientations Framework assessment supported a strategic alliance between a Dutch and a French firm. This assessment is typically followed by various coaching actions, particularly the coaching of the top team and of integration teams, which in turn contribute to infusing global coaching throughout the organization. Individual executive coaching is also a possibility, as I illustrated in the case of the successful Unilever and Bestfoods merger (Rosinski, 2003, 41–43). These actions allow organizations to proactively leverage cultural differences and achieve a synthesis, instead of destructive polarization.

IMPORTANT AND MEANINGFUL OBJECTIVES

Coaches are sometimes content to help their coachees achieve their objectives, regardless of the nature of these objectives. At worst, this "neutral" attitude helps coachees attain targets that are both harmful to themselves and to society. This is the case when coachees' objectives are *inauthentic* or *unsustainable*. Inauthentic goals are superficial desires that, when realized, bring only temporary satisfaction, not true joy. Unsustainable objectives are targets with which the individual and/or the planet cannot cope—for example, overstretching, or exerting too much pressure and pushing beyond personal limitations, which leads to anxiety and other mental and physical illnesses. Sadly, some coaches help companies achieve objectives that combine all these detrimental characteristics—by, for example, letting people work too hard to sell obscure toxic financial products; oversized, polluting cars; or unhealthy, greasy hamburgers.

I defined coaching as "the art of facilitating the unleashing of people's potential to reach meaningful, important objectives" (Rosinski, 2003, 4). This definition makes it clear that coaches need to be concerned with "what": objectives should be important and meaningful. The multiple perspectives framework can help us further contrast the notions of *important* and *meaningful*. *Important* refers to the physical, psychological, and cultural realms; *meaningful* is about the spiritual.

What is important? First come physical needs: it is important to sleep, drink, and eat adequately to survive. It is also important to exercise and stay in good physical shape, which will help us to perform our tasks. Second, what matters is a function of our personality. For example, it is important for extraverts to have plenty of social contacts to "charge their batteries" and for "introverts" to secure ample time alone for reflection and meditation. Third, at the cultural level, "values" designate by definition what is important for a group and its members. Profit, market share, and equality constitute examples.

What is meaningful? This refers to something deeper. It implies discovering a sense of meaning for oneself and in serving others. It entails living accordingly, in full conscience, "awakened."

Can *important* and *meaningful* be the same thing? I hope the answer is yes! This happens when what is important is *truly important*—in other words, when the physical, psychological, and cultural meet the spiritual. To live mindfully, we need to be present to ourselves and others. When it happens, we respect our physical and psychological needs. We honor our desires, at least those that can be turned into authentic and sustainable goals.[5] We serve others in the same spirit. We leave the "autopilot" mode, in which we passively let our existences be forged by society, acting out of habits, whether constructive or destructive. Instead, to achieve meaningful success, we reclaim our right, power, and responsibility in life.

I was at the movies during a summer night. In a commercial, the sun was plunging the streets into an oppressive heat. A thirsty man was searching for relief. Fortunately he found a coke dispenser. The man gulped a coke with intense pleasure, if not ecstatic rapture. The message is straightforward: coke is the ultimate thirst quencher! Coke is important then, is not it? Not really. While an occasional coke might be okay, regular consumption of sodas with excessive sugar content is damaging for your health (see Chapter 3). Fresh mineral water, freshly squeezed fruit juices, and summer fruits (such as watermelon, melon, apricots) constitute healthier refreshers. When you are used to these natural sources of liquid, you may find them much tastier than sodas. In our consumerist society, we are bombarded with advertisements that blur our notions of what is important and meaningful. Global coaching can help people keep a necessary distance from social conditioning and make more authentic choices.

SUSTAINABLE DEVELOPMENT

We face unprecedented global challenges. Mentalities are changing. Corporations are under increased pressure to seriously integrate sustainable development practices. I will mention research findings from the Boston College Center for Corporate Citizenship and McKinsey about these new trends. For example, 57 percent of executives cited "environmental issues, including climate change"[6] as one of three issues likely to gain the most public and political attention in the next five years. This figure has soared in the last few years; the environment is now the top issue (Bonini, 2008, 5).

But we have a long way to go before a majority of people, corporations, and societies engage in the necessary transformations. Global coaching is a necessity, not a luxury. It can help transform the individuals leading, working for, investing in, and buying from these corporations. By transformation, I am not suggesting turning anyone into somebody else. I am rather proposing to facilitate the unfolding of the heroic and noble qualities that reside in each of us. These qualities are seriously needed today!

However, while global coaches fervently believe in the strength of human potential, we don't ignore the real-life facts. We must work to transform a sometimes crude reality into something beautiful. Complacency would only help us dig our collective grave.

In the following sections, I will share some disturbing stories. I will follow with constructive examples that can give us hope and inspire us to take action.

General Motors: A Tale of Marketing Myopia

Peter Horton, a writer, director, actor, and EV1 enthusiast,[7] explains:

> In 1990, California found itself in danger of losing federal highway funds if it couldn't find a way to meet air quality targets set by the Clean Air Act. As the California Air Resources Board searched the hazy landscape for relief, its eyes landed on a prototype electric car coming out of GM called the Impact . . . so the air resources board proposed a mandate that by 1998, 2% of cars

sold in California would be zero-emission vehicles. By 2001 that would increase to 5%. And by 2003 a whopping 10% of all new automobiles sold in California would be emission free.

GM's first response was to dive in. The company committed millions of dollars and teams of designers and engineers, who emerged six years later with a sleek rocket ship of an electric car renamed the EV1. It then set out in search of a sales team, one that was not only good at selling cars, but that had the patience and passion to educate an interested but suspicious public. It ended up with a group of men and women in their 20s who were almost all single, determined, and enthusiastic about the electric car. GM titled them, rather dryly, "EV specialists." By the time I met them five years later, they could be more aptly called 'the Subversives.' They were battered and bitter, but fighting with almost religious fervor against GM, the company that had recruited them, for the survival of the EV1.

Peter Horton tells the story of these "Subversives" who did not feel that the company had given the car a chance to succeed and fought for the EV1.

The Subversives designed, printed and distributed their own brochures, took over all event marketing from the company GM had hired, and decided to go after their celebrity customers, who they knew would talk about the car publicly. 'We knew we had to show GM the product they were asking us to sell was worth making. But we knew at some point GM was going to get behind this. It had to. It was just too great a car.'

By the spring of 1999, the Subversives had done it. They had leased all 648 cars. And word was getting out, with requests for cars starting to flood in. Still, GM didn't reopen the plant. The Subversives got frustrated . . . . With no more cars to sell and demand rising, the Subversives took the initiative and started a waiting list.

Horton shows the tremendous commitment of these Subversives and the enthusiasm the EV1 had generated:

By the fall of 1999, the Subversives were feeling optimistic: There was talk of the much-improved Generation II EV1, which featured an advanced battery. GM and the state of California were starting to make headway with the infrastructure, placing charging stations throughout the state, and subsidies were kicking in, which brought the monthly lease payment in L.A. County down to a reasonable $275 a month. But GM had a problem. They had been able to persuade the air resources board to give them a pass on the 1998 2% requirement for zero-emission cars as long as they could get 186

Generation II vehicles on the road by the end of '99. It was now November, and after much delay, the cars had finally arrived—a year's worth that not only needed to be leased but on the road by New Year's Eve. The Subversives dove in. They worked straight through Thanksgiving and Christmas, 14- and 15-hour days, seven days a week . . . . And just hours before New Year's, they leased and delivered the last of the 182 cars.[8] They were elated. "That was our most hopeful. We had real traction then . . . ." But the silence from the top was deafening. Finally, GM's EV1 brand manager, Ken Stewart, sent out a letter: "I want to personally thank you for the wonderful job . . . your efforts and results were absolutely outstanding . . . . you were a part of one of the highest performing teams I have ever had the pleasure to work with." The use of the word "were" didn't escape them . . . .What was becoming clear to the Subversives, and anyone interested in the future of the EV1, was that it only had a future as long as there was a mandate. And the mandate was starting to crumble. The 2% and 5% zero-emission requirements had been eliminated entirely, and the 10% requirement for 2003 could now include low-emission gasoline vehicles.

A website dedicated to the EV1, "Electric car unplugged,"[9] explains:

In 2001, auto manufacturers sued, arguing the mandate conflicted with the federal government's sole right to regulate fuel economy. The Bush administration filed a brief siding with Detroit, and a federal court agreed, ruling the Zero Emissions Vehicle mandate could not be enforced. Soon after, General Motors cancelled its EV1 electric car program; GM Manager Dave Barthmuss says the company could not afford to lose any more money on it. To express their frustration with GM's decision, electric car owners organized [on July 24, 2003] the funeral for the EV1 to bid farewell to their beloved cars and to raise awareness for the advantages of zero-emission vehicles. Says film producer Chris Paine, "It's insane that an incredible advance like the EV1 commuter car has been pulled from the roads before most people ever had a chance to drive one."

Senator Tom Hayden had these words: "Our mistake in the beginning was believing that by mandating it, making it necessary, and giving them incentives to make it profitable, they would do it. We were mandating an unwilling party. Unwilling in the deepest sense. Unwilling to make a profit off an electric car because of an unwillingness to embrace the notion" (Horton, 2003).

It is shocking to know that GM continued to sell the huge and highly polluting four-wheel-drive Hummer. Eventually though, GM's workers and also its shareholders paid the price for these errors. GM filed for bankruptcy in 2009, having, in President Obama's words, "reached the end of that road."

You might remember Theodore Levitt's 1960 *Harvard Business Review* classic "Marketing Myopia." Obviously, GM ignored his advice: "Sustained growth depends on how broadly you define your business—and how carefully you gauge your customers' needs." He explained that the American railroads in the early twentieth century collapsed because they were thinking "railroads" rather than "transportation": "Even after the advent of automobiles, trucks, and airplanes, the railroad tycoons remained imperturbably self-confident. If you had told them sixty years ago that in thirty years they would be flat on their backs, broke, and pleading for government subsidies, they would have thought you totally demented. Such a future was simply not considered possible."

GM suffered from marketing myopia; it failed to notice that in the early twenty-first century, the future of transportation is once again with the train. Too bad GM did not facilitate the shift to clean modes of transportation, including the electric car and train. The fast electric train has already become a favorite mode of transportation in Western Europe. Like many others, I use the train from Brussels to Paris or London. It is a cleaner, more comfortable, and faster alternative to the car or the plane. California has engaged in a similar railroad liaison, initially between Los Angeles and San Francisco. This is the most ambitious train project in the U.S. in 80 years![10]

However, like the Sphinx rising from its ashes, General Motors is coming back to life. The company has announced the commercialization of its hybrid model Chevrolet Volt, which will consume 1.02 liter per 100km (235 miles per gallon)—four times less than the pioneer and industry leader Prius, from Toyota.[11] GM has seemingly learned at last.

Pharmaceutical Industry: Dirty Tactics

Several books have uncovered shameful practices by the pharmaceutical industry. A report called "Le Scandale de l'Industrie Pharmaceutique" (Books, 2009) reviews more than ten books on the subject and contains interviews with authorities in the U.S., the United Kingdom, and France. It notably mentions Melody Peterson's *Our Daily Meds: How the Pharmaceutical Companies Transformed Themselves into Slick Marketing Machines and Hooked the Nation on Prescription Drugs* (2008) and Marcia Angell's *The Truth About the Drug Companies: How They Deceive Us and What to Do About It* (Angell, 2004).[12]

Billions invested in advertising and funding for university research leading to conflicts of interests,[13] false marketing claims, old drugs repackaged as new, hidden health hazards and downplayed side effects, and more.

Janet Maslin (2008) summarizes the alarming trend in her review of Petersen's book:

Irate as [the author] is that in a period (1980–2003) when Americans dou-bled what they spent on cars they increased their spending on prescription drugs by 17 times, Ms. Petersen steps back to consider the long-term conse-quences of this shift in consumption. She notes that the first generation of children raised in front of ubiquitous, sunny drug-company advertisements (which became legal in 1997) has acquired the notions that prescription pills fix everything, and that they are less dangerous than street drugs. Then, look-ing to the elderly, she points out that increasing numbers of drugs are accu-mulating in these patients, with little regard for the consequences.

"As older patients move through time, often from physician to physi-cian," one doctor tells her, "they are at increasing risk of accumulating layer upon layer of drug therapy, as a reef accumulates layer upon layer of coral." And when the side effects of sleeping pills or antidepressants mean more el-derly people fall down, the solution is not likely to be the scaling back of such prescriptions. "Instead," she writes, "the companies have used the statistics on falls to create a new blockbuster pharmaceutical market for drugs they claim will reduce the chances of breaking a bone." The market for just two of these drugs, Fosamax and Actonel, is expected to be worth $10 billion by 2011.

Stephen Hall (2004) reports:

The reasons for the transformation of the industry's image from life-saving pioneer to robber baron are many. But at root is a profound shift in the hi-erarchy of influence and decision making within the companies themselves over the last two decades, as the traditional emphasis on research and devel-opment has given way to marketing. The change is everywhere apparent: in the background of many company executives, in the annual balance sheets (in 2001, Angell estimates industry-wide marketing budgets at $54 billion, almost double research-and-development outlays, which the industry lobby puts at $30 billion), in the army of 88,000 salesmen (or detailers), trained to bird-dog doctors and persuade them to prescribe their company's drugs. Though much drug industry research remains outstanding, the system re-wards what Avorn [Jerry Avorn, professor at Harvard Medical School] calls "trivial pseudo-innovation"; shifting the emphasis from research to marketing was, he says, "just responding rationally to the legal, regulatory and eco-nomic pressures of a marketplace that had become perverse."

Many of those in charge have apparently lost touch with their industry's mission. Drugs are meant to save and enhance lives. Nevertheless, people should only use them as a last resort.

David Servan-Schreiber (2007) recalls a dinner with cardiologists sponsored by a pharmaceutical company in a restaurant dedicated to the best beef in the U.S. One of the cardiologists asked for fish, saying that she was monitoring her cholesterol level. This request was met with kidding from her colleagues: "Just take your Lipitor and don't annoy us with your regime!" Incidentally, Servan-Schreiber notes, Lipitor is the all-time most profitable drug. At its peak, it was raking in a million dollars per hour, or nine billion dollars a year (193–194).

According to Philippe Even, physicians have not learned to exercise sufficient critical and scientific thinking (Books, 2009, 22). They don't recognize the pitfalls in the medical information they receive: a new "me too" drug may compare favorably to a placebo in the research findings but not necessarily to existing drugs using the same molecules. Many renowned university professors let themselves be bribed by pharmaceutical companies. Meanwhile, the Food and Drug Administration is financed largely by the pharmaceutical industry (Books, 2009, 19). The industry's powerful lobby has also succeeded in making advertising legal in the U.S. (fortunately not in Europe, though). Generic drugs would cost patients, as well as society, much less. And we all would be better off with fewer "lifestyle" and "me too" drugs and more research targeting serious diseases (including orphan diseases) and enhanced education for promoting healthier lifestyles.

To keep drugs at bay (as much as possible), people need to take care of themselves, notably through adequate nutrition, exercise, and life balance. For many this requires a courageous examination of one's physical, emotional, mental, and spiritual health. It implies disciplined actions rather than quick fixes. Global coaches can provide invaluable help by fostering autonomy rather than unnecessary dependency on drugs.

Despite the overall worrisome trends, there are some encouraging examples from the pharmaceutical industry. The Boston College Center for Corporate Citizenship (BCCCC) cites Novo Nordisk: "Their 'Changing Diabetes' platform supports the company's long-term aspiration to defeat this disease by finding better methods of prevention, detection, and treatment. Supporting the implementation of the UN Declaration on Diabetes, the company's efforts focus on encouraging health policymakers to put diabetes higher on their agendas, educating healthcare professionals and people with diabetes to improve diagnosis, care and self-management, and raise awareness in communities to drive prevention of diabetes" (2009, 33).

What strikes me is that, beyond selling its drugs against diabetes, Novo Nordisk promotes diabetes prevention by sponsoring education. This is a source of pride and meaning for employees, many of whom volunteer out-side work, reaching out to children with messages about preventing diabetes and discussing the UN Resolution on Diabetes (which particularly empha-sizes diet and physical activity).

Banking Sector: The 2008 Crash

The U.S. experienced a real estate bubble from 2001 until 2005. To increase their commissions, brokers resorted to giving credit to more and more people who could not afford to repay it. At the same time, investment banks pack-aged these credits into bonds. The prospect of high returns lured many inves-tors, who had forgotten that castles built in the sand are bound to collapse. Lehman Brothers vanished, and many banking institutions had to be res-cued by nation states. The financial crisis, and the economic recession that followed, made it painfully clear that we live in an interconnected world.

Citizens were shocked by the appalling greed, sense of entitlement, ir-responsibility, and hubris. *The Economist* asked, "What will it take for bank-ers to show a little remorse?" and noted, "It is telling that fully 79 percent of Wall Street workers who responded to a poll by eFinancialCareers.com said they received a bonus for 2008, despite the carnage. Almost half said they were dissatisfied with the amount received" ("Wall Street excess—Looting stars," 2009).

Bankers were not the only culprits, however. Regulators, too, were found wanting. For example, "the Securities and Exchange Commission (SEC), Wall Street's regulator in chief, overlooked [Bernard] Madoff's investment-advisory business, even though it had assets under management of $17.1 billion at the start of 2008. The outgoing head of the SEC has admitted the commission made a hash of the Madoff case, failing to act on warnings made nearly a decade ago" ("The Madoff Affair—Dumb Money and Dull Diligence," 2008).

The crisis was a complex phenomenon with multiple interconnected triggers, including inauspicious policy choices. "The Federal Reserve ig-nored the housing bubble and kept short-term interest rates too low for too long. The emerging world's determination to accumulate reserves, especially China's decision to hold down its exchange rate, sent a wash of capital into America. There was something of a perfect storm in which policy mistakes combined with Wall Street's excesses" ("Capitalism at Bay," 2008).

Insufficient regulation in the financial sector was a key factor. Even *The Economist*, relentless advocate of economic liberty, insisted:

Finance needs regulation. It has always been prone to panics, crashes and bubbles. Because the rest of the economy cannot work without it, governments have always been heavily involved. Without doubt, modern finance has been found seriously wanting. Some banks seemed to assume that markets would be constantly liquid. Risky behavior garnered huge rewards; caution was punished. Even the best bankers took crazy risks. For instance, by the end of 2007 Goldman Sachs, by no means the most daring, had $1 trillion of assets teetering atop $43 billion of equity. Lack of regulation encouraged this gambling. Financial innovation soared ahead of the rule-setters. Somehow the world ended up with $62 trillion-worth of credit-default swaps (CDSS), none of them traded on exchanges. Not even the most liberal libertarian could imagine that was sensible. ("Capitalism at Bay," 2008)

Somehow, many bankers and investors turned into speculators and gamblers, losing sight of a more basic and meaningful purpose. Banks should be at the crossroads between those individuals and companies who place their savings and are entitled to a reasonable return, and those who borrow money to fund projects. Ideally, these projects should provide real value to society: economic, environmental, and social.

I had the opportunity to coach a financial investment expert. We used the multiple perspectives framework as well as the "Global Coaching Process" described in my previous book. John's[14] coaching took place over several episodes and addressed various developmental challenges. In the process, John built a personal vision before the financial crisis. His authenticity, which John unfolded on his courageous developmental journey, contrasts with the shallowness of many of his peers, which the crisis brought to the fore.

John explains:

Our team [of investors] has always had a true passion for investing in spaces having a positive impact on the society, particularly the life sciences and renewable energies, and to a lesser extent information technology and the Internet.

Investments in these domains have, by nature, a substantial technological dimension. Consequently, they are riskier and have to be sized and handled appropriately.

We invest in start-ups and hire people to make projects happen. From a financial standpoint, this is distinct from what has been done in the recent years by buyout and hedge funds, respectively based on debt and trading.

Start-ups are private companies financed only with capital. Investing in them implies a long-term commitment to projects and managers. Performance is essential but takes a long time to materialize as these companies may not generate profits and even revenues for years.

While performance is key, confidence in managers comes first. Such con-
fidence is built, over time, through consistency and transparency. We have
also had to develop many tools and processes to select the managers and
projects. In the new environment, human qualities of integrity and dedica-
tion to long-term success suddenly happen to be of the essence and talent is
scarcer than one could think.

This noble vision, together with John's commitment to selecting the
right managers (leading start-up companies or managing funds investing in
these societies), being an excellent team leader, and ensuring that everyone
is fairly compensated, allowed him to attract and retain talented professionals. Pursuing meaningful objectives elicited the team's best efforts and enhanced their pride in their successes.

Research Findings: Doing Good to Do Well

There's more to be said about other sectors: oil, chemicals, food, to name but
a few—without forgetting the tobacco industry, whose deceptive ploys have
already been widely exposed.

While corporations bring many benefits, they can also cause much damage. From poisonous pesticides to greasy hamburgers, both unhealthy for
humans and for the environment, unsustainable habits seem hard to break.

The public's trust in business is at an all-time low. The 2009 Edelman
Trust Barometer shows that 62 percent of the public across 20 countries "say
they trust corporations less now than they did a year ago." In America, the
figure is 77 percent, which is the highest it has been in the ten years Edelman has tracked trust, (Boston College Center for Corporate Citizenship
2009, 2). The BCCCC remarks that "the appetite for government regulation
of business grows, and the expectation that businesses address global challenges increases."

This research (which notably includes "responses from 238 CFOs and
investment professionals from the full range of industries and regions") shows
that companies do better by doing good: "Overall, companies that excel in their
social, environmental, or governance programs see improved performance in
each of the standard dimensions that investors use to assess value: growth, return on capital, risk management, and management quality" (2009, 3).

In agreement with global coaching's holistic philosophy, the research
further reveals that to reap the full financial rewards

- environmental, social, and governance ("ESG") programs must align
closely with a company's core business and capabilities and

- companies must understand the value they are creating and communicate that value to the market.

This implies a clear vision, inspired by a genuine desire to serve society (rather than mere cynical opportunism). Practically, the research also shows that "it is critical for companies to establish metrics and track the impact of such programs on value—which few are able to do today" (2009, 3).

The following table[15] summarizes how ESG programs can create value.

Pathway to Value from ESG Along Four Dimensions		
Growth	New Markets	• Gain access to new markets and market share through exposure from ESG programs.
	New Products	• Create products to meet unmet social needs and increase differentiation.
	New Customers/Market Share	• Use ESG to engage consumers and build knowledge of expectations and behaviors.
	Innovation	• Develop cutting edge technology and innovative products and services for unmet social or environmental needs that could translate to business uses, patents, proprietary knowledge, etc.
	Reputation/Differentiation	• Foster brand loyalty, reputation, and goodwill with stakeholders by engaging with them on ESG programs.
Return on Capital	Operational Efficiency	• Enable bottom line cost savings through environmental operations and practices (e.g., energy and water efficiency, less raw materials needed).
	Workforce Efficiency	• Reduce costs generated by employee attraction and turnover by using ESG to build morale. • Develop employees' skills and increase productivity through participation in ESG activities.
	Reputation/Price Premium	• Develop reputation on ESG that garners customers' willingness to pay price increases or premium.

(continued on next page)

Pathway to Value from ESG Along Four Dimensions *(Continued)*		
Risk Management	Regulatory Risk	• Mitigate risks by complying with regulatory requirements, industry standards, and NGO demands.
	License to Operate	• Facilitate uninterrupted operations and entry in new markets using local ESG efforts and community dialogue to engage citizens and reduce local resistance.
	Supply Chain/Security of Supply	• Secure consistent, long-term, and sustainable access to safe, high quality raw materials and products by engaging in community welfare and development.
	Reputational Risk	• Avoid negative publicity and boycotts by addressing ESG issues.
Management Quality	Leadership Development	• Develop leadership skills and improve employee quality through ESG participation.
	Adaptability	• Build ability to adapt to changing political and social situations by engaging local communities.
	Long-Term Strategic View	• Develop long-term strategy encompassing ESG issues.

The BCCCC suggests articulating a "pathway to value" to "unwind the specific ways in which ESG activities contribute to the business, along the dimensions valued by the market: growth, return on capital, risk management, and management quality. Companies can then examine where their ESG programs have the most impact, and assess whether that impact is aligned with business priorities . . . . Articulating the pathway to value can also serve as a proxy when hard numbers are unavailable for assessing the impact of ESG programs" (2009, 26–27). The BCCCC notes, "Companies that understand the pathways to value, and identify the nature of the impacts from ESG programs (i.e., short or long term) will be able to define a few targeted measurements that will allow them to assess their efforts" (2009, 27). The report includes the example of Campbell Soup partnering with the American Heart Association to address the industry issues of nutrition and wellness, obesity, and food safety (2009, 25–28).

Global coaching's disciplined process is concerned both with unfolding the high view and facilitating the definition of concrete target objectives.

The Example of Philips Lighting: "Growth Through Sustainability"

I recall the joy and pride of one of my coachees, a senior executive working for Philips Lighting. He explained that by replacing current lighting systems with more efficient alternatives, we could reduce electricity consumption enormously. This would eliminate the need to build expensive power plants in Africa. The poor countries could ill afford these costly investments, which would have also been damaging for the environment.

My coachee had initially lost some of his old enthusiasm and spirit. Spending time in endless operational meetings, he had lost sight of the bigger picture and meaning of his work. By simply bringing his awareness to these questions, I was able to help him reconnect to his passion. He was particularly pleased to work for a company committed to sustainability and to feel his work was making a positive difference.

Philips has pioneered many of the key developments and breakthroughs in lighting technology. The company's booklet "Illuminating Ideas" highlights its philosophy and gives examples as well as figures (2008). Here are some excerpts that exemplify the company's commitment to sustainability and "meaningful innovation":

- *Sustainability for Philips Lighting is about much more than implementing and enforcing policies and systems. Sustainability is about growth. By empowering future generations to meet their needs, we open up a world of opportunity for our company.*
- *Lighting accounts for about 19 percent of worldwide electricity use. Our innovative lighting solutions can realistically save up to 40 percent energy on all today's installed lighting, whether outdoors, in offices or shops, or in the home. . . . We are also working to improve product lifetime and reliability in order to reduce waste and limit maintenance disruption.*
- *We adopt a sustainable approach in our production processes. All our manufacturing sites have achieved ISO 14001 certification and run environmental management systems. We make great efforts—in a variety of ways—to reduce energy consumption in each of our plants.*
- *Xenon saves lives: Xenon lights reduce serious night-time accidents on country roads by over 50 percent and by as much as 30 percent on motorways, according to a TUV Rhineland study (Germany, 2007). Compared to halogen lights, Xenon also saves 1.3g of CO_2 emissions for every kilometer driven.*
- *Helping birds migrate safely: Philips Lighting, together with NAM (the Dutch Oil Company), has developed a new type of lighting with a*

unique greenish color for offshore oil platforms; fewer birds are distracted by the light, which means fewer (frequently fatal) interruptions to migrations across the North.

DEMOCRACY AND THE MARKET ECONOMY

In *Coaching Across Cultures*, I advocated for leveraging liberal, ecological, and social political perspectives. This is consistent with sustainability's triple bottom-line approach: profit, planet, and people.

Communism, with its oppressive control and stifling regulations, has proved its limitations: preventing private enterprises, damping personal initiatives, promoting poverty, limiting freedom, and alienating citizens.

Liberalism has brought much richness and progress. Yet Adam Smith's invisible hand also appears more and more as a lure. Smith[16] is often remembered for his injunctions about "letting the market alone" and for saying "the least government, the better." We infrequently recall his messages about what the government should do and his aversion for the rising capitalist class. We forget that his system of "perfect liberty" was aimed at increasing the wealth of nations in the interest of everyone, especially the poor.

Robert Heilbroner (2000) explains: "Smith explicitly recognizes the usefulness of public investment for projects that cannot be undertaken by the private sector—he mentions roads and education as two examples" (69).

Concerning the rising capitalist class—Adam Smith's protagonists—Heilbroner argues that it was "the very class that Smith has excoriated for its 'mean rapacity,'" whose members "neither are, nor ought to be, the rulers of mankind" (66–67).

As the father of liberalism himself argued, we should avoid a simplistic liberalism in which the market is left alone and governments don't play their crucial part. We all can and should contribute to societal progress in the following ways:

- Ensure initiatives and actions are geared toward societal progress through appropriate regulations.
- Distinguish goods from merchandise.
- Appreciate the need for government intervention.
- Promote global governance to address global challenges.
- Encourage entrepreneurs and innovators.
- Embrace the complex multiple perspectives paradigm.

Ensure Initiatives and Actions are Geared Toward Societal Progress Through Appropriate Regulations

History repeats itself. Apparently we failed to learn the lessons from what caused the 1929 crash. Heilbroner (2000) explains what happened then: "The average American had used his prosperity in a suicidal way; he had mortgaged himself up to his neck, had extended his resources dangerously under the temptation of installment buying, and then had ensured his fate by eagerly buying fantastic quantities of stock—some 300 million shares, it is estimated—not outright, but on margin, that is, on borrowed money" (250–251). The parallel with the 2008 crash is evident.

André Comte-Sponville (2009) argues that "only the law can moralize capitalism. . . . What guided bankers was not the intelligent interest, but rather a blind and unreasonable passion: cupidity." Ethics is insufficient here. Law—that is, constraint—is needed. Meager regulation and over-reliance on the "invisible hand" led to the banking crisis in 2008, as even Alan Greenspan came to admit. Capitalism is dangerous when it becomes a capitalism of debt (i.e., you strive to become richer with money you don't have); it must be carefully regulated.

I agree that appropriate legislation is crucial. The laws should address potentially damaging conflicts of interest. For example, banks should be obliged to keep a sizeable percentage of the credit notes sold by their brokers (housing mortgages)—particularly the subprime assets—rather than hiding them in funds they sell to clients (who don't realize what's in their opaque portfolios). Top managers should be encouraged, with financial incentives, to create long-term value and should be penalized for destroying it. In late 2008, France legislated against golden parachutes that reward failure; this is a step in the right direction. We must ban sophisticated financial mechanisms that favor speculation over creation of value, opacity over clarity, and casino capitalism over entrepreneurship.

Global coaching can play a crucial role in increasing individuals' self-responsibility, which includes reflecting on the wider repercussions of our actions and realizing we have a choice and can make a difference. In other words, we can combine a political perspective (e.g., the coercive effect of law, in this case inspired by a commitment to serve) and a spiritual one (e.g., meaningful actions) to ensure the market works in the right direction.

Distinguish Goods from Merchandise

We must distinguish goods from merchandise. We need to relearn the value of many freely available goods, starting with nature itself. When we recognize their value, we are more motivated to preserve them. Other goods can (should?) be made available at a minimal cost, and perhaps even at no cost: these include healthcare, education, and public transportation.

Many natural products can promote health and fight disease, but they get little to no attention because they aren't patentable—and are therefore unprofitable for pharmaceutical companies. (See Chapter 3.) Pharmaceutical companies can play a useful role in promoting health and treating illness, but we should not over-rely on them. When the pharmaceutical industry finances university research (and substitutes for public funding), conflict of interest is inevitable, and researchers ignore potentially helpful non-drug treatments.

Merchandise and the market economy—with the appropriate regulations—still have their place; they generate the economic richness that contributes to financing and funding democracies, enabling them to provide other essential goods to citizens.

Inevitably, there is tension. The market economy produces wealth as well as consumerism's side effect: consuming more than necessary, to the detriment of our—and the planet's—health and well-being.

We should combat these excesses through legislation and education. Laws alone are not enough. We need to educate consumers, helping them make the shift from mindless buying to mindful decision-making based on what's truly best for them, and for the planet. My colleague See Luan Foo from Singapore sent a card with these words of wisdom: "The happiest people don't have the best of everything. They just make the best of everything they have! The richest person is not the one who has the most but the one who needs the least."[17]

Simplistic coaching merely focuses on larger sales and greater profits, confusing quantity with quality. It doesn't question the larger socio-political context, let alone attempt to change it. Global coaching aims to address the complexity head on, helping the coachee navigate through dilemmas and embrace the paradox that more can be less and less can be more.

Appreciate the Need for Government Intervention

Economist John Keynes theorized about the limitations of the market economy and the need for government intervention, particularly in a crisis. Franklin Roosevelt put some of those ideas in his New Deal when he became President in the depths of the Great Depression.

When consumer spending is depressed because of high unemployment and investment is low because business firms cannot see any prospect of good times returning, the economy as a whole is weak. For Keynes, the classical approach of reducing government spending at that time to balance the weaker tax revenues would only foster the downward spiral of depression. Instead, he argued that governments should increase spending, particularly on public works. This would 'prime the pump,' triggering growth in the economy with a 'multiplier' ripple effect: people who receive money spend most of it on products, increasing revenues that allow businesses to hire and pay more people, who can then spend more money on products, et cetera. Part of the government money injected goes back to the government in higher tax revenues. (See notably Smith, 2008, 163–169).

Keynes also explained "how the 'classical' remedy to unemployment, reducing wages to price workers back into jobs, would not work: apart from the fact that it is hard to get workers to accept wage cuts, even when prices are falling, wage cuts would, by reducing income, also mean lower spending power, or 'aggregate demand'" (Smith, 2008, 167).

Moreover, Keynes elucidated why the classical approach of stimulating the economy through cutting interest rates had lost its potency: "In his view a situation could develop where interest rates were as low as the authorities could push them but still too high to stimulate investment, because businesses were too gloomy about prospects—in Keynes's words, they lacked 'animal spirits.' In other words, it was possible for the economy to be caught in a so-called 'liquidity trap.' Even when interest rates were at their lowest practicable level, perhaps even zero, nobody wanted to borrow. In these circumstances, increasing money and credit would not help. All that would happen was that 'idle' balances would build up in banks" (167–168).

The market economy is not meant to satisfy human *needs* or human *wants*, but rather to provide merchandise to satisfy human *demand*. Some products may be demanded without being really needed (consumerism). Other products may be wanted without being demanded (because we cannot afford them): that is the issue Keynes's breakthrough helped to tackle by revitalizing the economy after the Great Depression.

In 2008, even George W. Bush, a proponent of leaving the market alone and minimizing government's intervention, had to advocate for government financing (i.e., socialistic nationalization) to rescue the banking sector and the whole market economy from collapse.

The market economy alone can't address the serious global challenges we face. But government involvement brings the risk of ineffective bureaucratic policies: public funding wasted in ill-chosen projects,[18] protected civil servants getting away with poor performance and low productivity. Yet social democracies (particularly in Northern Europe) have proved that economic prosperity can coexist with social protection, and a market economy can coexist with socialism. Governments and publicly owned companies *can* manage effectively and rigorously!

In 2008, Jean-Marc Nollet, a Belgian ecologist and politician, titled his book *Green Deal*, echoing Roosevelt's New Deal. We need government investments and business incentives to foster essential societal transition. When car makers feel constant pressure from Wall Street to deliver great quarterly results and cleaner vehicles are too expensive to produce, we will keep getting more of the same old thing. Governments need to invest in clean public transportations infrastructures (e.g., railroads) and create the right eco-incentives.

Nollet advocates the "polluter-payer" principle and "true-costing of pollutions" (94). Nature offers many vital services: water purification, flood prevention, cross-pollination of plants and fruits, soil fertility, and on and on. We should not take these services for granted. We should calculate their economic value and polluters should support the cost of destroying nature. This approach would favor sustainable enterprises and would eliminate many non-sustainable enterprises that are profitable today but would no longer be so under the "polluter-payer" regime. Similarly, *The Economist* (2009) argues that the "best way to curb global warming would be a carbon tax. . . . A tax on carbon dioxide (CO_2) would give everyone an incentive to emit less of it. It would be simple, direct, and transparent" (12).[19]

We need strong democracies to gear the economy toward meeting human needs rather than mere demands. If we leave the market alone, great financial profit is made by first inciting consumers to overeat junk food, and then by selling drugs to combat the multiple medical conditions related to this poor life hygiene. Instead, prevention, although less "profitable," is required to overcome the deleterious circle; this includes promoting healthy habits particularly through education (see Chapter 3), imposing stricter rules for advertisements, forbidding sodas and junk food in schools, et cetera. It would be foolish to rely on the "invisible hand" and expect business to meet human needs by promoting laisser-faire and an excessively free economy.

Promote Global Governance to Address Global Challenges

We should promote global governance to address global challenges such as destruction of biodiversity, depletion of Earth's resources, pollution, poverty, natural catastrophes, and terrorism. Jacques Attali (2004) notes that international corporations already have global governance and have the edge in the balance of power with democracies. Nations often are reluctant to give up parts of their national interests and sovereignty, but this is essential to forge solid global governance, establish and enforce international laws, and serve the interest of the world at large.

U.N. Secretary General Ban Ki-moon and Al Gore have urged countries to invest in renewable energies rather than keep alive dying industries and perpetuate bad habits (Ki-moon and Gore, 2009). They argue that continuing to invest billions of dollars in infrastructures that rely on carbon and subsidizing industries that rely on fossil fuels is equivalent to issuing risky mortgage bonds. To fight against poverty, they urge nations to increase public developmental aid. This includes investing in poor countries' agriculture by training farmers in sustainable practices and providing tools and seeds. Finally, they exhort governments to establish a real agreement about the climate, which would lead to massive investments and prompt innovations in clean energies.

The world crises represent opportunities to "kill two birds with one stone" (I prefer the French equivalent *faire d'une pierre deux coups*, which is kinder to birds): favoring business and employment while gearing these activities toward reducing carbon dependency, protecting ecosystems and water resources, and alleviating poverty. In other words, serving real human needs and averting future crises. Global governance is essential to avoid equivocation and haggling and adopt the ambitious measures the world needs, such as drastically reducing CO_2 emissions.

A report prepared for the United Nations Environment Program depicts this vision of a "Global Green New Deal," with a combination of actions and policies geared toward three objectives:

- Revive the world economy, create employment opportunities, and protect vulnerable groups.
- Reduce carbon dependency, ecosystem degradation, and water scarcity.
- End extreme world poverty by 2025. (Barbier, 2009, 8)

Some countries are showing the way. South Korea has announced a Green New Deal plan. At a cost of about U.S. $36 billion between 2009 and 2012, the initiative aims to create 960,000 jobs. The plan includes nine major projects: expanding mass transit and railroads, energy conservation (villages and schools), fuel-efficient vehicles and clean energy, environmentally friendly living space, river restoration, water resource management (small and midsize dams), resource recycling (including fuel from waste), and national green information infrastructure. (See Barbier, 2009, 17.)

Still, fragmentation is a key barrier to global action. As individuals we sense that addressing global challenges is beyond our control; as nations we tend to think that others should carry the burden. The holographic model can help us develop a global consciousness to promote progress.

Global coaches must be acutely alert to our interconnected world and aware that our actions have worldwide repercussions. We must ask ourselves and our coachees the difficult questions: how will our actions affect society and our planet? What legacy do we want to leave?

Encourage Entrepreneurs and Innovators

Another famous economist, Joseph Schumpeter, has highlighted the fundamental role of entrepreneurs and innovators. He has shown that "entrepreneurs and their innovating activity are the source of profit in the capitalistic system" (295).

"Innovations were usually the work of pioneers," notes Schumpeter, but whereas leading is rare and difficult, following is easy. On the heels of the innovator comes a swarm—the word is Schumpeter's—of imitators. The original improvement is generalized throughout the industry, and a rash of bank borrowing and investment spending gives rises to a boom. "But the very generalization of the innovation removes its differential advantage," Schumpeter says (296).

Schumpeter explains that "the entrepreneur is not himself necessarily a profit receiver, even though he is *the* profit generator. Profits go to the owner of the enterprise, just as rent goes to the owner of land" (296).

Why, then, would the entrepreneur take on an often thankless task? Schumpeter sees several possible reasons: the dream and the will to found a private kingdom, the will to conquer, and they joy of creating, of getting things done, or simply the urge to use one's energy and imagination (297).

Schumpeter has shown that, ironically, capitalism's success rests on the shoulders of leaders searching for meaning beyond profit. "Capitalism 'development' is not . . . intrinsic to capitalism as such. It is the dynamization of society at the hand of a noncapitalist elite!" (306). This paradox is only troubling under the habitual paradigm of simplicity. As I will explain, if we embrace the paradigm of complexity, it becomes clear that such breach is inevitable, consistent with Gödel's theorem.

According to Jacques Attali (2009), production, not growth per se, pollutes. He advocates for massive investment in technological innovation to save the day (while insisting that mentalities also need to evolve toward sustainable progress). *The Economist* (2009) cites the example of First Solar, an Arizona-based firm, which makes thin-film solar panels that are more cost-effective than most existing ones, and which doubled its production in 2009. This is of utmost importance since solar energy is more expensive than wind and relies on fat subsidies (13).

Jean-Claude Guillebaud (2009) points out that people are encouraged to consume but warned against squandering the earth's resources; he argues that we cannot simultaneously have our cake and have eaten it. Unfortunately, human happiness is associated with consumerism: replace your car, get a new phone, buy the latest fashions. For Guillebaud, consumerism is a mirage we have to abandon.

I believe we should best pursue the two goals concurrently: encourage entrepreneurs and innovators to create the clean, cost-effective energy solutions we desperately need and other technologies that enable societal progress, while at the same time changing our consumerist habits to reduce our "ecological footprint."[20]

Global coaching can help with both routes. In Chapter 10, you will discover how coaches can help awaken the heroes in each of us. For example, unfolding our Warrior and Explorer will liberate our entrepreneurial capacity. Contacting our Creator will reveal our innovative potential. The Caregiver and Sage will help us preserve Earth's resources, while our Destroyer will enable us to eliminate many wasteful habits. Multiple coaching perspectives can maximize our chances to address these formidable challenges.

Embrace the Complex Multiple Perspectives Paradigm

The Belgian newspaper *Le Soir* invited leading Belgian economists to analyze their collective failure to predict the 2008 crisis ("Les Économistes Surpris par la Crise," 2009). Few economists worldwide saw what was coming, and fancy economic theories were apparently of little help in thwarting the crash (even if economists helped to explain what happened and how to bounce back afterwards).

As the joke goes, "Put three economists together, and four opposite theories will come out!" *Le Soir* concludes, however, that these disagreements should not disturb us: "The multiplicity of theories is undoubtedly the condition allowing us to better understand reality's diverse facets; and the diversity of opinions is rather good news for our democratic societies" (2009).

Heilbroner's (2000) exploration of the great economic thinkers had already led him to several conclusions, all of which highlight the complexity.

- Interdependence

  "Today's economies are more interdependent than were the workers in Adam Smith's pin factory." (314)

- Complexity of human behaviors

  Traditional economics assumes "rational" and predictable human behaviors, in the form of automatic stimulus-response relations. However, we are not robots! "Human behavior cannot be understood without the concept of volition—the unpredictable capacity to change our minds up to the very last moment." (317)

- No truly neutral view

  "There is, of course, ample room for scientific method in analyzing many problems that economics seek to clarify, including the requirement that economists report the data they observe as scrupulously as possible. But when it comes to policy recommendations, it is impossible to present economic analyses as if they stemmed unchallengeably from the givens of society." (318)

  Heilbroner refers to Schumpeter: "The processes of economics are not sufficient in themselves to determine how the system goes." (305)

  The simplicity paradigm assumes a subject separate from the object (e.g., the economist as a distinct "subject" analyzing "objective" phenomena); the complexity paradigm considers that the subject is inseparable from the object.

- Multiple perspectives

  Heilbroner believes that economics needs to be deepened and enlarged with knowledge from the other branches of social inquiry and placed in the service of enlightened leadership toward meaningful ends. (321)

As we reach the end of Part I, I hope I have made clear the complexities we face as individuals (Chapter 1) and as collectivities (Chapter 2). We still need to go beyond mono-dimensional approaches and embrace our multilayered reality. We must also learn how to engage in complex multiple perspectives coaching in practice. Global coaching aims to prepare us for the journey and facilitate the transformation.

In Part II, we will first explore the six essential perspectives and ways to coach from each. In Part III, we will examine the links between these perspectives and between the different layers in our reality (from the individual to the societal). The holographic model and the complexity paradigm will help us understand this deep connectivity. We will then be equipped as coaches to address complex challenges and play our part in raising global consciousness and enabling sustainable progress.

NOTES

1. Furthermore, the reader interested in team coaching will find useful information in Clutterbuck, 2007. More has been published on one-to-one coaching in general and executive coaching in particular, including Stober and Grant, 2006; Passmore, 2006; Megginson and Clutterbuck, 2005; Wilson, 2007; Whitmore, 2002; and Downey, 2003.
2. Adapted from Rosinski, "The Applications of Coaching Across Cultures," 2003.
3. See Rosinski, 2003, 85–89.
4. The cynics might argue that the big size obliged the government to save the financial institution. It still resulted in thousands of job losses and costs for tax-paying citizens. See more in Engdahl, 2008.
5. These notions are neither neutral nor universal. Authenticity and sustainability are cultural values. Think for example of people (including great artists like the late Serge Gainsbourg) who indulge in unhealthy lifestyles, preferring to "live in the moment" without worrying about the long-term consequences. Some make a point of resisting the cultural "politically correct" health imperatives. That is what is meaningful to them. Coaches should be clear about what is truly important to them, what they can accept or not, and ensure there is sufficient alignment with their potential coachees' aspirations.
6. The prevailing theory that the earth's climate is changing dramatically due to human activity is increasingly challenged. *The Economist* argues that global warming is a serious threat and that politicians worldwide need to take steps to avert it, while also claiming that climate change is not a certainty. "Prevailing theories must be constantly tested against evidence, and refined, and more evidence collected, and the theories tested again. That is the job of the scientists" ("Climate Change—A Heated Debate," 2009). In any event, reducing pollution across the globe should remain an important goal, and the search for truth should continue.
7. Reprinted with permission of the author, Peter Horton, from "Peter Buys an Electric Car: When a Local Actor Falls in Love With the EV1, Little Does He Know He's About to Enter GM's Twilight Zone," *LA Times*, 8 July 2003.
8. Peter Horton could not recall the specific reason for the small 4-unit difference between the two figures. He told me the target for obtaining the pass kept diminishing as well, while the EV1 program was delayed. GM was the leader then and, instead, could have taken advantage of its technological advance. Phone conversation with the author. 19 April 2010.

9. See *www.generationev.com*. Retrieved 18 June 2009.
10. See Mailhes, 2009.
11. *Le Soir* 12 August 2009, p. 29.
12. Among the other books, let me mention Kassirer, 2004; Even and Debré, 2004; and Borch-Jacobsen, 2009.
13. See Wilson, 2009.
14. My coachee prefers to remain anonymous, which is why I have modified his first name. He is keen, however, that I share his view.
15. Reproduced with the kind permission of the BCCCC (granted on 17 August 2009 by Peggy Connolly, Director of Marketing and Communications).
16. See Smith, 1776/1937.
17. E-mail 23 December 2008. The text is from an unknown author.
18. In Belgium in the 1980s, journalist Jean-Claude Defossé launched a popular TV show called *Big Unnecessary Works*. Viewers discovered, for example, roads leading to nowhere, bridges disconnected from roads, and superfluous constructions.
19. But *The Economist* goes on: "For these reasons, it will never happen in America. Frank talk about energy policy is rare. Politicians hate to admit that anything they plan to do will cause pain to any voter . . . . The Congressional Budget Office estimates that a 15 percent cut in CO_2 emissions will cost the average American household $1,600 a year. If politicians pretend they can save the planet at no cost, they risk a backlash when people realize they were fibbing" (12).
20. Our ecological footprint is the measure of our human demand on the earth's ecosystems, compared with the earth's capacity to regenerate. The World Wildlife Fund has an online tool that allows us to calculate our ecological footprint and decide on specific actions to reduce it. See *http://footprint.wwf.org.uk*.

PART II

Exploring the Six Perspectives

CHAPTER 3

The Physical Perspective— Stimulating Health and Fitness

The physical perspective aims at actively nurturing the body, our precious yet fragile foundation.

Health and fitness are the foundation for all else. When we take good care of our bodies, we are fully alive and in contact with our vital energy. We are more resistant to illnesses and damaging stress. We are happier and can sustain high performance levels. We are more able to serve others.

Yet most tend to ignore the physical perspective altogether in coaching. (For example, when I ask workshop participants how they would help Marie—see Chapter 1—they seldom evoke the physical perspective.)

The problem sometimes begins with coaches themselves. Some even ignore their *own* physical well-being.

I have had the chance to coach several exceptions: one executive was an excellent tennis player, a second was running marathons, and another was jogging with colleagues at lunch. They all benefited from the serenity gained from these activities, not to mention the camaraderie built at work through sport.

I personally work with a fitness trainer twice a week to build muscular endurance, strength, and power, complemented with proprioception and stretching. My schedule is built around those sessions, which I manage to rarely cancel. Moreover, I regularly bike, typically with a 50–100 km ride during the weekend (except during the cold winter!). In addition but less frequently, I play tennis, kayak, swim, et cetera. I get plenty of sleep and carefully choose the food I eat. Far from restraining my freedom, this life hygiene actually opens new possibilities. Healthy food can be tasty and exercise is pleasant. Being in good shape makes life much easier and more enjoyable.

Sadly, many people miss out on this opportunity. Rather than living in a mindful fashion (see Chapter 8—spiritual perspective), they seem to be on autopilot mode. In a plane, I am struck that the majority, without thinking any further, simply eats whatever food is presented by the airline. This food is mostly junk made of trans-heavy and saturated fats, salt, and high-glycemic index sugar. Travelling in Australia, I experienced a rare occasion when apples were offered instead. People ate these nourishing fruits, as they would have eaten unhealthy cakes or crackers.

The figures are alarming: over 80 percent of adults over 30 in the U.S. are overweight or obese (over 50 percent obese), and respectively over 70 percent/30 percent in the UK and 50 percent/10 percent in France (about 30 percent/3 percent in Japan). It has become a worldwide crisis, concerning more and more children.

As global coaches, we can't be experts in fitness and nutrition but this domain is so important that we need to become more knowledgeable. We need to learn the specifics, beyond the usual advice—useful but too superficial: "You should exercise more"; "You should eat five servings of fruits and vegetables each day." Moreover, just as we refer to effective psychotherapists and psychiatrists when coaching is not the (only) answer, we should be able to collaborate with good nutritionists and effective fitness trainers to best serve our coachess.[2]

In this chapter, I will focus in particular on nutrition and fitness training. I will share solid evidence-based findings from reputable experts. However, the regimens I'll propose don't constitute the sole path to health and good shape. For example, strength and power training, when performed correctly, brings numerous benefits. It complements other sports that invariably emphasize certain muscles to the detriment of others. Still, your physician and fitness trainers may recommend other methods best adapted to your unique situation. Likewise, your nutritionist is best positioned to give you individualized advice. However, while some coaches might leave the matter completely up to experts, I want to share general principles and suggest a concrete possible path.

It is easy to become confused with the plethora of books and articles on nutrition. Ruthless businesspeople target the overweight, promising miracles with no effort thanks to supposedly wonder pills (which will sometimes lead to disasters—a case of kidney failure comes to mind). Some fanciful regimes may sound attractive but are not based on serious scientific evidence. For example, rather than burning fat, the low-carbohydrate diet eliminates body water, which will be regained afterwards with damaging effects: you may take a "swollen and puffy" appearance and in some cases be at risk for heart failure (Willcox, Willcox, and Suzuki, 2001, 51). Fortunately, an evidence-based approach has been developed, and leading researchers in nutrition worldwide tend to agree on some important basic principles.

LESSONS FROM OKINAWA

For centuries, humans have been looking in vain for the fountain of youth. Eternal life remains elusive, but there is one place where people consistently achieve a healthy longevity: Okinawa, an island in the southern part of Japan. This is where the highest proportion of centenarians and super-centenarians (110 years old and over) lives. Moreover, this is also where the highest proportion of elderly citizens can actually enjoy their old age without being plagued by debilitating diseases and lack of mobility. If you think that reaching a very old age necessarily means surviving bedridden, you may want to reconsider.

The Willcox brothers (Willcox, Willcox, and Suzuki, 2001, 13) were startled when they met their first centenarian, a man named Nakajimasan. When they reached his home, they found a sprightly man who appeared to be about 70, casually dressed and sorting through gardening tools. They asked to speak to his father. Mistake! This energetic man was Nakajimasan. A subsequent full geriatric assessment confirmed he was in outstanding health, to which the old man exclaimed "Chaganjuu," which in the Okinawan dialect means perfect health.

The karate master Seikichisensei became a hero when, at 96, he accepted a combat with Katsuo Tokashiki, a former world boxing champion (flyweight) now in his 30s. The old master, with remarkable agility, dodged all blows. After 20 minutes, the young champion slowed just a little and lowered his guard very briefly. That was enough for Seikichisensei to launch a decisive strike. The boxer, stunned and incredulous, uttered: "Yarareta, yarareta . . . !" (He beat me, he beat me!), to which the 96-year-old replied, jokingly: "He did not have enough experience yet to beat me . . ." (Curtay, 2006, 66–67).

If these individuals are particularly impressive, elders in Okinawa overall enjoy what may be the world's longest average life expectancy (81.2 years) as well as the longest health expectancy, delaying or sometimes escaping the chronic diseases of aging, including dementia, cardiovascular disease (coronary heart disease and stroke), and cancer (Okinawa Centenarian Study, 2008).

A 25-year scientific study led by Dr. Makoto Suzuki investigated the reasons for this exceptional record. The Willcox brothers brought this knowledge to America (Willcox, Willcox, and Suzuki, 2001) and Dr. Jean-Paul Curtay made it known in France (Curtay, 2006). In sum, four interconnected factors are at play:

- Nutrition: a low-calorie, plant-based diet high in unrefined carbohydrates
- Physical exercise: keeping fit in all components of fitness (anaerobic, flexibility, and aerobic) through the martial arts, traditional dance, gardening, and walking
- Community: personal relationships, solidarity, reciprocity
- Spirituality: living a balanced lifestyle in tune with nature's way, nurturing your "ki" or "life energy," deep respect for others, healing rituals that celebrate successful aging

Some might dismiss these findings and attribute Okinawan's lasting health to nature (genes) rather than nurture (lifestyle). But the research findings are unambiguous. When Okinawans live abroad and adopt a Western diet and lifestyle, their life expectancy drops dramatically and they become prone to illnesses like their fellow habitants. One of these numerous migration studies involved Okinawans in Brazil (Willcox, Willcox, and Suzuki, 2004). Sadly, younger generations in Okinawa have a lower life expectancy than their elders: the threshold corresponds to the Americanization that occurred after World War II when youngsters were seduced by greasy hamburgers, sweetened sodas, and other junk food.

The good news is that we can all do something about lifestyle factors, and make the most of the hand we have received by playing the cards wisely.

NUTRITION

Findings about Okinawan nutrition are remarkably consistent with other research, such as notably compiled by Dr. David Servan-Schreiber in his two French bestsellers: *Guérir* (*Heal*), which explains how nutrition and physical activity (among other non-pharmaceutical approaches) can combat stress, anxiety, and depression; and *Anticancer*, which describes how these lifestyle factors can help prevent and fight against cancer (complementing the traditional approaches of surgery, chemotherapy, and radiation therapy).

Serious research findings highlight the potent therapeutic properties of several foods. Servan-Schreiber explains how, for example, garlic, onions, and cabbage help inhibit the growth of cancer cells, and how curcuma and green tea block angiogenesis (new blood vessels feeding cancer cells). Many of these nutrients could make excellent drugs,[3] but, sadly, pharmaceutical companies cannot secure patents for these natural products and have little incentive to promote these "competitors." It is time for our governments and public institutions to play their part in educating the public (starting with children at school), funding healthcare research (rather than over-relying on the pharmaceutical industry), and regulating the food sector much more strictly, just as they have done (to some extent) with the tobacco industry: banning advertisement for unhealthy products, banning junk food from schools, obliging full transparency about content, forbidding false claims (sugar-laden cereals branded as fitness food), et cetera.

The good news is that the information is largely available to those who make the effort to find it. Coaching is invaluable in helping people learn self-responsibility and move from autopilot mode to living consciously and healthily.

The media are now raising awareness about nutrition. But since the market wants it, the food industry—by and large—continues to make junk food detrimental to the environment and to our health (using pesticides, hormones, antibiotics, trans fats, and other toxic products), taking advantage of lax legislation. See *Toxic* (Reymond, 2007).

Companies genuinely committed to do good may have an edge. A vision to promote health can inspire change and lead to seizing opportunities before the laggards who wait until change is demanded by the authorities or the public. The Alpro company's success exemplifies the former: "Alpro is the European pioneer in the development of mainstream soya-based food and drinks. For over 25 years, we have been championing a healthier, more sustainable way of producing and selling delicious products that conserve the unique nutritional value of soya beans."[4] The bio/organic lineage is booming in Western Europe and offers protection against harmful pesticides overused in industrial agriculture and insufficient quality of animal nutrition frequent in factory farming.

It is beyond the scope of this book to provide thorough nutrition advice. A nutritionist, along with the excellent books already mentioned, can help individuals devise a diet that takes their unique medical circumstances into account. However, let me briefly share some of the key conclusions from these experts, which are valid in most situations. Much more can be said but this will either get you started and/or serve as an essential reminder plus checklist.

- *Eat a variety of food, mainly from plant sources.* Notably "get five colors on your table" (red, yellow, blue-green, white, and black) to provide a variety of nutrients[5] as well as visual appeal inciting you to savor the food (rather than gulp it!).

- *Limit calorie intake.* This is "the healthiest approach to eating" (Willcox, Willcox, and Suzuki, 2004, 12). Cutting back on calories significantly reduces cancer risk and helps extend your life span. Low-calorie diets result in the lowered production of cell-damaging *free radicals*. When your body produces energy from food, it creates unstable molecules (free radicals, also called *oxidants*) that damage cells. Your body has natural defenses, including its own *antioxidants*, and other defenses come from the antioxidants in your food. However, the goal is not to be perpetually hungry or become anorexic! Instead, the trick is to eat a high-complex-carbohydrate, high-fiber diet. You get full on low-calorie, antioxidant-rich, minimally processed ("whole") food.[6]

- A useful concept is the *caloric density* (CD), which refers to "the number of calories in a specific amount of any given food," usually based on a 1-gram unit.[7] You can easily calculate the CD when looking at food labels. Divide the calorie count (expressed in kcal[8]) by the weight (expressed in grams). Often, the calorie count is already mentioned for 100 grams, which means you simply divide that number by 100 to obtain the CD. Furthermore, tables are available for non-packaged foods.[9]

  - *Featherweights* are foods with a CD of less than 0.7. You should build meals on a featherweight foundation. This includes many fruits, vegetables, and tofu.

  - *Lightweights* have a CD between 0.8 and 1.5. These foods should be eaten in moderation. This includes white flaky fish, cooked whole grains such as rice and pasta, and cooked beans.

  - *Middleweights* have a CD of 1.6 to 3.0. These should be eaten in relatively small portions. Fatty fish and hummus are examples.

  - *Heavyweights* have a CD of more than 3.0. They should be eaten sparingly. This includes many processed foods (processing frequently removes fiber and water, while adding sugar and fat) that can often best be avoided as well as some beneficial foods (such as nuts and omega-3-rich cooking oils).[10]

The brothers Willcox contrast the same 280 calories, typically eaten in North America in the form of a regular hamburger with cheese (100 grams, CD 2.8) and in Okinawa as stir-fried vegetables with rice and miso soup (500 grams, CD 0.6). In other words, you can eat more, feel fuller, and weigh less by adopting the Okinawa way!

Note also that muscles burn more calories at rest than fat,[11] which should encourage you to engage in strength and power training (which I will discuss later), and that "when more calories are consumed than expended, the excess calories are stored as fat."[12]

- *Eat at least seven servings of vegetables and fruits daily.* They are full of nutrients, yet contain few calories. They decrease your long-term risk for heart disease, cancer, stroke, hypertension, and obesity. As one of the main sources of antioxidants, they keep you looking younger.[13]

- *Eat six or more servings of grain-based foods daily.* Grain-based foods include whole-grain bread, brown (whole-grain) rice, quinoa, and bulgur.

- *Complex, whole carbohydrates found in grain-based foods, fruits, and vegetables should be the basis of your diet.* They contain more nutrients and more fiber, and are lower on the *Glycemic Index*[14] than processed food (white bread, refined sugar—mostly sucrose or table sugar, doughnuts, crackers, et cetera). Carbohydrates constitute the indispensable clean-burning fuel for your muscles.[15] The lower Glycemic Index variety will slow the absorption of glucose in your blood, which reduces the high-lows, is easier on your pancreas, lessens the risk of contracting Type II diabetes as well as hormone-dependent cancers and coronary heart diseases.

- *Eat good fats and avoid bad fats.* Good fats are essential, being notably vital for the healing and repair of cells and tissues, as backbone of all our body's hormones, and to absorb key vitamins. Incidentally, when fat circulates in the blood, it is called *cholesterol*.

    - The good fats come in two varieties: the *monounsaturated fatty acids* (MUFA) and the *polyunsaturated fats* (PUFA). The former (notably found in avocados, olive oil, and almonds) is most resistant to attack from free radicals. The latter come in two varieties: *omega-6* (in poultry, sunflower oil) and *omega-3* (in canola oil, walnuts, sardines, mackerel).

To be more precise PUFA are good when the *ratio omega-6/omega-3* is between 3 and 10 (which is the case with elderly Okinawans 3–4/1 but not with Americans 10–20/1). This unhealthy ratio promotes *inflammation*,[16] blood clotting, and possibly cancer growth. This means you typically have to lower your omega-6 intake and increase your omega-3 intake.

- The bad fats include the *saturated fatty acids* (SFA) and the "ugliest" fats, the *trans fatty acids* (TFA). It is unsaturated fat *trans*formed into saturated fat by the chemical process of hydrogenation (hence the appellation *hydrogenated fats*). You should avoid this potent artery clogger (raising your bad cholesterol LDL and lowering your good cholesterol HDL[17]), which is hidden in most cookies, margarine, deep-fried fast food, and potato chips. The saturated fats found notably in red meat, whole dairy products, and palm oil are still harmful, raising the bad cholesterol. Besides increasing the risk for cardiovascular diseases, evidence suggests a link with hormone-dependent cancers as well.

- *Eat three flavonoid foods daily.* These plant compounds are powerful antioxidants. They are notably found in soy products (e.g., tofu), onions, and Japanese green tea.

- *Eat three calcium foods daily.* Calcium is known to strengthen the bones and prevent osteoporosis. If dairy products are excellent sources of calcium, they are best consumed in moderation and in the low-fat or non-fat versions. The Willcox brothers mention research showing how too much protein in dairy products tends to leach calcium out of bones. Calcium-fortified foods and some green vegetables (kale, broccoli, cabbage) provide an excellent source of calcium.[18]

- *Eat reasonable amounts of proteins.* The amino acids that make up proteins are necessary for the body to build and repair tissues.[19] They are found in meat, fish, dairy products, soy, and nuts. Westerners (and particularly the Americans with the large portions often served in restaurants) tend to eat way too much protein, which can lead to common health concerns such as high blood pressure and arterial aging. Protein by-products such as ammonia and urea are highly toxic. This being said, the appropriate amount depends on your stage of life, muscle mass, and activity level. If you regularly work out in a gym and want to build up your muscles, you will certainly need more protein than if you don't. Proper balance is essential, neither too little (malnutrition), nor too much. You can also get healthier proteins, from fish and tofu[20] (and chicken to a lesser extent) rather than red meat. Proteins help with satiety[21] and help you feel fuller longer.[22]

- *Eat unsalted; instead, spice up your food with healing herbs.* Salt is one of the scandals of industrialized food. It is typically added to packaged food as a flavor enhancer (which I guess is understandable to make bad food somehow more palatable!). Salt tends to raise blood pressure, which is harmful for arteries.[23] Salt can advantageously be replaced by a variety of tasty and healing herbs: curcuma, ginger, and galanga have potent antioxidant and anti-inflammatory properties. (Small amounts of pepper and olive oil help absorb their active principles. You should best add the herbs when the food is cooked.) Mint, thyme, marjoram, basil, rosemary, parsley, celery, garlic, onions, cinnamon, ginger, as well as lemon juice, all have interesting properties. You can use tops (e.g., carrot tops) rather than throw them away.

- *Drink fresh water and tea; Avoid sodas and alcohol.*
  - Regularly drink water and carry a small bottle with you. In water, you usually want high levels of magnesium, calcium, and bicarbonates; low levels of fluorine and sodium (except if hypotension); and as little nitrates as possible. Japanese green teas are richest in antioxidant. Jasmin tea is appreciated in Okinawa (you can add curcuma, lemon, cinnamon, et cetera.). Avoid drinking extremely hot tea (cancer of the oropharynx and esophagus is likely due to recurrent heat injury). Herbal teas have good properties too: chamomile helps alleviate heartburn, indigestion, and insomnia.
  - Avoid sugar-laden sodas.[24] Freshly squeezed fruit juices (i.e., squeezed right before you drink it versus hours ago) are more valuable. Decline industrialized juices with anything less than 100 percent fruits (i.e., with added sugar).
  - Opinions differ regarding wine. A glass of red wine at lunch is good for you according to Servan-Schreiber and Curtay (antioxidant polyphenols and resveratrol protect against cardiovascular diseases and cancer) but is not recommended by the Willcox brothers for whom the French paradox (less cardiovascular diseases despite a diet that is not ideal and smoking) is still inexplicable. Could cultural differences be at play here? In general, alcohol is best avoided. It is high in calories (with risk of excess weight and accelerating aging), damages tissues, and destroys neurons when consumed in excess.

Alcohol suppresses inhibition and temporarily reduces stress, which explains its bleak appeal for those who abuse this substance in place of dealing head on with their difficulties and seeking help.

- *Eat in reasonable quantities.* Okinawans eat until they are 80 percent full. This prevents overeating. (It takes about twenty minutes for the stretch receptors in the stomach to tell the brain how full you really are.) It avoids a vicious circle of stretching your stomach each time to accommodate the extra food. However, since I personally don't know when my stomach is 80 percent full and don't like to feel hungry, I prefer to adhere to the following recommendation: stop eating "when you feel that first twinge of fullness."[25] You can still eat plenty of food (without excess) by favoring low calorie foods as discussed earlier. Moreover, opt for light meals in the evening. This will enhance the quality of your sleep.[26]

Incidentally, realizing that good food brings you life, carefully choosing what you will eat and not eat to respect your body, and taking the time to prepare and enjoy the food (presenting it in an aesthetic manner, savoring its taste before swallowing it) all have to do with the spiritual perspective, which we will discuss in Chapter 8. This attitude entails abandoning autopilot mode and taking responsibility for your health, cultivating a loving attitude and a mindful presence, and making thoughtful choices.

Choice means that when you dine out in restaurants, you can ask that sauce is placed on the side, that fish is cooked in olive oil, that vegetables are steamed, that no salt is added, et cetera. You can ask for fruits instead of the cake that is normally on the menu. If you feel embarrassed in front of your friends, you might consider turning to Chapter 5, where we will discuss how to develop an assertive outlook! Some restaurants will do their best to accommodate your requests and others might be more reluctant. You will know where to go back or not in the future.

Importantly, you should not turn your discipline and rigor about healthy eating into an obsession. For example, avoiding saturated fats does not mean that you have to give up all products that contain some saturated fat. I do enjoy eating Belgian dark chocolate (86 percent cacao)[27] and occasional waffles. Likewise, during my last visit to Prague, I did not renounce an incredibly delicious cheesecake. Moderation is the key. Striving for perfection is a battle you can only lose, and which can paradoxically lead to disorders. This maniacal obsession for healthy foods has actually a name, *orthorexia*. I am not advocating austerity. Reasonably healthy eating is a pleasure. Meals constitute ideal occasions to take the time and share a privileged moment with family, friends, or colleagues. Meals can be a ceremony.

You will find much more information in the books I have recommended. Let me mention here the importance of *magnesium* (found in mineral water, whole cereals, soy, green vegetables, nuts and almonds, et cetera). Curtay (2006) places this nutrient alongside antioxidants and omega-3 fatty acids in their crucial role against degradation and illnesses associated with aging. Magnesium is particularly helpful for managing psychological stress (another example of mind-material connection), for regulating what penetrates in our cells, and for protecting us against inflammation.

The good news is that many dietary habits are easy to change. For example, if you stop adding salt and sugar to your foods, your body eventually will stop craving them, and you will develop a heightened appreciation for food's natural flavors.

FITNESS TRAINING

As a coach, I often meet with executives who don't play sports or engage in any kind of exercise at all. Some enjoyed sports when they were young but claim they don't have time anymore. For them, the first step is to gradually pick it up again, after a medical checkup. For example, a female senior executive is now swimming again, twice a week, as a result of our coaching. Although it requires a personal discipline, she feels better and less stressed-out. Of course, other executives exercise regularly. Either way, coachees do not often evoke spontaneously the importance of physical exercise and its link to their well-being and professional performance. The global coaching framework allows coaches to suggest that connection and to encourage coachees to undertake a program of overall fitness training in addition to any sports they may already be practicing.

Fitness training includes several components, each with its own benefits. Many people ignore one or more of these components. For example, some people jog regularly to develop or maintain their cardiovascular endurance, but they ignore strength training for their muscles, which become weaker.

Coaches should have a good understanding of general fitness principles, engage in training themselves, and be able to recommend personal trainers, whose physical work with the coachee can complement the executive coaching process. Practically, this comprehensive approach is reserved for executives eager to make the most of their potential to reach higher levels of well-being and performance at work.

Next I will explore the following interconnected domains: cardiovascular training, strength and power training, balance training, and stretching.

Cardiovascular Training

First, we need to distinguish *aerobic* from *anaerobic* training. Aerobic exercise is intended to "improve the efficiency of the body's cardiovascular system in absorbing and transporting oxygen" (*The New Oxford Dictionary of English*, 1998). In anaerobic exercise, muscles obtain their energy from sources other than oxygen, particularly adenosine tri-phosphate, creatine phosphate and glycogen. This energy accumulated in the muscles is readily available but quickly consumed (Bosch, 2007, 31). Running long distance at a moderate pace, which you can sustain, is an aerobic activity; sprinting at high speed is an anaerobic exercise.

Regular and adequate aerobic exercise increases endurance level: the cardiovascular system transports more oxygen to the muscles, and exercisers can keep going for a longer period and at a higher intensity. Conversely, I am shocked to see some middle-aged people so unfit that they are already out of breath when they climb a few stairs or walk uphill.

Cardiac frequency indicates training intensity. It is also an indication of your physical shape. When you can achieve the same performance with an inferior level of cardiac pulses, you are generally in better shape. Of course, other factors can influence the cardiac frequency. For example, warm weather (particularly above 25°C) implies an additional charge for the body and leads to higher cardiac frequencies (at rest and during the effort). Similarly, insufficient hydrating raises the cardiac frequency during the exercise, which should incidentally remind us to drink sufficiently (Bosch, 2007, 42).

Doctors use an effort test to determine maximal cardiac frequency (CF), also called heart rate (HR).[28] During the test, a person undertakes progressively more strenuous exercise on a treadmill or stationary bike, from an easy walk/pedaling to exhaustion. CF max appears to be a genetic individual characteristic; it diminishes with age[29] but does not change with fitness training. (See Bosch, 2007, 34.) However, training can help lower resting CF.

Karvonen's formula can be used to determine targeted CF during the effort:

percent (CF max – CF rest) + CF rest = CF effort

CF effort can actually best be measured using a cardio-frequency meter (comprising a sensor and a watch).

The following example shows how training intensity can be calculated using Karvonen's formula. If someone's CF rest is 52 and CF max is 200, and if he or she wants to train at 70 percent of maximum capacity, the targeted CF effort should be 156 (i.e., 70 percent × (200 − 52) + 52 = 156).

Different training intensities offer specific benefits.

Type of training[30]	Approximate percentage of maximum cardiac frequency capacity
Recovery /warm up	Below 60%
Aerobic endurance	60%–80% Green zone
Aerobic–anaerobic endurance	80%–90% Orange zone
Anaerobic endurance	Over 90% Red zone

To appreciate the differences, you will find a brief (and simplified) physiological explanation in the following table.[31]

Chemical reactions in the green, orange, and red zones

The energy needed to run, bike, or perform any other endurance activity is produced through chemical reactions that transform the adenosine triphosphate (ATP) into adenosine diphosphate (ADP), which liberates one phosphate atom. There are two main types of chemical reactions:

- The *aerobic reactions*, in which the ATP are produced using lipids (fats) and oxygen

  $Lipids + O_2 + ADP \rightarrow CO_2 + ATP + H_2O$

  CO_2 as you exhale and H_2O (water) as you sweat are produced alongside the necessary energy.

  This is the *green zone*. The lipids are a sort of diesel fuel: we can sustain our effort for a long time as we typically have a lot of lipids available. As with all these equations, reality is more complex. We also use glucides (carbohydrates) particularly at the beginning; the reaction with lipids takes some time to be in place; but the point is that lipids eventually constitute the primary fuel in the green zone. Furthermore no lactic acid (almost none) is produced, so muscles don't become stiff.

- The *anaerobic reactions*, in which the ATP is produced with glucides and without oxygen

  $Glucides + ADP \rightarrow lactic\ acid + ATP$

  This is the *red zone*. Lactic acid is the side product. Muscles stiffen and contract. Furthermore, the reserves of glucides are fairly limited (first in the blood, then the glycogen). This effort can therefore not be sustained for very long. The glucides are a sort of super-fuel, which is quickly available for rapid runs and accelerations but inadequate for long distances.

Furthermore, there is an *orange zone* in between the green and the red:

- In the aerobic–anaerobic zone, the lactic acid produced by the anaerobic reaction is recycled

Lactid acid $+ O_2 + ADP \rightarrow CO_2 + ATP + H_2O$

The combination of the two reactions when the recycling exactly compensates the production of the lactic acid is

Glucides $+ O_2 + ADP \rightarrow CO_2 + ATP + H_2O$

In the orange zone, the limited reserves of glucides are used but the absence of lactic acids allows us to sustain the effort for longer than in the red zone. The effort can also be prolonged because, in this in-between zone, fats are burned as well: the aerobic reaction takes place alongside the two reactions above.

The cardiac frequencies corresponding to these zones are not absolutes.[32] The percentages in this table are typical for a well-trained sportsperson.[33] The red zone threshold could be reached at 65–70 percent for untrained individuals[34] rather than 90 percent.

The heart rate method is recommended for monitoring exercise intensity.[35] As a rule of thumb, 80 percent of the cardiovascular training should be in the green zone, 15 percent in the orange zone and 5 percent in the red zone. However, a jogger will instinctually run only 10 percent in the green zone, 70 percent in the orange, and 10 percent in the red.[36] More is not always better. When training too much and too hard, there is a danger of *overtraining*, which actually leads to a decline in performance and can cause fatigue (that is not simply remedied with rest and dietary manipulation), emotional instability, depressed immune function and so on.[37] Pushing too hard is largely a cultural phenomenon (spurred by a propensity for control and competition, as defined in Chapter 7). Kenyan runners, on the other hand, are more in touch with pleasure and tend to avoid this pitfall.[38]

Training in the green zone promotes a healthy cardiovascular foundation and endurance by[39]

- strengthening and enlarging the heart muscle,[40] to improve its pumping efficiency and reduce the resting heart rate
- improving blood circulation and reducing blood pressure
- improving capillarization of the heart and skeletal muscles, by increasing the absolute number of capillaries and the capillary density (number of capillaries for a given cross-sectional area of muscle).[41] (Experienced runners have about 40 percent more capillarization than people who don't train.)

- allowing muscular fibers to increase their stock of oxidative enzymes (which facilitate the necessary chemical reactions using oxygen), glycogen, and functional fat
- increasing the number of mitochondria[42]
- burning fat
- improving muscles' ability to use fats during exercise and preserve intramuscular glycogen
- enhancing the speed at which muscles recover from high-intensity exercise

Training in the orange zone is beneficial for[43]

- adding fun and variety in training: you accelerate without sprinting
- adapting the body to the faster, yet still comfortable, pace used in long-distance competition (e.g., marathons and half marathons)
- training the body to smoothly transition from fat metabolism to carbohydrate metabolism (the latter is used primarily in the red zone)

Training in the red zone is useful for[44]

- developing the body for high-intensity and short-duration efforts (e.g., sprinting, closing up a gap, accelerating on a hill)
- helping the body to better tolerate the presence of lactic acid[45]
- building up the heart (Your left ventricle pumps blood to your body. Your heart must pump harder to supply blood to your muscles. The muscular wall of your left ventricle will thicken so your heart can deal with the increased blood pressure.)

However, this anaerobic training

- consumes glucides and quickly depletes glycogen reserves
- is reserved for experienced sportsmen and sportswomen; endurance should be developed first

Several activities can be considered for cardiovascular training, either indoor or outdoor. I prefer bicycling over jogging. It is smoother on my knees than high-impact running. You need to choose what is right for you and may want to consult a sport's physician or orthopedist to determine that. Vary the activities: swimming, cross-country skiing, skating, Nordic walking, et cetera. Try the stationary bicycle, which you might use while listening to music, watching sports on television, or a movie on an iPod. A friend of mine devised that effective and pleasant method, which allows her to train regularly for about 90 minutes each time. When the weather is good though, she will train outside and enjoy the sights, sounds, and smells of nature. Indoors, I also recommend the rowing machine and elliptical trainer. If you use the treadmill, beware of its danger: avoid distractions that might take you off track and cause serious injury! And of course some will fancy aerobics classes (high– or low-impact) with its rapid stepping patterns performed to music.

Strength and Power Training

Strength and power training (also referred to as *weight training* or *resistance training* (RT)) is the use of resistance to muscular movement to develop the endurance, size, strength, and power of skeletal muscles.[46]

Muscular *strength* is "the maximal force that a muscle or muscle group can generate" while "maximal power (generally referred to as *power*), the explosive aspect of strength, is the product of strength and speed of movement." In other words:

power = force × distance/time where force = strength and distance/time = where force = speed

"Maximal muscular power is the functional application of both strength and speed of movement. It is the key component in most athletic performance."[47]

RT used to be performed by select athletes and body builders and has now grown in popularity. American health organizations, including the American College of Sports Medicine and the American Heart Association recommend resistance training "for most populations including adolescents, healthy adults, the elderly, and clinical populations (e.g., those individuals with cardiovascular disease, neuromuscular disease)" (Kraemer and Ratamess, 2004, 674).

In 2009, the American College of Sports Medicine (ACSM) articulated the multiple health benefits of RT and proposed progression guidelines. (See Ratamess et al., 2009.) They chose a rigorous evidence-based approach, classifying each recommendation with a grade of A, B, C, or D based on the quantity and quality of evidence.

RT, when incorporated into a comprehensive fitness program, improves cardiovascular function, reduces the risk factors associated with coronary

heart disease and non-insulin-dependent diabetes, prevents osteoporosis, may reduce the risk of colon cancer, promotes weight loss and maintenance, improves dynamic stability and preserves functional capacity, and fosters psychological well-being.

These impressive benefits explain why I advocate RT as well as cardiovascular training to complement executive coaching. "Mens sana in corpore sano" as the Greeks said long ago! And here again, coaches should set the example, so we have both the credibility and the experience to make the case.

However, engaging in RT should not be done lightly. There are many interconnected variables to consider in RT. This complexity requires calling upon an expert to optimize your training and avoid injuries. I prefer professionals with a general physical therapy degree and a specialization in RT. A competent personal trainer should also demonstrate good global coaching qualities, particularly effective time management (managerial perspective), relational qualities (psychological perspective), intercultural expertise (e.g., leveraging control and humility—see Chapter 7), and even spiritual intelligence (teaching presence to oneself when exercising by being fully present him- or herself). Incidentally, this exemplifies the holographic principle of the whole being in the part (the emotional, cultural, and spiritual intelligences within the physical frame).

The ACSM stresses that RT "needs to be *individualized*" (ACSM's italics, Kraemer and Ratamess, 2004, 674). The individualization involves several steps.

1. At-risk individuals (e.g., those with a physical ailment) should obtain *medical clearance*. This will ensure that "RT is beneficial rather than harmful to those individuals with predisposing injuries or illnesses" (675). The clearance may not be a simple yes or no but could highlight those exercises that could (and should) be included and those that should be avoided. I have practiced RT with injuries and have been amazed by what can still be trained. Some physicians with insufficient competence in this area might unfortunately recommend stopping altogether when selectivity would be more effective.

2. The second step involves a *needs analysis*. What health/injury concerns should be taken into account? What type of equipment should be favored? What training frequency and time constraints? What muscle groups should be trained in particular? What type of muscle actions are needed (e.g., concentric, eccentric, isometric, plyometric)?

3. The *program goals* should be determined next. Since, in this book, RT is integrated with global coaching aimed at leaders and professionals rather than professional athletes, moderate improvements rather than maximization in endurance, hypertrophy (increasing the size of muscles), strength, and power will be sought. RT sessions, completed with balance training and stretching, will also enable greater stability (hence reduced risk of falls and injuries) and flexibility. Additional goals might be improvement in general health (e.g., reduce body fat, lower blood pressure, reduce stress) and rehabilitation from injuries.

4. The *program design* is finally established. Just like with sound coaching, the design is meant to be flexibly and creatively adapted during sessions to adjust to particular circumstances (e.g., form of the day, availability of equipment).

The ACSM highlights three foremost principles of RT progression[48]:

1. *Progressive overload*: the gradual increase of stress placed upon the body during exercise training

2. *Specificity*: all training adaptations are "specific" to the stimulus applied

3. *Variation or periodization*: entails the systematic process of altering one or more program variable(s) over time to allow for the training stimulus to remain challenging and effective. (Because the human body adapts quickly to an RT program, at least some changes are needed for continual progression to occur.)

Your personal trainer can adjust multiple variables for optimum results. The following table highlights some of the important variables.[49]

Key Program Variables in Resistance Training

- Intensity: refers to the amount of work required to achieve the exercise, and is proportional to the mass of the weight being lifted. The intensity is usually measured as a percentage of 1RM (*1RM* or *one repetition maximum*, representing the maximum weight you can lift just once for a given exercise).[50]

- Volume: "is a summation of the total number of repetitions performed during a training session multiplied by the resistance used (kg) and is reflective of the duration of which muscles are being stressed. Altering training volume can be accomplished by changing the number of exercises performed per session, the number of repetitions (reps) performed per set, or the number of sets per exercise."

(continued on next page)

- Rep(etition): is a single cycle of lifting and lowering a weight in a controlled manner, moving through the form of the exercise (i.e., the topography of movement designed to maximize safety and muscle strength gains).

- Set: consists of several repetitions performed one after another with no break between them with the number of reps per set and sets per exercise depending on the goal of the individual. Incidentally, "X"RM (repetition maximum) is the highest weight one can lift with a maximum number of X repetitions. For example, 10RM = 70 kg means one could perform ten reps maximum at 70 kg.[51]

- Session frequency: refers to how many training sessions are performed per week.

- Muscle actions involved: *isotonic* (dynamic) if a body part is moving against the force, either *concentric* (e.g., going upstairs—squeezing) or *eccentric* (e.g., going downstairs—stretching); *isometric* (static) if a body part is holding still against the force. Let me also mention *plyometrics*, a dynamic action that involves contracting the muscle eccentricly and then immediately after, concentricly.[52]

- Repetition speed/tempo: refers to the contraction velocity. For example a moderate speed could be 1–2 seconds concentric (e.g., bending your biceps against gravity) followed by 1–2 seconds eccentric (e.g., extending it back, resisting gravity).

- Rest periods: recuperation period between sets, exercises, et cetera.

- Muscles: several muscle groups are usually trained including shoulder, chest, back (upper and lower), biceps, triceps, abdominals, thighs, hamstring, and calves. Smaller muscles are typically trained while training these major groups.

- Range of motion: the measurement of the achievable distance between the flexed position and the extended position of a particular joint or muscle group.[53] In RT, the targeted range of motion can vary from the full range to a fixed position.

- Bilateral and unilateral exercises. For example, a two-handed pull-up is a bilateral movement, while a one-arm pull-up is a unilateral movement.

- Single and multi-joint exercises. "Single-joint exercises, such as knee extensions and knee curls, have been used to target specific muscle groups and pose a reduced level of skill and technical involvement. Multiple-joint exercises, such as bench press and squat, require complex neural responses and have generally been regarded more effective for increasing overall muscular strength because they enable a greater magnitude of weight to be lifted" (Ratamess, 200, 691).

- Fixed and free-weight exercises. "A fixed form training device has a fixed range of motion in which a user is unable to deviate from the intended range. Such an example is a leg extension machine in which the movement arm of the equipment only allows a range of motion from extension to flexion and additional movements are restricted by the equipment. A free-form training device allows multiple planes of motion within the intended exercise movement of the machine, although free weight would also qualify as free-form of equipment."[54]

- Energy system involved: strength training exercise is primarily anaerobic. Even while training at a lower intensity (training loads of ~20 RM), anaerobic glycolysis is still the major source of power, although aerobic metabolism makes a small contribution (Knuttgen, 2003). For goals such as rehabilitation, weight loss, and body shaping, lower weights are typically used and aerobic character is added to the exercise.

The ACSM offers general evidence-based guidelines for different category practitioners, from novice (untrained individuals with no RT experience or who have not trained for several years), to intermediate (approximately six months of consistent RT experience) to advanced (years of RT experience). For example, and just referring to intensity, it is recommended that, for the novice, loads correspond to a repetition range of 8–12 RM while intermediate and advanced users should use a wider loading range from 1 to 12 RM.

I am impressed by the variety my personal trainer, Chris Richartz, brings to my workouts. RT, much like coaching, is a science (great trainers are aware of research findings and can put these evidence-based recommendations into practice) and an art (they creatively adapt to situations). Chris is making the one-hour training sessions most productive and enjoyable.

I had done RT before but started again in January 2006 at a basic level, having lost much muscle after an unusual ailment. As a novice again, the emphasis was placed on building endurance. I was very prone to minor injuries and inflammation, and it was very important to tread carefully. If you are out of shape, you will need to be equally careful but the good news is that progression can be spectacular at the beginning. These days, and despite a serious knee injury contracted in early 2007 (falling off a treadmill), which required the graft of a tendon to replace my cross-anterior ligament and a long rehabilitation, I have become much stronger. Chris is able to provide the right challenge so that I keep improving, while respecting my limitations to avoid injuries. My goal is simply, yet imperatively, to be in very good physical shape and to enjoy these sessions, rather than prepare for the Olympic games! Improvement at the advanced stage ("advanced" being always relative of course) is harder to achieve and this is when being capable to play with all training variables is critical. I am surprised to now be able to achieve a 1RM of about 300 kg on the leg press, often training at the maximum weight available on the machine. I am 49 years old and could not have done this at 20, even though I was regularly playing sports. Importantly, this strength improvement materializes in power gain when I am bicycling. Climbing hills is easier, faster, and done with higher gear ratios (i.e., more power, since my circumferential pedal velocity is the same as before).

Although most of your coachees probably don't care about increasing their muscular strength per se, you might want to remember the various health benefits RT entails. In addition to improving the cardiovascular function and enhancing bone density, it does increase your metabolism[55] rate (more so than aerobics), which promotes fat loss. You become less frail and therefore able to avoid some types of physical ailments and disabilities. You improve your posture, muscle tone, and appearance, and feel better.

RT, as a preventive practice, is aligned with coaching aimed at improving performance and well-being. It should be distinguished from physical therapy, which much like psychotherapy, is meant to heal wounds. RT implies a reasonable cost but its benefits make it a sound investment not just for yourself, but also for your organization and for society overall. Like the proverbial apple, RT, as well as cardiovascular training, keeps the doctor away, reducing both medical costs and time away from work to combat illnesses and injuries. These physical activities can be considered good citizenship contributions, at least in countries where the state is covering most of the medical bills!

It is beyond the scope of this book to enter into more details but, to give you a more concrete sense, let me share some of the methods I have experienced with Chris:

- Variety: concentric followed by slower eccentric movement (and even more focus on the eccentric movement if a tendon is slightly inflamed), bilateral and unilateral, various set structures (e.g., pyramid set in which the weight is first increased and then decreased over a series of sets, providing a combination of volume and intensity), et cetera.

- Power training: after doing a series of movements on the leg or bench press at high loads, Chris often gets me to continue the set with a lower intensity but at high velocity. This situation is closer to what I would encounter playing sports: bicycling, tennis, kayak, et cetera. His goal is to help me transfer more muscular strength into functional power.

- Circuit training: while one group of muscles recovers from one set, I train another group. Not only do I accomplish more within one hour, but this swift (yet not hurried) pace provides some aerobic exercise as well.

- Balance training: I perform many exercises in unstable environments using Swiss balls, wobble boards, and BOSU balls. The rationale is the following:

  The body has sensors all around it which sense where parts of the body are even without looking. These sensors are called proprioceptors. If the ankle or lower leg is damaged then the proprioceptors can be damaged also. If you have ever started to turn your ankle over and it has automatically righted itself then this is the proprioceptors working automatically to prevent further injury. In the injured athlete these sensors will not work so well, increasing the chance of re-injuring the leg or ankle. This is why some people once they sprain their ankle, continue to sprain it repeatedly. Using a wobble board on a regular basis can help retrain the proprioceptors and improve coordination, hence preventing further injury. All the athlete has to do is stand on the board and try to keep it horizontal—without the edges touching the floor.[56]

I would add that you don't need to wait to be injured to train the proprioceptors: your stability will be improved. For example, I often exercise my biceps with two feet or just one on the BOSU (furthermore, bilaterally and unilaterally), building up strength and balance at the same time.

- Functional training: this involves training the body for the activities performed in daily life (which includes work and the sports you practice). It helps to perform these activities more easily and without injuries. Free-weight exercises are favored and proprioceptors are often trained. Chris takes into account my profession (often seated[57]) and the sports I practice.

- Stretching: is meant to increase flexibility. In addition to some stretching throughout the RT session, Chris ends up by stretching several muscles and muscle chains. Stretching is often a separate component altogether in a fitness program, which could be done in addition to RT sessions.

Hopefully, by now, you have acquired a sense of the benefits of RT to consider it, and you realize its complexity to call upon an expert for you or your coachee.

Stretching

We can learn from cats among other animals who don't neglect their stretching routine. Another feline, the cheetah, the fastest of all, exemplifies the complementary nature of strength and flexibility.[58]

Philippe Souchard (1996) and Norbert Grau (2002) make the case for stretching and propose specific exercises, which can either be performed alone or with someone's help. Our various activities call upon our muscles, which tend to retract. This is true for static muscles, which allow us to stay erect by "fighting" against gravity, and to restore balance when we oscillate from a centered position. These static muscles rarely rest and stiffen without the counter effect of stretching. A stiff muscle is also weaker. Dynamic muscles perform wide amplitude movements and can become overly relaxed through lack of use (e.g., abdominals). With physical activity, they will retract as well if not properly stretched.

In some joints, we have dynamic muscles in opposition with static muscles. For example, the dynamic quadriceps (agonist muscle—extend the knee) oppose the static hamstrings (antagonist muscle—flex the knee). Often when we strengthen muscles, the hamstrings stiffen even more, creating a disequilibrium that hampers the knee extension, which reduces performance and can lead to injuries.

Maintaining or even increasing muscles' flexibility is essential for ease of movement and maximum range of motion. It also helps prevent detrimental disequilibrium. General stretching is important but it is worth emphasizing areas that are particularly retracted so all movements can be performed smoothly, damaging compensations can be avoided, and an ideal posture can be maintained.

Furthermore, stretching also induces a pleasant relaxation and fosters well-being. Again, however, moderation is key; the tension of stretching should not hurt.

There are different modes and techniques of stretching (e.g., passive, active, contract-relax, contract-relax-antagonist-contract, muscular chains[59]). Competent personal trainers are familiar with stretching and integrate it within RT sessions.

A Global Approach

Finally, let me stress importance of a global approach. Whatever the physical activities you select, make sure to develop your endurance and your strength, without forgetting your flexibility and balance. In other words, cardiovascular exercise, RT, and stretching are all crucial. I would add balance training to these fundamentals. You can then engage in specialized activities such as tennis or basketball. Most sports require adequate physical preparation. This becomes even more critical as we get older.

Coachees often complain that they don't have the time to exercise. They have myriad responsibilities and heavy workloads. I invite you to challenge this limiting belief. I sometimes teasingly remind my coachees that world leaders such as Barack Obama and Nicolas Sarkozy[60] manage to dedicate time to physical exercise every day!

Help your coachees set specific goals (engaging gradually with physical activity) and build a discipline around physical exercise. But it should be a pleasure, too. We all have hopefully enough challenges and opportunities to excel at work. So we shouldn't worry if we don't set any new sports records!

Fitness for Enhancing Leadership Competence

Exercise does more than help people achieve optimal health and prevent debilitating diseases. The Center for Creative Leadership's (CCL) research (*Fitness for Leadership*, 2005) reveals that exercise also improves leadership performance. In this research, exercisers (those who exercised regularly for at least six months) were compared with those who exercised sporadically or not at all. They were rated by observers using two psychometric tools, Executive Dimensions and the Campbell Leadership Index.

"Exercisers were rated significantly higher by their observers on Leading Others (specifically Inspiring Commitment, Forging Synergy, and Interpersonal Savvy), Leading by Personal Example (specifically Credibility), and Results Orientation. The Overall score was also higher for the exercisers. Similar results were found for the Campbell Leadership Index. Here the observers rated the exercising executives significantly higher on Energy, Organized, Productive, Thrifty, Optimistic, Dependable, Resilient, Calm, Flexible, Optimistic, and Trusting. The Overall score was also higher for the exercisers." (2005, 12)

The correlation between exercise and leadership competence is clear. However, as CCL remarks, it is difficult to imply cause and effect: "Do executives lead better when they exercise because exercise leads to being less stressed, more energetic, and feeling better about themselves, or conversely, do they exercise because they are less stressed, more energetic, and feel better about themselves?" (2005, 13)

Global coaches only need to know that the correlation exists. We can then foster a virtuous circle of progress: exercising, feeling better, leading better, being encouraged to do more and better exercise, feeling even better, leading even better, et cetera.

Global coaches also need to uncover reasons for not exercising (What prevents you from exercising?). We can help coachees reevaluate their reasons (lack of motivation and lack of time most frequently cited[61]) in light of the potential benefits. We can also help remove these obstacles, for example through better time management (managerial perspective) or greater self-care (psychological perspective).

Regular exercise, even a limited amount, already provides substantial health[62] and leadership benefits. CCL's research does not delve into the type and amount of exercise. For the non-exercisers, just changing and sticking to a regular exercise routine (after a medical checkup) will bring high dividends. However, in this chapter, I have advocated going beyond a bare minimum and becoming much more sophisticated and ambitious. The increased health and fitness benefits will ensue.

COMMUNITY AND SPIRITUALITY

The Okinawa research reveals two other essential factors that affect health and fitness: community and spirituality.

In Chapters 5 through 8, I will discuss coaching's role in developing constructive and fulfilling relationships. The psychological, cultural, and spiritual realms covered in the next chapters remind us once more that everything is connected. Our relationships with others and with nature enable us to be healthier and fitter. Conversely, isolation and separation are damaging for our bodies as well as our minds.

SLEEP[63]

In my experience, executives often sacrifice sleep to squeeze more time into their busy days. A vicious circle of chronic sleep deprivation follows, leading to fatigue, irritability, and loss of productivity.

As a coach, I challenge my coachees to get the sleep they need and to let something else go instead. They must carefully examine of how they spend their time and then reprioritize, focusing on what really matters and striving for effectiveness.

Preserving sleep is not only a matter of setting aside sufficient time. It means creating a sanctuary, a pleasant and relaxing environment that favors sleep. Conversely, noise pollution can cause stressful disturbances.

Sleep is the indispensable base for performance and fulfillment. I make sure to cover this topic in coaching, and my coachees regularly set one objective in this area.

HUMOR AND LAUGHTER

Although not primarily physical—it belongs also to the emotional, mental, and spiritual realms—humor's favorite consequence, laughter, can be self-induced through physical techniques.[64] Laughter is enjoyable, of course, and it is also healthy. The poet Edward Estlin Cummings wisely said, "The most wasted of all days is one without laughter." Okinawan elders know how to keep an amused and smiling attitude.

I find that lightness and laughter help coachees enjoy and benefit from the coaching process. As global coaches, we need to cultivate a light heart, learn to spontaneously laugh at bizarre situations (which occur regularly in this world), not take ourselves too seriously, and stay in contact with our childlike qualities. Humor may arise in many coaching situations, such as role plays. Laughing helps people view difficult interactions and situations from new perspectives. At the same time, it does not keep us from exploring serious issues and connecting with buried and unpleasant emotions. Humor reveals our humanity and gives us the courage to face adversity with a smile.

As we will see in Chapter 10, the Fool and the Sage are inseparable. How wise can a person really be if he or she is always mired in gravitas? I have noticed that coaches (as well as psychotherapists) who lack a touch of lightness and humor are far less effective at building relationships and fostering change.

NOTES

1. See notably World Health Organizations *https://apps.who.int/infobase/compare. aspx?dm=5&countries=184%2c583%2c520%2c570%2c776&year=2005&sf1= cd.0704&sex=all&agegrou* (accessed on 10 June 2010). "Overweight" means a body mass index (BMI) ≥25, while "obese" means a BMI ≥30.
2. I usually prefer nutritionists with a medical degree and fitness trainers with a physical therapy degree.
3. For example, Dr. David Jenkins found that a diet based on Okinawan habits adapted to foods available in a Western context, which he called the "Garden of Eden Diet," allowed a dramatic 29 percent level decrease in LDL (bad) cholesterol after just a week. These findings suggest that this diet "may be as effective as the class of drugs known as statins, which have been the standard drug therapy for high cholesterol for the last fifteen years." The diet also brought a host of other benefits: reduced weight, inflammation, and insulin levels (Willcox, Willcox, and Suzuki, 2004, 42).
4. *http://corporate.alpro.com/en/organic-food-company.html*.
5. Likewise, Dr. Fuhrman observes: "Nutritional science in the last twenty years has demonstrated that colorful plant foods contain a huge assortment of protective compounds, mostly unnamed at this point" *www.drfuhrman.com/library/ article17.aspx*, accessed on 22 January 2010.
6. Adapted from Willcox, Willcox, and Suzuki, 2001, 28–29.
7. Willcox, Willcox, and Suzuki, 2004, 12.
8. When people speak about calories, such as Okinawans eating 1,600 calories per day and Americans 2,100 (Willcox, Willcox, and Suzuki, 2004, 12), they

really mean kilo calories (kcal). On packages you will typically see the number of kcal, for example 97 kcal for 100 grams (which would correspond to a CD of 0.97).

9. See notably Willcox, Willcox, and Suzuki, 2004, 59–60.

10. Adapted from Willcox, Willcox, and Suzuki, 2004, 53.

11. Willcox, Willcox, and Suzuki, 2004, 25.

12. Willcox, Willcox, and Suzuki, 2004, 29.

13. More antioxidants means less cell damage from free radicals. Less damage to collagen in the skin means fewer wrinkles; less damage to the internal organs means they wear out slower. From Willcox, Willcox, and Suzuki, 2001, 115.

14. The Glycemic Index (GI) is the rate of conversion from carbohydrates to blood sugar. "Very simply, the GI tells us how much our blood sugar rises after we eat a particular kind of carb food. Rapidly converted carbs cause a large rise in blood sugar levels—which is not a good thing. Increases in blood sugar lead to increases in insulin levels, which have been linked to a host of problems including obesity, diabetes, cardiovascular disease, certain cancers, and even aging itself. Bottom line: Any food that gets your insulin levels too high is bad news." Note also that "certain protein-heavy and fat-heavy foods can also cause large insulin spikes" (Willcox, Willcox, and Suzuki, 2004, 34–35).

15. Their main function is to "provide immediate energy use and short-term energy storage (glycogen) in the liver and muscles." They can take the shape of simple sugars like fructose (fruit sugar) and sucrose (table sugar), and more complex forms: starch—amylopectin and amylose, which converts more slowly to blood sugar than amylopectin—and fiber (Willcox, Willcox, and Suzuki, 2004, 34).

16. Inflammation is the mechanism that allows the reparation of tissues after an injury. The Greek physician Dioscorides described its manifestation already in the first century AC: "Rubor, tumor, calor, dolor" (red, swollen, warm, painful). This corresponds to a complex healing mechanism. Inflammation is a double-edged sword: more than one cancer out of six is directly connected to chronic inflammation, when the mechanism is diverted to fuel the growth of cancer cells. See Servan-Schreiber, 2007, 69–72.

17. A simple way of remembering which is which consists of thinking of L as in "lethal" and H as in "healthy."

18. Moreover Curtay argues that the most important factor for preventing osteoporosis is not milk, but—and by far—physical activity. See Curtay, 2006, 145.

19. The Willcox brothers summarize: "Simply put, your body prefers protein for growth and repair, carbs for fuel (immediate use and short-term storage in the liver), and fat to make body fat (long-term energy storage)." See Willcox, Willcox, and Suzuki, 2004, 38.

20. The Willcox brothers recommend soy as a principal protein. See Willcox, Willcox, and Suzuki, 2004, 70–78. They advise choosing vegetable protein over animal, at least some of the time. "A cup of cooked lentils has 34 grams of protein, but less than 1 gram of fat—and that fat is of the healthy kind" (67).

21. Willcox, Willcox, and Suzuki, 2004, 37.

22. Willcox, Willcox, and Suzuki, 2004, 65.

23. In areas of high pressure, small cracks eventually appear in the walls of your body's arteries. Cholesterol is used to repair the cracks. If you have too much cholesterol, your body liberally slaps it onto any small arteries it finds; pretty soon the artery walls thicken and you are set up for a heart attack or embolic (cholesterol plug) stroke. Taken from Willcox, Willcox, and Suzuki, 2001, 24.

24. I recall my trip to Nepal in 1986. I admired the healthy-looking teeth of several young and mid-age women, beautiful yet very poor. At the same time I was shocked by kids begging tourists for candies. Likewise many kids in third-world countries have become hooked on American cola beverages, with damaging consequences for their dentition (not to mention all the other more harmful health effects). This is a sad example of America exporting its worst part, in an area where the U.S. should best learn instead from these people's healthier eating habits.

25. Willcox, Willcox, and Suzuki, 2004, 61.

26. Curtay agrees with the popular wisdom: you should eat as a prince for breakfast, as a bourgeois for lunch, and as a beggar for dinner (Curtay, 2006, 246).

27. Apart from the saturated fats and the sugar (at a reasonable level when 86 percent is cacao), dark chocolate is also fortunately a potent antioxidant.

28. See Wilmore, Costill, and Kenney, 2008.

29. Wilmore et al. explain that CF max (or HR max) is higher in children than in adults, and decreases linearly with age: frequently over 210 beats/min under the age of 10, approximately 195 at 20, and decreases of 0.5 to 1 beat per minute each year with further aging (25–30 years old and older). See Wilmore, Costill, and Kenney, 2008, 388–389.

30. Terminology for the various training intensity ranges according to Professor Jacques Duchateau (Institut des Sciences de la Motricité, University of Brussels). Correspondence with the author, July 2009.

31. This explanation is adapted from Van Rensbergen, 1996.

32. See notably Cooman, 1991, 11–14. Actually, these zones can be determined in several ways: during an effort test, as the intensity of the effort increases, the cardiac frequency is measured while the production of lactic acid or the ratio volume of CO_2 exhaled/ O_2 inhaled is monitored.

    Minimal lactic acid is produced in the green zone. The quantity starts to rise in the orange zone and then augments sharply in the red zone. As far as exhaled air, it rises linearly with the increased intensity and then, at the threshold, the line begins to shift to a more vertical direction. There is certainly a correlation between the two methods, even if the correspondence is not exactly perfect.

33. See Cooman, 1991, 13.

34. According to Professor Jacques Duchateau (Institut des Sciences de la Motricité) and Chris Richartz, my physical trainer. Conversations with the author on 6 and 20 July 2009. For trained individuals (rather than well-trained sportsmen), 85 percent is typical.

35. See Wilmore, Costill, and Kenney, 2008, 461.

36. Eddy Cuypers (former physical coach of tennis champion Justine Henin), presentation 16 April 2007, "Connaissance de Son Potentiel Physique."

37. See Wilmore, Costill, and Kenney, 2008, 301–308.
38. Steffny and Pramann, 2005, 29.
39. See notably Steffny and Pramann, 2005, 28; and Wikipedia "Aerobic exercise" *http://en.wikipedia.org/wiki/Aerobic_exercise*. Viewed on 20 June 2009.
40. When one trains in the green zone, dilatation occurs and the heart volume/capacity increases. Consequently, more blood can be expelled for each heart beat (or, in other words, pumping can occur at a lower rate to expel a similar quantity of blood). Training in the red zone strengthens the heart muscle. The heart is able to pump harder, which is also more tiring. Conversation with Professor Duchateau on 6 July 2009.
41. *The Oxford Dictionary of Sports Science & Medicine*. Michael Kent, 2007.
42. "Mitochondrion: an organelle found in large number in most cells, in which the biochemical processes of respiration and energy production occur" (*The New Oxford Dictionary of English*, 1998).
43. See notably Steffny and Pramann, 2005, 34, 36.
44. See notably Van Den Bosch, 2007, 31.
45. The production of lactic acid is minimal in the green zone, starts to go up in the orange zone, and rises sharply, exponentially in the red zone (Steffny and Pramann, 2005, 31).

    Too much lactic acid slows down the burning of fat. Carbohydrates are consumed instead. This is what often happens for amateurs who train too hard (Steffny and Pramann, 2005, 26).
46. Definition adapted from Kraemer and Ratamess, 2004, 674. The endurance we refer to here is the local muscular endurance (LME).
47. Wilmore, Costill, and Kenney, 2008, 188.
48. Ratamess et al., 2009, 688.
49. Sources include: Ratamess et al., 2009, 688, 687, 690; and "Strength training" Wikipedia *http://en.wikipedia.org/wiki/Strength_training*. Retrieved on 20 June 2009, pages 3, 6, 11.
50. See *www.build-muscle-and-burn-fat.com/one-rep-max.html* (See how easily you can calculate your one rep max. Retrieved on 20 June 2009): for example, "When you hear someone ask, 'How much do you bench?', they are asking specifically what is the maximum amount of weight you can bench press." It is often not feasible or safe to "max out" (i.e., test one's 1RM). Formulas exist to give us estimates of 1RM. A simple formula is 1RM = ((Number of repetitions performed/30) +1) × weight used. For example, if you are able to bench press 13 reps at 70kg, you should be able to lift 100 kg, but just once.
51. Incidentally rather than establishing 1RM directly, a safer way consists in determining 3RM, which roughly corresponds to 90 percent of 1RM. The previous formula is consistent with this remark by Chris Richartz (correspondence with the author in July 2009).
52. See Bender, 1995:"In plain English, the muscle is stretched (i.e., loaded) before it is contracted. A good example is push-ups with a clap in-between each push-up. Your muscle (pectorals in this case) is elongated and loaded by the downward force of your body, then immediately you must contract the muscle

to push yourself back up . . . . Plyometrics is one of the best ways . . . to improve power."

53. See Wikipedia: range of motion *http://en.wikipedia.org/wili/Range_of_motion*. Retrieved on 24 June 2009.

54. Adapted from Spennewyn, 2008, 75–76.

55. "Metabolism is the chemical and physical processes in the body that build and destroy tissue and release energy, thereby generating heat." "Reduced muscle mass [rather than age per se] causes slowing metabolism." In Clarence Bass: "The Metabolism Myth—There's No Biologic Reason to Get Fatter as You Grow Older" (1997). *www.cbass.com*. Retrieved on 21 June 2009. Hartman et al. come to a similar conclusion: "resistance training improves metabolic economy during functional tasks in older adults, thereby providing a possible mechanism for increasing quality of life in older population" (Hartman et al., 2007, 91).

It is suggested that "the variables that mostly influence energy expenditure of resistance exercise are volume and intensity, during the exercise session itself and excess post-exercise oxygen consumption, respectively" (de Mello Meirelles and Gomes, 2004).

56. See "Why Use a Wobble Board or Balance Board?" *www.sportsinjuryclinic.net*. Retrieved on 24 June 2009.

57. Incidentally, a Swiss ball or Swedish seat (which I use in front of the computer), is healthier for the back. Ergonomics is another area worth exploring.

58. As Philippe Souchard suggested. See Grau, 2002, 8.

59. Guissard and Dejaeger, 2004.

60. However, even French president Sarkozy (fifty-four years old), by fainting while jogging in July 2009, found out that you should not train too hard (particularly in the intensive summer heat) and that you should eat adequately. Sarkozy too must learn moderation, avoiding excess in sports and an overly draconian diet. See Algalarrondo, 2009.

61. (2005, 8)

62. See Haskell et al., 2007.

63. Alain Goudsmet evokes seven mechanisms to recuperate, to recharge our batteries (2002):

   1. Sleep
   2. Nutrition
   3. Physical exercise
   4. Humor
   5. Relaxation
   6. Motivation factors
   7. Social contacts

The perspectives are clearly interconnected. Human contacts clearly fill a psychological need as well but we will explain in Chapter 5 how we actually have a biological need to communicate with others. Sleep is the first mechanism on his list. Sleep is the recuperation time *par excellence* and a time to dream.

64. See laughing clubs (Rosinski, 2003, 171).

CHAPTER 4

The Managerial Perspective—
Fostering Productivity and
Results

Management is a task that consists in focusing resources on the
organization's goals, and then monitoring and managing the use of these
resources. (Campbell, 1991)

The managerial perspective is one of two pillars of traditional coaching
(alongside the psychological perspective). Numerous coaching and
management books cover areas such as time management, personal organization, and project management. Typical management training focuses
on disciplines aimed at increasing results and productivity. These fields include strategy, marketing, human resources (i.e., humans as resources), ac-
counting, and finance.

For example, personal coach Talane Miedaner advises coachees to clear
their plate before taking on new objectives (Miedaner, 2000). People often
overlook this simple, commonsense idea. As a coach, I challenge coachees
to leave behind what is no longer a priority (or what is simply unnecessary)
to make room for new projects. As we will see in Chapter 10, it's necessary to
unfold the Destroyer archetype here. In my previous book (Rosinski, 2003),
I mentioned more time-management approaches as well as diverse organizational arrangements inspired by various cultures.

Certain management tools specify target objectives, such as the Tab-
leau de Bord, the Balanced Scorecard (Kaplan and Norton, 1996), and the
EFQM Model (European Foundation for Quality Management, 1999).[1]

The Balanced Scorecard also highlights cause-and-effect relations between measures. Unfortunately, this may exclude factors whose importance for the business unit's strategy cannot be established in such a linear fashion. I introduced the Global Scorecard to extend the scope of possible objectives, broadening the definition of traditional business success to encompass realms that are beyond business and yet interconnected with it: self (self-care), family and friends (sharing love and friendship), and community and world (improving the world). The Balanced Scorecard introduced a multiple perspectives approach within the managerial perspective (linking marketing, finance, et cetera); the Global Scorecard connects multiple perspectives that go beyond management. See Rosinski, 2003, Chapter 12.

In this chapter, rather than elaborating on tips or management metrics, I would like to focus on a classical model by Hersey and Blanchard: situational leadership. It provides a concrete method for fostering responsibility and helping people access their own resources for tackling various tasks. Good managerial intentions and discourses are not sufficient to build workers' sense of ownership. And as we have discussed before, when workers have a sense of self-responsibility and individual power, they can take proactive good care of themselves and of others, thereby playing their part in forging thriving organizations and promoting sustainable progress. Managers can become more effective at empowering subordinates simply by becoming aware of their leadership styles and by adapting their style to each situation. The situational leadership model continues to prove very useful in my coaching, and I invite you to consider it in yours as well, not as a stand-alone model but in combination with other perspectives.

TASK AND RELATIONSHIP BEHAVIORS

In the late 1940s, researchers at Ohio State University launched a comprehensive research project to identify independent dimensions of leader behavior. They began with more than 1,000 dimensions of behavior, and they found that just two categories accounted for most of them. They called these two dimensions *initiating structure* and *consideration*.

> *Initiating structure refers to the extent to which a leader is likely to define and structure his or her role and those of subordinates in the search for goal attainment.*
>
> *Consideration is described as the extent to which a person is likely to have job relationships characterized by mutual trust, respect for subordinates' ideas, and regard for their feelings. (Robbins, 1989, 306)*

Researchers at the University of Michigan's Survey Research Center began a leadership study at about the same time. It revealed two similar dimensions of leadership behavior related to performance effectiveness. The researchers labeled these *employee oriented* (emphasis on interpersonal relations) and *production oriented* (emphasis on technical or task aspects of the job).[2]

In the early 1960s, Robert Blake and Jane Mouton outlined a two-dimensional view of leadership style called the Managerial Grid. They called their dimensions *concern for people* and *concern for production*.

That dichotomy later became the foundation of situational leadership, which I will explore next.

These two fundamental types of leadership behaviors are often simply referred to as *task* and *relationship*. A task behavior occurs anytime you help someone complete an assignment—for example, by saying what to do, how to do it, or with whom to do it. A relationship behavior happens anytime you make someone feel important, significant, valued, or appreciated. It means providing socio-emotional support (e.g., saying "good comment!" or "good point!").

SITUATIONAL LEADERSHIP

The two dimensions, task and relationship behaviors, can constitute the axes of a two-by-two matrix, a simple tool fancied by consultants.

This yields four leadership styles, based on whether the behavior is manifested frequently (high) or rarely (low). Paul Hersey and Ken Blanchard argue that the best leadership style depends on the follower's readiness for a particular task.

High		
	S3 ENCOURAGING	S2 COACHING
RELATIONSHIP **behavior**		
	S4 DELEGATING	S1 TELLING/ STRUCTURING
Low		
	Low	**TASK** **High** **behavior**

The follower's readiness level is one-dimensional and consists of two factors: ability and willingness. The assumption is that these two factors will evolve together over time. R1 (first level) refers to people who are both unable to perform and unwilling to take responsibility for performing the task. They are neither competent nor confident. R4 (most advanced level) refers to people both able and willing to do what is asked of them. They combine a sense of ownership with the skills to deliver. The explanations provided for R2 and R3 seem less straightforward. For example, Hersey refers to R2 as "unable but willing or confident" and R3 as "able but unwilling or insecure" (Hersey, 1979–1993). However, in my experience, willingness and confidence don't necessarily decrease as ability increases. It is often the opposite!

In any event, I find it useful to think of the readiness level as a combination of ability and willingness, in which willingness comprises motivation and sense of responsibility. The readiness level refers to somebody for a particular task. Hersey and Blanchard suggest that to maximize productivity, leadership style S1 is best suited for readiness level R1, S2 for R2, et cetera.

Managers often use the wrong style for a given situation. Delegating (S4) is ideal when the follower is able and willing to do the task and can be relied upon to deliver with minimal involvement from his manager. However, this style would be inadequate if the follower is inexperienced; she might feel confused or abandoned with too little direction.

The typical progression can be represented by a bell-shape curve: at the R1 level, the follower needs precise instructions to perform the task, which is an S1 style. Coaching[3] (S2) would be less efficient here: the manager would need to spend a great deal of time asking questions and drawing answers from the follower, who lacks the expertise that comes from experience.

Once the follower achieves initial successes, she de facto moves to the R2 level. It is time for the manager to capitalize on these first successes by acknowledging them and congratulating the follower (relationship behavior). This praise provides a positive reinforcement, which will promote a virtuous circle of progress. The manager can also give less advice and ask more questions, enabling the follower to find his own answers, building on the experience he has acquired by now (task behavior): how would you do this? What do you propose? What are the advantages and disadvantages of the solution you propose? The S2 leadership style is most time consuming, being high both on task and relationship behavior.

Typically, both ability and willingness will continue to evolve. At the R3 level, the follower can ask herself questions and become her own coach. The manager can devote less time to the process, saying simply, "If you have any questions or need some help, just let me know!"

However, the manager should keep encouraging (S3) the follower, recognizing progress and providing positive reinforcement. This will build trust. Eventually, the follower can work on the task fairly autonomously (R4). The manager can leave the follower alone after they agree on specific deliverables and timelines. The delegation (S4) will now feel right to both parties: the follower has established the ability and willingness to perform the task, and the relationship has solidified.

Non-mindful managers tend to apply the same style (unconsciously dictated by their psychological and cultural preferences) in all situations. Those caught in a telling mode (S1) will miss opportunities to develop their subordinates through coaching. I have encountered numerous managers who fall into this category and complain that their subordinates never take any initiative! They will find that shifting to S2 makes a big difference: when their style evolves, the subordinates' hidden qualities emerge.

Delegation becomes more effective as well. Managers don't have to take a chance by hastily entrusting a subordinate with an important task. Trust is built over time, as the follower's readiness level gradually increases. Consequently, managers can really count on people who work for them. When they delegate, they are confident that the work will be completed competently and delivered on time. Managers can dedicate their time and energy to areas they should focus on. For senior executives, this might include strategic thinking and mobilizing people around the company's vision. Middle managers might have more time to concentrate on improving processes and developing their subordinates.

As a coach operating from a managerial perspective, you can invite coachees/managers to map out their subordinates and assess their readiness for various critical tasks. You can then ask your coachees to compare their current leadership style with the model's recommended style, based on your interpretation of the explanations I have just given. It is merely an estimate to identify critical gaps. The table below illustrates this process. Give a title and brief description for each task.

Subordinates	Tasks	Subordinate's readiness level	Your current leadership style	Recommended leadership style
John	Task Jo1	R2	S1	S2
John	Task Jo2	R2	S1	S2
John	Task Jo3	R1	S1	S1
Sara	Task Sa1	R3	S4	S3

You can focus your coaching art on helping to bridge the gaps—for example by helping the manager to move from S1 to S2 (e.g., John for his first two tasks). This will involve the usual coaching questioning and role plays to give the manager a chance to practice. You can play the role of his subordinate, or, if the manager has difficulties dealing with the subordinate, you might invite him to play the subordinate part while you demonstrate how to do S2 in practice.

I use this process regularly, and managers are often amazed by the progress they can make with this simple tool.

Can leadership development be reduced to the situational leadership model? The answer is no. Leadership is complex. Situational leadership, despite its usefulness, doesn't cover every facet. Used alone, it may mislead leaders into thinking that the myriad challenges can be treated from this single managerial perspective.

I see situational leadership fitting under the managerial perspective because it is mainly instrumental and reduces relationship behaviors to positive reinforcement. Furthermore, one only needs to employ rudimentary psychology to use the model. Martin Buber probably would refer to "relations" rather than "relationships" here. Mere positive reinforcement hardly qualifies as the authentic relationships and genuine meetings Buber writes about. The relational part of the situational leadership model, by its utilitarian nature, is of the *I-It* type. *I-Thou* relationships, crucial in global coaching, are of a different quality and will be discussed in Chapter 11.

To best apply the situational leadership model, coaches should take psychological and cultural preferences into account. In other words, they should weave other perspectives into the process. For example, a telling (S1) approach might bear fruits in a hierarchical environment, even if the model recommends S2 in that situation. Insights into personality and culture will help determine preferred styles and indicate ways to move outside one's comfort zone. Moving to S2, for instance, would imply adapting to a more egalitarian approach, assuming the subordinate has the potential to take responsibility and become gradually empowered.

Once we understand that the ideal leadership style (assuming it even exists) should take different realities into account, including the physical, psychological, political, cultural, and spiritual, we can choose to zoom in on the managerial perspective.

Let me illustrate how I have done so with an executive named Marc.[4] Marc was struggling. Unlike many others, he was not into micro-management. He preferred to give plenty of autonomy to his employees. He provided broad instructions and readily delegated tasks. Some fared well under his leadership, but others were not performing. I introduced the situational leadership model and invited him to "map out" his challenging employees on the simple chart for their given jobs, evaluating their ability and willingness (i.e., readiness level). His leadership style was not a good match with one new employee, Robert. The model made that clear, and showed Marc what he needed to do. It immediately made sense to Marc: delegating was counterproductive; he needed to give direct instructions. We also were able to envision the next step and prepare Marc for that coaching style.

During our second session, Marc proudly reported that Robert was making quick progress. As we had discussed, Marc had started by giving instructions. The job was new to Robert, and he lacked the knowledge to perform his work. A month later, Robert was becoming more adept at his task. Marc decided to shift to a coaching style, which we had rehearsed during the first session. Rather than telling Robert what to do, Marc asked questions: what can you do? How can you solve this? What is your proposition? I also congratulated Marc for (mostly) resisting the temptation to answer Robert's questions, inviting him to learn to find his own answers.

I asked Marc about the "relationship" behaviors. Marc smiled: he could still make progress there! He decided to acknowledge Robert's successes— even small ones—more consistently. It was clear to Marc that this would motivate Robert and stimulate his progress. The psychological perspective proved helpful here. Marc saw that his perfectionism led him to set the bar very high. Consequently, his employees' work was rarely good enough to justify praise. By giving himself the permission to seek effectiveness rather than perfection, Marc could praise Robert more consistently, thereby fostering his progress.

During the third coaching session, Marc reported further progress. To his credit, Marc's commitment had manifested itself in his disciplined and consistent approach. Robert had moved to an R3 level, and Marc shifted his style accordingly. Marc began to say, "When do you want us to discuss the project next?" Marc empowered Robert to initiate the contact if he needed support along the way. Marc also acknowledged Robert's success on a regular basis. He and Robert developed a solid relationship. Marc was very open about using the situational leadership model. Sharing the model allowed him to talk with Robert about leadership style and exchange feedback. Furthermore, the tool pointed to a goal they shared: full delegation. Getting there might require Marc to make comments such as "You are doing fine!" (or better still, praising specific behaviors and accomplishments); "I don't want to annoy you and make you feel as if you don't know what you are doing. Let us agree on some objectives, and then just go and do it!" (recognizing achievements and encouraging autonomy); "How did you feel about that experience? What did you learn from it?" (fostering learning and being prepared to learn from your subordinate as well); "Do you have any concerns about your next project meeting?" (asking for concerns).

As I write these lines, I expect that during our next coaching session, Marc might report reaching the S4 level. (Our sessions usually take place every four to five weeks.) It will be important then to discuss how he can best engage in delegation. Delegation does not imply abdication. Marc is still accountable and needs to decide, with Robert's input, how best to get progress updates. Beyond this, Marc needs to be open to new and innovative approaches, as long as Robert delivers. With additional experience, Robert is likely to find novel methods to achieve the targeted outcomes. Still, Marc has to be prepared to defend Robert's work, taking the heat from upper management if he doesn't meet expectations. The relational aspect can be minimal at this stage: an occasional thumbs-up from Marc might provide enough encouragement.

The following table summarizes typical behaviors for each style.

S3: ENCOURAGING	S2: COACHING
Recognize achievements	Celebrate first successes
Encourage autonomy	Give more opportunities to practice and improve
Engage in dialogue and be ready to learn as well	Ask questions enabling the follower to find her solutions
Discuss ways to refine performance	Before a challenging task: discuss how to do it
Ask for concerns	During: if present, be ready to jump in
Cement a trusting and respectful relationship	After: provide performance feedback
S4: DELEGATING	**S1: TELLING/STRUCTURING**
Empower the person (information + resources + authority + accountability)	Say what is expected
Be open to innovative approaches	Explain how to do it
Be aware of your accountability	Provide example
Get synthetic information on progress	Follow execution very closely
Be ready to act as "heat shield"	

Robert proved an excellent choice. He was ambitious, ready to work diligently, and eager to learn to move up the corporate ladder. In this case, Marc had a fairly easy time applying situational leadership.

Some other subordinates proved more challenging. Frank had an overly favorable view of his abilities. He would either do what Marc wanted immediately or not at all. In our coaching session, Marc realized that he needed to coach Frank more closely. Marc had started dialogues with questions, but when he hit Frank's resistance, he reverted to a telling mode: "You should do this and that." Referring to coaching fundamental communication tools, such as transactional analysis and neuro-linguistic programming,[5] Marc discovered how to continue the coaching dialogue until Frank could find a solution and commit to specific actions.

Dirk was even more challenging. He had been in the company for more than thirty years and was just a few years away from retirement. He was knowledgeable, committed to the point of refusing to take most of his holidays, and a perfectionist. On the other hand, he would only work on tasks he chose himself, and his precision often came at the expense of productivity. Marc had given up on changing the situation. The psychological perspective, and particularly the "I am OK–You are OK" model we will discuss in the next chapter, helped Marc to change his attitude and beliefs. Through our role play, Marc became convinced that something could be done and that even Dirk could change. Marc realized he could acknowledge Dirk's professional commitment and rigor while also providing honest feedback about areas that needed improvement. He decided to state his expectations and have a conversation with Dirk in which they could agree on the best way forward.

Managers need more advanced coaching skills to handle such situations constructively. They must call on an array of perspectives if the dialogue goes in various directions. Managers may have to deal with psychological resistances, decipher cultural orientations, and elicit a renewed sense of meaning. Situational leadership alone can't properly address these issues. In the next chapter, we will turn to psychology.

NOTES

1. See Rosinski, 2003, 211–212.
2. See Robbins, 1989, 301–337, for a review of classical leadership models.

3. In this context, coaching is simply defined as a style that is high both on task and relationship behaviors.
4. I have changed the names to preserve anonymity.
5. See Chapter 5 and also Rosinski, 2003, Appendixes 1 and 2.

CHAPTER 5

The Psychological Perspective—Developing Emotional and Relational Qualities

Psychology is the study of individual personality, behaviors, emotions, and mental processes. Psychology differs from culture in that its primary focus is the individual rather than the collective.

In this chapter, I would like to revisit a powerful theory, transactional analysis (TA). TA was developed in the 1960s by Dr. Eric Berne. Yet its richness is still largely untapped by coaches. I have used TA for almost 20 years. My clients and I are amazed at the positive changes we can achieve with it. I will also touch on other useful theories: positive psychology and psychoanalytically informed coaching.

The HR director of an international company recently called me. The company was astonished by the quick progress of one of its executives after I coached him. This manager was technically very competent and reliable. But he lacked executive presence. His self-confidence was so poor that he would get flustered and fall silent when challenged in executive meetings. He seemed dismounted, lost. I used TA in my coaching to help him raise his self-confidence and become assertive. The HR director wanted to send me another executive with similar issues; local coaching had not had the same dramatic impact.

In my first executive coaching assignment with this company, I worked with an executive who had received twice official complaints. He too was a technically competent and dedicated manager, and a valuable contributor. In his case, the issue wasn't lack of presence but lack of self-control, and over-emotionalism. He often got worked up and shouted at employees. TA again proved invaluable; it helped him shift from aggressiveness to assertiveness, and develop a calm and serene presence. His manager, skeptical that anything could be done to change these deeply engrained habits and patterns, was grateful after the coaching process. A few years later, the executive was still maintaining more productive relationships at work.

In all these cases, which I will discuss in this chapter, the executives I coached seemed engaged and genuinely eager to embark on the coaching process. It takes two to tango. Coachees need to play a critical part in achieving their own success. I can only facilitate the process.

In *Coaching Across Cultures* (Rosinski, 2003), I described the OK–OK mindset that is conducive to productive and fulfilling communication, contrasting it with the other mental combinations: not OK–OK characterizes the Victim (Submissive); OK–not OK is associated with the Persecutor, Rescuer, and Victim (Rebellious); and the not OK–not OK is worst of all.

I also discussed the concepts of constraining messages, centers of resources (ego states), contamination, and transactions.

In this chapter, I would like to emphasize key related TA concepts:[1]

- We are 100 percent responsible for how we communicate.
- We need "strokes." Communication is a biological necessity. We can meet this need either positively or negatively.
- How can we structure time to receive the strokes we need?
- What does the OK–OK mindset mean?

Most of all, I will explain how coaches can put these concepts into practice to effectively promote assertiveness and an OK–OK mindset.

I usually share the transactional analysis theory upfront with my coachees. By doing so, I help coachees equip themselves to handle their challenges autonomously. Furthermore, this explanation seems to act as a form of metaphor, suggesting—consciously and unconsciously—transformational possibilities for the coachees.

Michel Chalude said that TA changed his life; I tell my coaches, in all honesty, that it changed mine as well.

According to TA, we are 100 percent responsible for how we communicate. This may not be a fact, but it is a powerful belief that fosters self-responsibility. We have choices, and we have much more power than we usually realize. TA provides easily accessible tools (meant to be understandable by an eight-year-old) to uncover these choices, overcome obstacles, and tap into our power. As coaches, we don't need to spend time understanding *why* others communicate in a certain fashion. We can focus instead on *how* we communicate. How does our communication affect others? What else can we do?

TA is well suited for coaching, which is action-oriented. Coaches can explore new options systematically during sessions, trying out the communications in role plays within the safe coaching environment. Then the coachees can practice this in the real world. I ask them to journal what happens, recording both pluses (successes) that will be celebrated in the next coaching session (reinforcing the new habits and coachee's confidence), or minuses (outcomes below target) that will allow us to learn further from the interactions.

Although we are 100 percent responsible for how we communicate, we only bear 50 percent of the responsibility for successfully communicating with someone. It takes two. However, we can increase the odds of success when we do the best at our end, notably by maintaining an OK–OK attitude even when we are invited to "play games" (a concept I will explain shortly).

HUNGER FOR STROKES

Eric Berne uses the word *stroke* to refer to "the fundamental unit of social action." [2] A stroke may be words we say to someone or a nonverbal recognition of someone's presence (for example, a smile or a frown).

I ask my coachees to imagine a rat in three different situations. In all cases, the rat is well fed. In the first situation, the rat receives a caress, a gentle handling. In the second situation, the rat gets an electric shock from the experimenter. It is painful but not really dangerous. In the final situation, the rat is left alone. I ask coachees how they think the rats will evolve. Usually, participants say that the first rat will do well; the second rat will be "stressed out," will eat very little, and will grow thin; and the third rat will be all right, even if it doesn't do as well as the first rat.

I then reveal the research findings: the first two rats turn out healthy, and the third rat quickly dies (Berne, 1964, 15).

These findings apply to humans as well. In the first part of the twentieth century, doctors separated infants from their mothers and kept them in a nursery environment with strict hygiene, good nutrition, and excellent medical treatment. To prevent contamination, doctors minimized interaction between babies and staff; infants were left alone. Despite all these precautions, the infants began wasting away. Finally, psychiatrist René Spitz hypothesized that lack of human contact was the problem. He had noticed that infants in a penitentiary nursery did much better; there, the hygiene was far from ideal but convicted mothers could take care of their babies. As soon as nurses started to cajole the babies in the regular nursery, the condition named "hospitalism" vanished.

This suggests that communication is far more than an exchange of information. It is not even merely a psychological requirement. We have a biological need for contacts, for human strokes. If we can't meet this need positively, we will manage somehow to obtain the strokes negatively. That's preferable to no interaction at all. Observe, for example, what happens when a child wants to play with her parent. If the parent says "I'm busy right now" and ignores the child, she is likely to do something silly or become angry. Then what? The parent might scold the child or even shout. This way, the child gets attention—albeit negative rather than positive.

The implication is profound and applies to all human activities. We simply cannot expect to get rid of the negative by merely demanding it. Negative strokes serve a vital purpose. We need to replace the negative strokes with positive ones. In other words, to eliminate war and destructive behaviors, we need love and constructive behaviors instead. This is true at home, at work, and in international relations.

How can we achieve this? TA, again, has an elegant and useful model to answer the question.

TIME STRUCTURING

There are six ways to obtain the strokes we vitally need. They increase in intensity as we move from the first to the sixth. You can compare this to moving from basic food to a refined gourmet dinner.

1. Withdrawal

   Withdrawal refers to the communication we have with ourselves. This internal dialogue can be very rich, but is not recommended in meetings: it can lead us to miss what is going on.

2. Ritual

Rituals refer to the "'Hello, how are you?' 'Fine, thank you'" type of routine we engage in when we meet someone. The film A *Fish Called Wanda* (1988) ridiculed the superficiality of these exchanges in an amusing scene involving fishes greeting each other in a fishbowl. You could argue that "How are you?" is not always genuine: you typically don't expect people to tell you how they really are. Yet these rituals are quite important: they provide basic strokes, which we absolutely need. If your colleague leaves for a few days, you are likely to say more to her when she is back: "How are you? How was your trip?" It is as if you are both entitled to more units of energy to compensate for the absence of strokes in the last days. Furthermore, rituals serve as the first gear that allows people to shift to the next ones.

3. Pastime/Conversation

Conversations refer to casual discussions about anything: vacations, restaurants (a favorite topic in Belgium, alongside football), sports, politics, et cetera.

The conversation is a goal in itself. Talking about politics, in this instance, is not about creating change but about entertaining one another (even if participants might not admit this).

Work meetings can be conversations when there are no objectives in sight. In my early days as a trainer, I worked with an unproductive bureaucratic organization that was starting a journey toward more professional management. One topic was how to conduct more effective meetings. In a role play, a participant said at the end of the meeting, "We had a good debate. Let's continue it next time!" Nothing had been decided and nothing had been accomplished. This meeting was useful in that it allowed crucial exchanges of strokes. Gradually, participants learned a new way to obtain this energy. They realized that meetings could become activities rather than mere conversations.

4. Activity

An activity is a project carried out with other people. It involves an overall purpose and specific objectives. Activities offer invaluable opportunities to obtain positive strokes by engaging in constructive interactions.

5. Game

Games are negative exchanges of energy. I previously explained and illustrated the mechanism (Rosinski, 2003, 260–261): it invariably starts with one person entering the *dramatic triangle* either as a Persecutor, a Rescuer, or a Victim. The *game* occurs and the negative energy begins to flow when the second person takes the bait and enters the triangle as well. This is a waste of human energy; it increases uneasiness, sterile conflicts, and damage. Yet let us remember that negative strokes are better than no strokes at all. This is why these games are prevalent, particularly when energy is not exchanged positively.

6. Intimacy

Intimacy is the highest gear, which we normally reach after using all the previous gears (except gear five, which we can best skip!). It is the richest way to exchange positive energy. It refers to authentic relationships. We are ready to make ourselves vulnerable because we trust the other person. We open up ourselves, and reveal our hopes, dreams, and feelings. This enables us to bond deeply with the other person. We get in touch with our humanity. These moments are fulfilling. Effective coaching is powerful because it primarily involves a combination of intimacy and activity.

OK–OK MINDSET

This TA model refers to how we view ourselves, how we see others, and the resulting impact. OK–OK is a mindset all coaches need to develop. It is also a tool to replace destructive or ineffective communications with productive and enriching ones.

We can choose, regardless of the situation, to adopt an "OK (self)–OK (others)" mindset. This means we will tend to trust ourselves and others. OK means worthy of respect, having positive intentions, and able to make a difference. OK does not mean perfect or faultless. This mental outlook will naturally lead us to engage in constructive communications and actions, and develop richer and more productive relationships.

The important point is that OK–OK is a subjective choice, independent of "objective" reality. It doesn't matter that we can make a rational case for the other mental combinations (OK–not OK, not OK–OK, not OK–not OK). For example, if we distrust people, our attitude will typically alienate them or lower their self-confidence. We foster vicious circles when we interpret their lack of commitment and poor results as a validation of our initial beliefs. Coaches prefer the OK–OK perspective, because self-fulfilling prophecies also work positively: when we trust ourselves and others, we enable virtuous circles of respect, productive behaviors, and creativity.

Two of my coachees, whom I evoked when starting this chapter, were trapped in "playing games," much like Marie (see Chapter 1). Like Jean,[3] many people in the not OK–OK position automatically cast themselves in the submissive Victim role, unconsciously inviting others to play the Persecutor or Rescuer part. Like Jacques, people in the OK–not OK position often play the Persecutor role, inviting others to respond as Victims (submissive or rebellious).

When Jean and Jacques recognized this simple dynamic and realized they had the power to change their position to OK–OK, they were on their way to quick and amazing progress.

The OK–OK position is one of assertiveness, calmness, and serenity combined with firmness. It exudes quiet strength and a reassuring presence.

Coaches can help coachees recognize that they most likely adopt the OK–OK position already. Knowing that they are capable should help build coachees' confidence. The challenge is to maintain the OK–OK position under stressful circumstances.

Coaches should help coachees explore what prevents them from adopting the OK–OK position. In Jean's case, it was a self-imposed perfectionism he could not possibly live up to; this perfectionism made it difficult for him to feel OK. Moreover, he had learned as a child to suppress his anger. Jean needed to make a twofold resolution. At a cognitive level, Jean started to give himself permission to make mistakes and not be perfect. He allowed himself simply to do his best, accepting that he could not always control the final outcome. At an emotional level, Jean learned to access his anger and to find his voice (a deeper voice than the high-pitched and soft one he had been using). Anger is a useful emotion aimed to protect our boundaries.

I warned him that an intellectual understanding of the dynamic was not enough. To move from not OK to OK, he needed to access his anger or risk what TA refers to as *racket*: instead of experiencing anger when being abused, he would feel another emotion—in his case, fear. Fear is useful when it prompts us to avoid danger, but it is inadequate when it replaces anger. Anger can lead us to stand for what is right.

Jean identified permissions that would help him raise his confidence and effectiveness in dealing with unfair situations: "I have the right to assert myself!," "I stop considering that what I have done is never good enough!," "I congratulate myself for what I do well!," et cetera.

I challenged Jean to voice these permissions while accessing his anger. Intimidated at first, Jean gained confidence when he realized that I did not judge his attempts to unfold his anger. I told him how commonplace this situation is. Still, Jean was not ready to do it but agreed to try it out alone. The next session, Jean dared saying these words with anger in my presence. All he could achieve initially was a soft version. This was a progress. I then mustered the anger I could find in me and said the words with rage. Jean repeated after me. I went deeper and deeper. He followed, his anger becoming stronger and stronger. Afterwards, he felt more serene. He got the message in these permissions, which sunk in at an emotional and gut level. Jean regularly practiced between our sessions. The next time, Jean was able to contact anger on his own. He became more assertive and effective at work.

Note that Jean quickly remembered situations in which he had suppressed anger vis-à-vis his parents. Rather than inviting him to express his anger toward his mythical parents (as can be the case in psychotherapy), I encouraged him to voice genuine rage referring to his current situation. This proved sufficient for Jean to replace his old "tapes," unproductive internal dialogues, with constructive new ones.

Jacques, on the other hand, had no problem accessing anger. In fact, his angry outbursts had gotten him into trouble. Our exploration using the "Global Coaching Process" (Rosinski, 2003) involved tools such as the Myers-Briggs Type Indicator® (MBTI®)[4] and the Fundamental Interpersonal Relations Orientation–Behavior™ (FIRO-B®).[5]

After studying the MBTI® booklet (Briggs Myers, 2000, 25), Jacques decided he had an ENTJ (Extraverted, iNtuitive, Thinking, Judging) type. He underlined the following "potential areas for growth" passage in the booklet because it felt spot on:

- If ENTJs do not find a place where they can use their gifts and be appreciated for their contributions, they usually feel frustrated and may
  - Become too impersonal and critical
  - Be intrusive and directive
  - Become abrasive and verbally aggressive.
- It is natural for ENTJs to give less attention to Feeling and Sensing parts. If neglected too much, however, they may
  - Fail to notice or value another's need for personal rapport, appreciation, and praise
  - Fail to factor into their plans the needs of others for support.[6]

His FIRO-B® scores showed that he put his highest energy (need and behavior) in Expressed Control, way above Affection.

This was consistent with the ideals Jacques talked about when we investigated his desires. His accomplishments were of utmost importance: "I summarize my life by what I do and not what I am. I make all required efforts to reach the goals."

He was highly motivated to win (at work and in sports) and be recognized as a true professional. His enthusiasm, drive, and dedication came at the expense of relationships, which he viewed as merely instrumental. He was impatient with subpar performance and quality.

As it turns out, Jacques prided himself on being fair and honest with people. And although he had not realized it, he was a sensitive and caring person. But he had learned over the years to conceal this nurturing side. The complaints about his verbal abuses served as a wake-up call. He was genuinely affected and saddened. Tools such as the MBTI®, FIRO-B®, and COF (which emphasized his penchant for direct communication, doing, and competition, and which we will examine in Chapter 7) made him aware of his natural (and cultural) pitfalls. His ego was preserved: all personalities have pitfalls. More important, he could do something about the problem.

Jacques took several routes to move from OK–not OK under stress to OK–OK.

One was to reduce his overall stress level through regular meditation sessions during the day: simply breathing in, breathing out, and focusing on the here and now. By stepping back from the frenzy, albeit momentarily, Jacques could remember his intention to stay in an OK–OK mode.

Jacques also started to build relationships, talking to people not only for business but also to find out about them.

In meetings, he began paying closer attention to his own feelings, to others' feelings, and to nonverbal manifestations. In other words, he stopped simply focusing on the content and became conscious of the process. He developed a mindful presence. When he noticed he was becoming angry and impatient, he got into the habit of taking a deep breath. Initially, he chose not to speak to avoid making a hostile remark he would later regret. Gradually, as he felt more at ease with listening and maintaining his composure, he started to speak up again, assertively rather than aggressively. He learned to ask questions in a calm yet determined way, rather than judging and telling people what to do.

The journaling process proved very useful: Jacques used it to capture his successful interactions and the remaining challenges. We acknowledged the former and explored the latter together. I typically asked, "What prevented you from . . . ?" He identified new obstacles. Then I asked, "What can you do about this?" Or "How could you overcome this difficulty?" I offered suggestions if he could not figure out what to do differently. I also reminded him of insights he had gained earlier. I shared tools along the way. This included a more detailed description of transactional analysis's centers of resources (ego states): he learned to speak more often with his Adult (e.g., asking genuine questions) and avoid overusing his normative Parent (e.g., proffering judgments). It also included NLP's meta-model.[7] Role plays gave him a chance to practice and leave the coaching session with concrete new tactics for handling the remaining challenges.

Eventually, Jacques was able to manage his emotions, avoid counterproductive behaviors, and show his caring side while retaining his emphasis on business results. His manager later confided in me that he hadn't believed such drastic positive change was possible.

As coaches, we need to live in the OK–OK region. Had I seen Jacques as fundamentally not OK—that is, unable to change his ineffective behaviors— had I failed to notice the positive intentions behind the unflattering mask, I would have reinforced the OK–not OK position and propagated the vicious circle.

WEAVING MULTIPLE PERSPECTIVES INTO TRANSACTIONAL ANALYSIS

The previous examples should make apparent that even when we choose TA (or any other psychological approach) as the prime method, we shouldn't exclude other approaches. Quite the contrary.

In Jean's case, the emotional work complemented TA. In his book *Au Coeur de la Relation d'Aide* (*At the Heart of the Helping Relationship*), Vincent Lenhardt describes a similar approach that combines TA and bioenergy (2008).[8] He advocates for integrative psychotherapy and coaching and is dismayed by the petty-minded quarrels between various schools in psychology.

In Jacques's case, psychometric tools such as the MBTI® and FIRO-B®, and NLP proved useful. Multiple perspectives within psychology were augmented by perspectives outside psychology. In particular, the political perspective (see Chapter 6) served Jacques well. He learned to map out his various stakeholders and began building alliances with noteworthy discipline.

As far as psychology is concerned, I regularly refer to other theories as well. Let us now delve into some of these.

POSITIVE PSYCHOLOGY[9]

Psychology is essential for both coaching and psychotherapy. At their core, these practices differ thusly:

1. Psychotherapy typically aims at relieving clients (often referred to as "patients") from suffering, which can take various forms (e.g., anxiety, phobia, depression, lack of confidence, relationship difficulties). Psychotherapy is, fundamentally, about reducing or removing pain.

2. Coaching helps people who already feel reasonably well and successful to be even more fulfilled and successful. Coaching is, fundamentally, about increasing joy.

In practice, the boundaries are not always sharply drawn, and coaching and psychotherapy can overlap, in part because of the wide range of approaches within psychotherapy itself (e.g., behavioral psychology versus psychoanalysis) (Rosinski, 2004).

Still, psychotherapy is generally associated with diminishing deficiencies, curing illness, and solving problems, and coaching focuses on deploying human potential and addressing challenges.

The deficiency outlook has long dominated psychology. However, a new current, positive psychology, is starting to change the problem-fixing mindset (Seligman and Csikszentmihalyi, 2000). Capturing the essence of the positive psychology movement, Seligman describes a full life as "experiencing positive emotions about the past and future, savoring positive feelings from the pleasures, deriving abundant gratification from your signature strengths, and using these strengths in the service of something larger to obtain meaning" (Seligman, 2002). This relatively recent trend takes psychology back to the humanistic movement of Carl Rogers and Abraham Maslow, who based their approaches on a fundamental belief that people have the innate capacity for growth and development. The counselor's role is to encourage the unleashing or revealing of potential rather than to "fix" or "change" the client.

Carol Kauffman's chapter in the *Evidence Based Coaching Handbook* (Kauffman, 2006, 221) shows how positive psychology can help scientifically ground the field of coaching, which has emerged through the work of practitioners rather than in academic circles: "It is our belief that positive psychology theory and research will provide the scientific legs upon which the field of coaching can firmly stand." Kauffman offers positive psychology research that shows the merits of building on the positive (which is, in my view, the essence of coaching and does not exclude dealing with difficulties). It is comforting to notice this trend in psychotherapy, and to entertain the idea that psychotherapy is starting to learn lessons from effective coaching!

That said, neither psychologists nor coaches should take credit for the underlying idea in positive psychology, which dates back several centuries. The great philosopher Baruch Spinoza argued in the seventeenth century that joy, positive energy *par excellence*, is the path to human development: "Joy is a man's passage from a lesser to a greater perfection. Sadness is a man's passage from a greater to a lesser perfection" (Spinoza, 1677/1996, 104). Spinoza's writing had deep resonance. I discovered his Ethics after I wrote *Leading for Joy* (1998), in which I shared a similar insight:

> *The ultimate goal is not measured in terms of shareholder value, nor is it about customer or employee satisfaction. These may be valuable targets, calling for estimable achievements but the real indicator is whether joy has been created (and pain reduced) through your enterprise, whether happiness has been fostered (and misery alleviated) thanks to your efforts.*
>
> *Joy unleashes a flow of positive energy, liberates the human potential, creates a virtuous circle for the customers, for the employees, for society and the world overall. The joy we refer to has a broad scope. It includes simple things such as laughing with friends, enjoying a good meal in good company, dancing or physical pleasure. Joy is a spontaneous expression of a soul and a body in peace. Happiness is achieved when you start understanding your real needs and motives, those of others and you embark on a journey to discover all these further and serve them.*

In her chapter, Kauffman notably discusses

- positive emotions and their multifold benefits
- royal roads to happiness
- the notion and condition of flow; being vitally engaged in one's life and grounded in a sense of meaning and purpose
- the triumph of hope based in reality
- diagnosing strengths
- authentic happiness

Positive emotions "broaden and build" access to personal competencies. In the physical realm, positive emotions have been shown to increase immune function, improve resilience to adversity, reduce inflammatory response to stress, increase resistance to rhinoviruses, lower cortisol, and a number of studies show they predict longevity. Positive emotions are central to psychological flourishing and have been found to have a significant impact on increasing intuition and creativity, and attention span.

Positive emotions increase our capacity to use multiple social, cognitive, and affective resources and to take an integrated, long-term perspective. Also, positive emotions have been found to have a powerful effect on work teams, which translates into profitability. Research data suggest that negative emotions serve to quickly negotiate life/death challenges, but positive emotions are connected to competencies we need most of the time.

Mihalyi Csikszentmihalyi's research shows that beyond meeting our survival and safety needs, what we have doesn't matter. What matters is how mindfully we experience things. Some studies reveal a "hedonic treadmill" phenomenon—in which individuals quickly acclimate to their new possessions or positions without finding happiness in these—and a negative relationship between materialism and happiness.

Research confirms that being vitally engaged in one's life and grounded in a sense of meaning and purpose is a powerful route to happiness. Csikszentmihalyi discusses the notion of flow, or *état de grace*, or being in the zone, and most interestingly describes the "conditions of flow."

Coaches should become familiar with this theory, particularly the link between happiness and a sense of meaning and purpose. (Research connects the psychological and spiritual perspectives.) We can apply the theory during coaching sessions, helping clients find their own ways to access the high-performance state of flow. These findings from positive psychology provide, *a posteriori*, additional validation of the Global Scorecard model (Rosinski, 2003), which includes internal objectives (e.g., experiencing flow, serenity, and joy, and building on one's strengths) and external objectives such as "improving the world" as a potentially rich source of meaning and purpose. The Global Scorecard emphasizes the interplay between the various categories for fostering success for self and others. See Chapter 12 (Rosinski, 2003).

Other useful research in Kauffman's chapter includes Peterson and Seligman's classification system of strengths. Their findings point once again in the same direction as global coaching. For example, "wisdom and knowledge" is the first category, and it includes these five subcategories: creativity, curiosity, open-mindedness, love of learning, and perspective.

Overall, global coaching can help promote "authentic happiness" (characterized by a joyful, engaged, and meaningful life) while utilizing positive psychology research on the ingredients of "authentic happiness."[10]

PSYCHOANALYSIS

Psychoanalysis was developed by Sigmund Freud and his followers. It can be defined as "a system of psychological theory and therapy which aims to treat mental disorders by investigating the interaction of conscious and unconscious elements in the mind and bringing repressed fears and conflicts into the conscious mind by techniques such as dream interpretation and free association" (*The New Oxford Dictionary of English*, 1998).

Coaches cannot be expected to master this large body of ideas. However, we do want to pay particular attention to what is referred to as "defense mechanisms."

Defense Mechanisms

In psychoanalytic theory, defense mechanisms are "any of a group of mental processes that enables the mind to reach compromise solutions to conflicts that it is unable to resolve. The process is usually unconscious, and the compromise generally involves concealing from oneself internal drives or feelings that threaten to lower self-esteem or provoke anxiety. The concept derives from the psychoanalytic hypothesis that there are forces in the mind that oppose and battle against each other."[11]

George Vaillant (1977) classifies defense mechanisms in a hierarchy corresponding to the person's psychoanalytical developmental level.[12]

Level IV refers to mature defenses, which are commonly found among healthy adults. This is what coaches will often deal with, since, unlike psychotherapists, they primarily work with healthy and successful adults. Mature defenses include

- humor: connecting with the funny side inherent in an event that might be unpleasant
- anticipation: realistic planning for future discomfort
- altruism: constructive service to others that brings pleasure and personal satisfaction
- identification: the unconscious modeling of one's self upon another person's character and behavior
- sublimation: transformation of negative emotions or instincts into positive actions, behavior, or emotion
- suppression: the conscious decision to delay paying attention to an emotion or need in order to cope with the present reality; the ability to later access uncomfortable or distressing emotions and accept them

However, reality is not black-and-white. Even if our coachees (and we ourselves) are doing reasonably well and seem healthy overall, we need to prepare ourselves to encounter less favorable defense mechanisms. Then we will not be surprised when our coachees manifest these reactions. We will be equipped to appreciate the dynamics at play rather than remain confused and clueless about what happened. We will also learn to monitor our own reactions when we are confronted with these dynamics.

Level III defense mechanisms are considered neurotic, albeit still fairly common. They include:

- intellectualization: separation of emotion from ideas (for example, Jean, who was not in touch with his anger)

- displacement: redirecting emotion from its real object to a safer outlet (e.g., not voicing frustration with one's boss *to* one's boss and instead shouting at employees or family members)

- reaction formation: converting "dangerous" or anxiety-provoking unconscious wishes or impulses into their opposites (e.g., becoming a strong advocate for ethics, while being tempted to act unethically); the problem is that the impulse may eventually prevail

- repression: burying painful or dangerous thoughts in the unconscious; the emotion is conscious, but the idea behind it is absent (e.g., wanting to beat a colleague instead of sharing best practices despite one's rhetoric about collaboration, and failing to deal with the contradiction)

- regression: temporarily reverting to an earlier stage of ego development rather than handling unacceptable impulses in a more adult way (e.g., succumbing to irrational fears, being unable to maintain a confident face, and impulsively leaving or giving up)

At this stage, coaches should be able to help coachees become aware of the dynamic so they can handle the difficult situation and make informed choices. Coachees might recognize that the way they dealt with problems earlier in life no longer works in the current context. They might recognize their power and choice to act differently today. However, coaches need to tread carefully here. If coachees seem unable to take the actions they set, expressing that this is beyond their will, it may be the sign of a resistance at a deeper level. Painful emotions linked with past trauma may be reemerging; perhaps the new circumstances have somehow triggered associations with the past. When this happens (very rarely, in my experience), I typically gently suggest that my coachee sees a psychotherapist or even a psychiatrist if they show symptoms of severe anxiety or depression. I remember referring an executive once to a psychiatrist who confirmed the depression I suspected. We stopped the coaching and the process was resumed several months afterwards when the coachee felt well again after having been treated by the psychiatrist.

Level II defense mechanisms have been called immature defenses by Vaillant. They include

- projection: attributing one's own unacknowledged unacceptable/unwanted thoughts and emotions to another
- hypochondriasis: the transformation of negative feelings toward others into negative feelings toward the self—pain, illness, and anxiety
- passive aggression: aggression toward others expressed indirectly or passively
- idealization: subconsciously choosing to perceive another individual as having more positive qualities than he or she may have

These defenses often occur during adolescence, but they become very problematic for the adult. They may accompany severe depression and personality disorders. These mechanisms may temporarily lessen distress, but if a coachee is pathologically unable to take ownership of such defenses, coaching becomes ineffective and inadequate, and the coachee will be better served by therapy. However, if the coachee has a strong enough ego, she may recognize some of these mechanisms and feel confident about her ability to change. Thus she can move to an OK–OK position. This regularly happens in coaching, since most coachees begin from a place of strength. Executive coaching provides a benevolent and safe environment for this authentic exploration and ensures that the confrontation is always constructive. The coachee's courage, determination, and humility to question herself does the rest—that is, it enables personal growth and transformation.

Level I refers to psychotic defenses and includes

- denial: refusal to accept external reality because it is too threatening
- distortion: a gross reshaping of external reality to meet internal needs

In my experience, these manifestations are uncommon among executives who voluntarily enter the coaching process. The main merit of the psychoanalytical perspective in coaching is to prepare the coach for seemingly irrational and paradoxical reactions. Let me share a personal example. A company asked me to help them promote diversity. I met with certain managers who boasted that they had traveled to and lived in several countries;

some claimed to speak several languages. At a dinner in a local restaurant (in the U.S.), two of them displayed their knowledge of French wines. Yet when I introduced the concept of attitudes vis-à-vis cultural differences (differentiating between ethnocentrism and ethnorelativism), the managers met my remarks with unusual resistance: frustration, even anger. They felt I was wasting their time, telling them things they already knew.

After further conversation, I realized the company was only paying lip service to diversity. A senior executive said, for example, "Asians we deal with should simply adapt to our processes." Fortunately for him, his customers were multinational corporations, many of which were already making sure the local Asian businesses followed U.S. headquarters' processes. The executives could maintain a U.S.-centric attitude while superficially adapting to some local customs. I realized many of these executives were not emotionally ready to question their "diversity as a politically correct gimmick" approach and to engage instead on a genuine path of appreciating diversity. Most of them were in denial.

The denial came with projection: rather than acknowledging their limited competence around diversity, the executives projected it onto me, their coach.

Coaches often risk becoming the "ritual pig," sacrificed to preserve the team's cohesion and the status quo. Coaches risk entering the not OK–OK zone, feeling embarrassed, guilty and incompetent. We may not always be able to turn around the situation (it takes two to tango), but we must at least learn to deal productively with the counter-transference dynamic. As Lenhardt (2008, 68) explains, "[The coach] needs to be able to manage his own emotional and affective reactions, which have been reactivated by the transfer upon him from the person he is helping." In other words, we need to be open to feedback and have the humility to accept our inevitable mistakes, but we should not succumb to negative projections. Rather than taking the criticism personally, lamenting the unfair treatment, and playing the Victim, we should instead maintain the OK–OK assertive and constructive position.

Complex situations spanning multiple cultures create a particular fertile terrain for psychoanalytical manifestations such as denial and projection. These unconscious dynamics represent formidable learning opportunities for the coachee; global coaching offers many tools to enable successful confrontations that will foster new insights and effective transformation. Masterful coaching helps coachees reclaim their consciousness and their freedom to make authentic choices.

Coaches should resist the temptation to abandon coachees and refer them to a therapist (unless serious emotional pain prevents the coachees from functioning normally and they seem likely to suffer an emotional collapse if the coach brings unconscious motives to the surface). At the same time, coaches should refrain from trying to "do it all," acknowledging and respecting their own limitations. Coaches should refer the coachee to therapists if the situation demands it.

The Case of Psychopaths

Coaches believe in human potential and assume positive intentions; therefore, they have a hard time facing the stark reality of intentionally evil behaviors. In their book *Snakes in Suits* (2006), Paul Babiak and Robert Hare uncovered the ways in which psychopaths operate in the workplace; they also explain how to defend oneself against them.

Psychopathy is a personality disorder. Psychopaths are "without conscience and incapable of empathy, guilt, or loyalty to anyone but themselves," write Babiak and Hare. They refer to psychopaths' "emotional disconnect": "an inability to experience or express normal feelings concerning the effects their actions have had on other people."

This emotional disconnect is also a strength of sorts: psychopaths don't have to deal with the compassion, guilt, and remorse that the vast majority of us feel if we harm someone. They have no qualms about inflicting suffering. They look for excitement, which involves taking unreasonable risks and manipulating and conning people to get their way. They abuse trust and behave like predators. They can come across as very charming and exude a sense of confidence, which make them attractive to potential employers looking for charismatic leaders. Although previous research suggested that psychopathic types could not survive in the corporate world, Babiak and Hare have found that the modern corporation provides an excellent breeding ground for such employees. Indeed, in a culture that values high risk, image over substance, and short-term performance, they feel at home. Smart psychopaths often get away with their abusive behaviors.

Psychopaths' inability to experience deep human emotions, especially love and compassion, or to build genuine relationships with others, puts them out of touch with the holographic universe, which assumes the dynamic interconnection of all things. Disconnected psychopaths represent the antithesis of the whole person, who is united with himself and with the world at large. Emotional cut-off is at odds with the developed self, which can only be achieved when one's ego has embraced one's shadow.

Can one apply the OK–OK mindset when dealing with psychopaths? I believe so, but we need to clarify what "OK" means in this situation. "I am OK" means I remain self-confident, maintain self-esteem despite the psychopath's attempts to destabilize me, and forgive myself if I fall into the psychopath's trap or fail to expose him. OK–OK means that I will deal assertively with the psychopath: firmly but without overt aggression (which would likely backfire anyway), calmly but with determination. Keep in mind that OK–OK never means blind and naïve acceptance and trust.

That said, the psychological perspective is usually insufficient to confront psychopaths. These are master players of the political game, which they practice in a negative and destructive fashion. To protect oneself and one's organization from these predators requires engaging in constructive politics, notably by building alliances. We will examine how to do this in the next chapter.

It is likely that there were several psychopaths among the reckless top executives who precipitated the fall of major banks in the 2008 financial crisis and who felt no remorse or responsibility for their foolish actions.

These are not the type of people who would engage in personal development work with a global coach. However, coaches may encounter psychopaths on occasion. In such cases, the psychoanalytical perspective will help warn you about the danger. However, don't assume that someone is a psychopath simply because she is displaying some of these characteristics. When in doubt, you might want to refer to Babiak and Hare's description and advice.

FREEDOM

Let me end this chapter with a contradictory view. The French philosopher Jean-Paul Sartre refused the Freudian concept of the unconscious, preferring the notion of "bad faith" of the conscience. The executives I discussed earlier probably knew deep inside that they were not honest and that they were only paying lip service to the value of diversity. According to Sartre,[13] man is not the puppet of his unconscious mind. As Sartre puts it, "man is condemned to be free." Unlike an inanimate object, whose essence (raison d'être) precedes its existence (e.g., a glass is built to hold a liquid), "man's existence precedes its essence." In other words, man is free to choose that essence. The executives I discussed could either live as "bastards" (literally translating Sartre's expression "salauds," which I would not use with my clients!), contented with their "bad faith," or choose to make their actions consistent with their words. They could overcome their negative mental conditioning to develop an authentic way of being, taking advantage of the coaching help available.

Global coaches, who embrace complexity and its paradoxes, are not disturbed by the contradiction. If the unconscious exists, it can be unfolded; it should not be an excuse for avoiding responsibility.

Global coaching gives us the multiple perspectives and interconnected tools to help people become aware of their biases, expand their worldviews, discover new options, embrace complexity, and, consequently, exercise their freedom. Because transactional analysis so simply and brilliantly enables people to face their responsibility and choices in any situation, it has become my favorite psychological tool.

NOTES

1. I would like to acknowledge Michel Chalude, who trained me and was one of the first psychologists to bring TA in Europe. I am also grateful to Janine Somers, who successfully used TA as a psychotherapist, and gave me a chance to learn it as part of my own personal development.
2. Moreover, "an exchange of strokes constitutes a *transaction*, which is the unit of social intercourse" (Berne, 1964, 15); hence *transactional analysis*.
3. Names of coachees have been modified and the name of the corporate client is not divulged to preserve anonymity.
4. See Briggs Myers, 2000.
5. See Waterman and Rogers, 2007. See also the individual executive coaching study in Chapter 7.
6. Jacques chose these two "Feeling"-related items, Feeling being actually his inferior function. Naomi Quenk offers this explanation about the inferior function: "We are all capable of using our tertiary and inferior functions when a particular task requires them. When our least preferred process is being used consciously, we might think of it as our *fourth* or *least preferred function*. When this process is engaged unconsciously and operates outside our control, it serves as our *inferior* function . . . [The] deliberate use of the least preferred functions is quite different from the involuntary occurrence, or 'attack,' that we describe as being in the grip of one's inferior function" (Quenk, 1993, 47–48).
7. I have described how to use these two tools in Appendixes 1 and 2 of my first book, *Coaching Across Cultures*.
8. See Chapter 2. Lenhardt holds a PhD in psychology. He is a psychotherapist as well as a coach.
9. This section is adapted from Abbott and Rosinski, 2007.
10. Intercultural research can add to the evidence base of positive psychology research with insights on cultural variations in how people conceive happiness.

Further, such research can have relevance in coaching across cultures. For example, the American-Taiwanese researcher Jeanne Tsai has done numerous studies that show striking variations in what sort of happiness people want. She found that European-Americans aspire more often to a high-energy elation—perhaps because American culture is so individualistic and prizes the ability to influence others. However, people raised in more collectivist Asian cultures—which prioritize adjusting to others—aspire more often to a tranquil joy. Asian Americans, influenced by both cultures, tend to fall somewhere in the middle (Tsai, 2006).

Coaches need to consider coachees' cultural background as they seek to facilitate reflection and engage in dialogue about aspirations and joys.

11. *www.britannica.com/EBchecked/topic/155704/defense-mechanism*. Retrieved on 15 May 2009.
12. Some of the explanations in the following text are adapted from "Defence mechanism," Wikipedia *http://en.wikipedia.org/wiki/Defence_mechanism*. Viewed on 15 and 18 May 2009. The examples are mine.
13. See notably Sartre, 1946.

CHAPTER 6

The Political Perspective— Building Power and Service

Politics is an activity that builds and maintains your power so that you can achieve your goals.

In 1998, I made the case for "constructive politics," arguing that it is essential for leadership:[1]

> Go into any organization and say the word *politics*, and you will see most people shake their heads disdainfully. It has largely a negative connotation, suggesting hidden agendas, manipulation, deceit, alienation, struggling, and jockeying for positions. At worst, it is seen as destructive; at best, a necessary evil.
>
> In my view, however, organizational politics does not have to be destructive. In fact, it is fundamental, essential to having an impact as a leader. In order for it to be constructive, though, leaders must put aside their negative view, approach it systematically, and engage in it with a sense of purpose.
>
> In my work coaching executives and senior management teams, I have found that it is helpful to think about constructive politics in terms of two dimensions: *power and service.*

Coaches can help coachees systematically examine their sources of power and power dynamics. The notion of constructive politics is consistent with the basic values of coaching. I have defined *politics* as "an activity that builds and maintains your power so that you can achieve your goals." Accordingly, *power* can be understood as "the ability to achieve your meaningful, important goals." Politics is a process. Power is potential, and it comes from many sources. In *Constructive Politics*, I refer to the following sources of power: external networks, internal allies, knowledge, credibility, the ability to generate choices, formal authority, interpersonal skills, and intrapersonal skills. Politics becomes constructive when it also works in the service of others—when we attempt to understand the hopes, needs, and dreams of people and to creatively seek common ground between their goals and ours. We want to be open to their wishes while staying true to ours, looking for synergies or for innovative, win-win situations. One goal may be to help others achieve *their* goals (Rosinski, 2003, 123).

SOURCES OF POWER[2]

As we review habitual sources of power, I invite you to think about a challenging situation you face. You might want to rate the relative power you have in the situation, considering each source separately on a scale of 0 (no power available) to 5 (great power available). This simple assessment may help you uncover important sources of power you've overlooked. For example, you may have failed to identify allies who could support you; without other options available, you might feel constrained to put up with an unpleasant situation. Conversely, you may realize that you have more power than you think, and reflect on ways to leverage this power. As a global coach, you can help your coachees use this systematic assessment. The next step is to devise ways to build more power, ensuring that it is broad-based by developing as many sources as possible, and capitalizing on the power you already have available.

External Network

There is power in knowing and having access to key people in the environment outside the organization, people who may be able to help the organization in some significant way—for instance, a potential large customer, an influential political figure, or a useful expert.

Internal Allies

Interdependency is inherent to organizational life. We need others to achieve our goals. Therefore, we need to build and maintain a strong network of internal allies. Power comes from developing a good relationship with key people inside the organization. One effective way to do this is to contribute substantively to their work. Another is to contribute in some way to their lives—for instance, giving people the opportunity to take part in a project that is especially important to them because it relates to a personal goal.

Knowledge

Physical power and material wealth were once the dominant sources of power. In *Powershift*, Alvin Toffler argued that knowledge has overtaken them (1990). He explains that organizations avidly seek pertinent information that will help them take the edge over competitors. The same idea applies to individuals and teams.

Quantity of information is not the issue. We are awash in information. What we need is synthesized, up-to-date information—that is, knowledge—that is specifically pertinent to organizational challenges.

Credibility

If leaders (and workers in general) are believable and trustworthy, and if they consistently perform well, their ability to achieve their goals is increased.

Others will want to call upon such workers. That puts them in demand and increases their power—as long as they meet (or exceed) expectations and honor the trust that's been put in them.

Just as companies advertise the merits of their products and brands, workers need to recognize the importance of marketing themselves to reinforce their credibility. I regularly work with high-performing executives who consider that their results should speak for themselves. This works until they are passed over for promotion by a colleague with fewer accomplishments but more political activities.

Choice

Providing oneself with alternatives in any situation can be a source of power. This is a basic negotiation principle. Roger Fisher and William Ury (1981) refer to it as the BATNA (best alternative to a negotiated agreement). For example, consider a situation in which a manager is negotiating with a computer vendor; if a range of models meets the manager's quality requirements but the vendor has to meet sales targets, then the manager is in a position of relative power. Thus it is best to avoid, consequently, becoming overly dependent on a superior, subordinate, customer, or supplier.

Formal Authority

This is the source of power most people are familiar with: having control of resources and decisions. The growing appreciation of leadership without authority notwithstanding, formal authority remains politically important, certainly in hierarchical cultures but even in equalitarian ones. Although authority alone is no guarantee that one's goals will be accomplished, it does typically provide more resources and opportunities to put ideas into actions. This can facilitate bigger success and increased visibility, which in turn can lead to further opportunities to achieve important goals.

Interpersonal Skills

Leadership study and training often focus on interpersonal skills as a source of power. Persuasiveness, humor, assertiveness, respect for others, and the ability to embrace different perspectives are skills that increase one's capacity to work effectively with others to foster support and commitment to organizational goals (especially those aligned with one's personal goals).

Intrapersonal Skills

Power can also come from abilities such as individual creativity (the capacity to see problems from various perspectives and to frame issues in advantageous ways), physical fitness (energy and endurance), optimism, and mental skills (for instance, a good memory for facts).

Former Belgium Prime Minister Wilfried Maertens often won negotiations late in the night, when everybody else got tired and was ready to leave.

U.S. Presidents Bill Clinton and Barack Obama projected an impressive and contagious optimism. "Yes, we can" symbolizes this confidence amid great challenges.

DYNAMIC APPROACH

Coaches can provide invaluable help by considering sources of power in a systematic fashion, identifying the key areas to focus on and concrete ways for building that power.

In my previous book, I explained how managers can build internal alliances by identifying key stakeholders, assessing their proximity to each key stakeholder (both from a strategic alignment and a relational closeness standpoint), getting to know their key stakeholders and finding synergies, and dealing with challenging situations.[3]

Simply mapping out the stakeholders during a coaching session often reveals important gaps: coachees, despite their seniority, might barely know certain colleagues with considerable clout who can affect outcomes of important projects. Proactively building select relationships becomes a goal.

Coaches might help coachees identify or create the best opportunities for doing so, including being prepared for brief and sometimes impromptu encounters with these powerful stakeholders.

Coaches can also help uncover stakeholders' motives and find constructive ways to address strategic differences by devising a way to leverage the diversity and synthesize viewpoints. This usually involves tapping into the other global coaching perspectives, particularly psychology, culture, and spirituality.

This approach can go a long way, and nothing else is usually required. However, for the politically minded, or those who want to unearth and defend themselves against damaging political tactics, let me mention an amusing and cultivated guide for modern Machiavellians, *The 48 Laws of Power* (Greene and Elfers, 1998). For example, their advice to "make use of the cat's paw" is cynical, inviting workers to build their power at a colleague's expense.

> *In the fable, the Monkey grabs the paw of his friend, the Cat, and uses it to fish chestnuts out of the fire, thus getting the nuts he craves without hurting himself.*
>
> *If there is something unpleasant or unpopular that needs to be done, it is far too risky for you to do the work yourself. You need a cat's-paw—someone who does the dirty, dangerous work for you. The cat's-paw grabs what you need, hurts whom you need hurt, and keeps people from noticing you are the one responsible. (1998, 206)*

This would not qualify as constructive politics! Yet the recommendation may be appropriate for anyone regularly caught in the ingrate executioner role. In this case, it makes sense to call upon others to do their share. However, aside from any moral considerations, the advice will not be politically savvy in all cases. Taking a courageous, albeit unpopular, stand can earn you respect and thus power. The example of former French President François Mitterand comes to mind. In 1981, he ensured capital punishment would be abolished at a time when a majority still favored it. Quickly, though, this decision contributed to building Mitterand's statesman stature.

SERVICE[4]

Politics cannot be constructive if it is only for the benefit of the leader. It must work in the service of others—superiors, subordinates, peers, customers, and shareholders—as well as society in general. Power gives impact and leverage;

service guides our actions. In my experience, accessing the spiritual perspective is an effective way to embrace a larger purpose and become genuinely dedicated to serving others.

Leaders vary in their relative orientation toward service, depending not only on the strength of their commitment to others but also on how many others they are trying to help. At the highest level, leaders are devoted to serving the world at large, not just their constituencies or immediate stakeholders. They are ready to sacrifice selfish interests if they go against the greater common good. Failing to address these serious issues would eventually mean loss of power for everyone.

Leaders vary in their eagerness and capacity to listen, empathize, trust, respect, share, and care. By developing emotional, cultural, and spiritual intelligence with the help of global coaching perspectives, leaders can unfold these qualities.

Listen

The ability to hear people out, without assuming that we know what they are going to say or interrupting them to advance our own view, is crucial to constructive politics. It means accepting and honoring disagreement and having faith that we will be able to work out a shared position at some point.

Empathize

In addition to listening to other people's positions and understanding them intellectually, empathizing means imagine ourselves in their situation and understanding their feelings and what causes them. Sometimes feelings, not just ideas, must be addressed.

Trust

Trust is crucial to constructive politics. That doesn't mean blind acceptance. Rather, we need to develop the ability to tell when people are being authentic and likely to be consistent in their actions, and factor this into our plan for achieving our goals.

Respect

Respecting people and the work they do is key to service. This can be difficult in organizations that particularly value certain kinds of work, such as financial analysis or strategizing, and downplay others, such as support functions.

Share

Although we shouldn't make the mistake of trying to convince everyone to take our view of a situation, we also need to let them know what our position is. This makes it possible for other people to understand and evaluate our words and actions.

Care

Probably the most important capacity we can bring to service is the choice to care. Without it, the other capacities may be merely instrumental. In the words of the psychologist Alfred Adler, caring is "a deep feeling of identification, sympathy, and affection in spite of occasional anger, impatience, or disgust" and "a genuine desire to help the human race."[5] Care is beyond morality, in the domain of love.

Taken together, these qualities can give direction to building and using power.

THE FOUR BASIC POLITICAL TYPES[6]

To understand the interaction of the two dimensions of Constructive Politics, power and service, think of four basic political types, which can be arranged in a two-by-two matrix (see table): the Individual Achiever, the Idealist, the Prince, and the Enlightened Builder. The four political types can help you assess your situation and set developmental goals for constructive politics. Power enables you to make your goals happen; service ensures that others too are better off as a result.

	High		
	THE IDEALIST		THE ENLIGHTENED BUILDER
SERVICE			
	THE INDIVIDUAL ACHIEVER		THE PRINCE
Low			
	Low	**POWER**	**High**

The Individual Achiever

With a low service orientation and not much power, individual achievers are seen as self-centered. This type can have a high technical competence and be very successful at some activities—think of a lone rock climber who can negotiate a long vertical ascent. If the conditions are right—with a protective boss or in a situation with few interdependencies—individual achievers likely will not feel powerless or feel the need to engage in politics. In an interdependent situation, however, they may be frustrated by the inability to focus on and productively engage in the technical work.

The Idealist

The idealist has a genuine desire to serve others but has little power. Often seen as a crusader, this type may succeed through perseverance but is often frustrated by bureaucratic obstacles. Idealists tend to resent politics; often this is because they avoid conflict. Because they focus on others, idealists may also devalue self-affirming activities that relate to personal goals. In some cases, they may end up blaming others for their failures and unconsciously play the victim.

The Prince

The prince, as described in the classic work by Machiavelli, has a lot of power but is largely committed to—or is *seen* as being largely committed to—self advancement. Although often viewed negatively, this type can make things happen and achieve objectives. However, the prince runs a high risk of alienating people, which in the long run can erode power.

The Enlightened Builder

With a desire to serve others and well-developed power, the enlightened builder is the type most likely to be described as a leader. This type can use politics to help people identify and respond to challenges en route to achieving the organization's mission. Enlightened builders have personal goals and accept that other people do too. They tap into these personal motivations to serve people in general.

DEVELOPING CONSTRUCTIVE POLITICS

Coaches and coachees can use the matrix to assess their current situation and identify gaps they need to bridge so that their power matches their ambition and so their actions have a positive, or at the very least a neutral, impact on society.

The matrix makes it clear, for example, that if coachees' generous and noble actions have only a frustrating paltry impact, they need to build power, moving from the Idealist quadrant to the Enlightened Builder position. Likewise, if coachees enjoy a power position but wonder about the legacy they will leave and aspire to create meaning in their life, they will need more service, to shift from the Prince to the Enlightened Builder.

The corresponding coaching questions can be open: What important sources of power have you overlooked? What can you do to build that particular source of power? Coachees can offer freewheeling ideas that coaches can follow with the usual checks: what would prevent you from doing this? Or: what would happen if you developed that capacity?[7]

Beyond these traditional coaching questions, the coach can offer tools and methodologies to systematically build alliances, a crucial source of power.

However, interacting at a cognitive level may not be sufficient. Accessing emotions is often critical. Contacting anger can be a potent way to reclaim power. Likewise, being in touch with sadness may facilitate the grieving process, leading one to give up futile pursuits in favor of a more fulfilling service-oriented path. Instinctual, emotional, and spiritual levels complete the cognitive exploration.

Archetypes

To facilitate this deeper journey, as you will discover in Chapter 10, global coaches can explicitly refer to the archetypes in our collective unconscious. The coach's role is to help unfold these necessary heroes that are within us all. At this stage, let me simply mention certain archetypes that are particularly relevant. Their names should give you a feel for what these archetypes represent and what they can contribute.

The Caregiver and Lover are clearly alive in the Idealist. The Warrior and Magician are present in the Prince. Together with the Ruler (guided by the Sage and derided by the Fool), they make up the Enlightened Builder. Other archetypes can also come into the picture. For example, the Explorer helps us to acquire new knowledge, and the Creator allows us to devise new solutions, thereby enhancing our power.

Progressing on the journey toward the Enlightened Builder (as much as necessary) becomes a matter of identifying the archetypes we need and developing these (as explained in Chapter 10). We unleash more of our potential by bringing these enfolded heroes to the fore. We facilitate this process with our coachees as well.

NOTES

1. Rosinski, 1998.
2. Adapted from Rosinski, 1998, 1–2.
3. See Rosinski, 2003, 138–140.
4. Adapted from Rosinski, 1998, 2–3.
5. See Adler, 1979, 15; Heinz Ansbacher notes that when "Maslow studied people of ideal mental health, he found that one of their characteristics was *Gemeinschaftsgefül* (social interest), which was Adler's criterion for mental health." Incidentally, we will refer again to *Gemeinschaft* in Chapter 11 when exploring Martin Buber's view.
6. Adapted from Rosinski, 1998, 3–4 and Rosinski 2003, 123–125.
7. The meta-model from neuro-linguistic programming is very useful in this sort of dialogue. See Rosinski, 2003, 267–271.

CHAPTER 7

The Cultural Perspective—
Promoting Diversity and
Creativity

A group's culture is the set of unique characteristics that distinguishes its members from another group.[1]

oaching, defined as "the art of facilitating the unleashing of people's potential to reach meaningful, important objectives" (Rosinski, 2003, 4), has developed essentially from common sense (e.g., setting priorities, managing time) and psychology (e.g., behavioral psychology, emotional intelligence). For many years, the cultural dimension was ignored or, at best, given anecdotal and superficial attention. Coaching, originating from the U.S., assumed a worldview that was not universally applicable. In *Coaching Across Cultures* (Rosinski, 2003), I aimed to help unleash more human potential by tapping into the richness of cultural diversity.

Coaching across cultures (also referred to as "intercultural coaching") has two goals:

- to enable more effective work across cultures (internationally and also when working with people from various organizations and backgrounds); and

- to offer in essence a more creative form of coaching. The approach challenges cultural assumptions. It propels you, the coach, and your coachees beyond previous limitations. It offers new options in the form of alternative ways of thinking, communicating, managing time, and engaging in our various activities.

A group's culture can be defined as the set of unique characteristics that distinguishes its members from another group (Rosinski, 2003, 20). These characteristics include external/visible behaviors as well as internal/buried traits such as norms, values, and basic assumptions. The poet David Whyte once said, "difficulties can fall away when we make our inner territory larger, while simplifying our outer work."[2] Intercultural coaches help their coachees raise their awareness and expand their worldview (internal reality) to address complex challenges and enable effective actions (external reality). In turn, these experiences enrich coachees' cultural repertoire, fostering an upward learning spiral.

Since the publication of *Coaching Across Cultures*, more people have recognized that culture should be taken into account.

A 2008 study by Andrew Lambert from the Corporate Research Forum among 50 companies in the United Kingdom (including several international organizations), highlighted coaching across cultures as a new trend: "The pace of globalization has quickened considerably since 2001, with few organizations unaffected. Many are now tacking the challenges of cross-border integration and relocation in order to fight for market position and cost-effectiveness" (63). Lambert explains, "In building what has been referred to as 'cultural intelligence', coaching works as a tailored adjunct to training in cultural awareness and integration activities." He gives me credit for "having provided the first comprehensive examination of this topic." Lambert also notes, "A cardinal point he makes is to consider more than just national cultures. Increasing cross-border M&As and joint ventures pose challenges of combining corporate as well as national cultures. Professional cultures represent another dimension. An organization may cover many professional disciplines . . ."

Several universities and business schools have started to weave coaching across cultures into their curriculum and research projects: these include Oxford Brookes University (Kate Gilbert) and Surrey University (Almuth McDowell and Céline Rojon) in the United Kingdom, and the University of Sydney (Anthony Grant and Geoffrey Abbott) in Australia. It is also the case at the Kenichi Ohmae Graduate School of Business in Tokyo, where I teach coaching across cultures for managers in the MBA in globalization.

But although Harvard Business School chose *Coaching Across Cultures* as its featured recommendation in the category of business leadership, U.S.

coaching (professional as well as leadership) seems slower to embrace cultural diversity. Maybe President Obama's multicultural background and openness in reaching out to other cultures (particularly nations and religions) will influence U.S. coaching, placing culture on the radar screen.

In 2006, several colleagues and I[3] started to offer a three-day advanced international coaching across cultures seminar. Participants are seasoned professional coaches, experienced leaders who are adept at using coaching, and skilled interculturalists. During the seminar, they learn experientially how to integrate the cultural dimension into coaching, and how to maximize opportunities from diversity.[4] In 2006, I also started to develop the COF online assessment, which I will elaborate on in this chapter.

However, despite these positive signals, we still have a long way to go before culture is systematically integrated into coaching and all coaches make an effort to learn about the cultural perspective and weave it into their practice, and before mainstream corporations and institutions become aware of intercultural coaching's benefits and start adopting it. The good news is that culture still represents a largely untapped opportunity.

THE CULTURAL ORIENTATIONS FRAMEWORK

To systematically integrate culture into coaching, we need a language with which to talk about culture—a vocabulary to describe cultural characteristics. The task may appear daunting: there is an almost infinite number of possible behaviors, norms, values, and basic assumptions. The good news is that we can take a pragmatic approach and focus on the most relevant and salient aspects, building upon the work of eminent interculturalists. The Cultural Orientations Framework (COF) (Rosinski, 2003, Part II) is meant to serve that purpose. The COF is *an integrative framework designed to assess and compare cultures*. The COF assessment is a coaching-specific measurement tool that can be invaluable for introducing meaningful dialogue about culture into coaching and coach training. It can be used to establish individual and collective COF profiles, while providing the scope for creating new cultural dimensions that reflect unique contexts.

The COF includes a range of cultural dimensions/orientations, grouped into seven categories of practical importance to leaders, professional coaches, and anyone striving to unleash human potential in organizations:

- sense of power and responsibility
- time management approaches

- definitions of identity and purpose
- organizational arrangements
- notions of territory and boundaries
- communication patterns
- modes of thinking

The COF builds upon the findings of anthropologists, communication experts, and cross-cultural consultants, including Florence Kluckhohn and Fred Strodtbeck (1961), Edward Hall (1976), Geert Hofstede (2001), and Fons Trompenaars (1997), among others.[5] A *cultural orientation* is an inclination to think, feel, or act in a way that is culturally determined, or at least influenced by culture. For example, in the United States, people tend to communicate directly, saying what they mean and meaning what they say. The message is clear, but it can also be perceived as offensive. Their cultural orientation, then, is direct communication, in contrast with Asians' typical indirectness. Asians don't necessarily spell out what they mean, at the risk of being misunderstood, because they wish to avoid hurting someone's feelings.

Cultural orientations are not black-and-white. In other words, no one is always direct or indirect; individuals and cultures lie somewhere on a continuum bounded by the extreme on both ends. For example, you may be inclined to be direct 75 percent of the time and indirect the rest of the time (see figure below). In other words, your cultural orientation, on the "direct-indirect communication" *cultural dimension*, is primarily "direct communication."

Example: Direct - Indirect communication cultural dimension

| 100% | 75% | 50% | 25% | 0% |
| direct | | | | direct |

Direct communication orientation   **Indirect communication orientation**

The COF has a number of uses:

Assess cultures. The COF provides a language to describe the salient traits of a culture and focus attention on key cultural variables and tendencies.

Discover new cultural choices. We may recognize an orientation for, say, hierarchical organization and compare it with a preference for a flat structure. Patterns that seemed natural and universal suddenly appear relative and even biased when contrasted with their opposites. Orientations that were overlooked or undiscovered offer new options for dealing with challenging situations.

Assess cultural differences. As Stewart and Bennett's research indicated, "The core difficulty in cross-cultural interaction is—simply stated—a failure to recognize relevant cultural differences" (1991, 6). When several cultures are involved, the COF provides a systematic approach to identify cultural differences as well as similarities among them.

Bridge different cultures. After pinpointing specific cultural differences, we can focus energy on bridging the gaps.

Envision a desired culture. The COF provides a vocabulary to describe an ideal culture. It then becomes a matter of building a bridge from the current culture to the desired one. The challenge is still great, but it becomes manageable.

Leverage cultural diversity. With cultural alternatives clearly identified, we can choose the best of the two or three viewpoints for each dimension. Whenever possible, we can make the most of cultural differences and achieve synergy.

Several important nuances distinguish the COF from previous models. Among these nuances:

Merit. The choice of words should convey the potential merit of each orientation. For example, I chose the term *humility* instead of *subjugation to nature* coined by Kluckhohn and Stodtbeck (1961).

Essence. I adhered to the essence of dimensions, which lies in their etymology. For example, I defined *monochronic time* simply as "concentrate on one activity and/or relationship at a time" in contrast with *polychronic time*, "concentrate simultaneously on multiple tasks and/or relationships." Hall's original concept (1976) includes other notions, such as scheduling and compartmentalization, which do not necessarily relate to the duality monochronic/polychronic time per se (Rosinski, 2003, 96).

Dialectics. Most important, I am less interested in describing static and binary traits of a culture (e.g., the French are like this, the Americans are like that) than in having a vocabulary to depict dynamic and complex cultural features. Aristotle declared that "out of two contradictory propositions, if one is true, the other must be false."[6] Ironically, this is true and false at the same time! *Binary thinking (or)* tends to promote

Cultural Orientations Framework

Categories	Dimensions	Description
Sense of Power and Responsibility	Control/ Harmony/ Humility	Control: People have a determinant power and responsibility to forge the life they want. Harmony: Strive for balance and harmony with nature. Humility: Accept inevitable natural limitations.
Time Management Approaches	Scarce/ Plentiful	Scarce: Time is a scarce resource. Manage time carefully! Plentiful: Time is abundant. Relax!
	Monochronic/ Polychronic	Monochronic: Concentrate on one activity and/or relationship at a time. Polychronic: Concentrate simultaneously on multiple tasks and/or people.
	Past/ Present/ Future	Past: Learn from the past. The present is essentially a continuation or a repetition of past occurrences. Present: Focus on the "here and now" and short-term benefits. Future: Have a bias towards long-term benefits. Promote a far-reaching vision.
Definitions of Identity and Purpose	Being/ Doing	Being: Stress living itself and the development of talents and relationships. Doing: Focus on accomplishments and visible achievements.
	Individualistic/ Collectivistic	Individualistic: Emphasize individual attributes and projects. Collectivistic: Emphasize affiliation with a group.
Organizational Arrangements	Hierarchy/ Equality	Hierarchy: Society and organizations must be socially stratified to function properly. Equality: People are equals who often happen to play different roles.
	Universalist/ Particularist	Universalist: All cases should be treated in the same universal manner. Adopt common processes for consistency and economies of scale. Particularist: Emphasize particular circumstances. Favor decentralization and tailored solutions.

	Stability/ Change	Stability: Value a static and orderly environment. Encourage efficiency through systematic and disciplined work. Minimize change and ambiguity, perceived as disruptive.
		Change: Value a dynamic and flexible environment. Promote effectiveness through adaptability and innovation. Avoid routine, perceived as boring.
	Competitive/ Collaborative	Competitive: Promote success and progress through competitive stimulation.
		Collaborative: Promote success and progress through mutual support, sharing of best practices and solidarity.
Notions of Territory and Boundaries	Protective/ Sharing	Protective: Protect oneself by keeping personal life and feelings private (mental boundaries), and by minimizing intrusions in one's physical space (physical boundaries).
		Sharing: Build closer relationships by sharing one's psychological and physical domains.
Communication Patterns	High-Context/ Low-Context	High-Context: Rely on implicit communication. Appreciate the meaning of gestures, postures, voice and context.
		Low-Context: Rely on explicit communication. Favor clear and detailed instructions.
	Direct/ Indirect	Direct: In a conflict or with a tough message to deliver, get your point across clearly at the risk of offending or hurting.
		Indirect: In a conflict or with a tough message to deliver, favor maintaining a cordial relationship at the risk of misunderstanding.
	Affective/ Neutral	Affective: Display emotions and warmth when communicating. Establishing and maintaining personal and social connections is key.
		Neutral: Stress conciseness, precision and detachment when communicating.
	Formal/ Informal	Formal: Observe strict protocols and rituals.
		Informal: Favor familiarity and spontaneity.
Modes of Thinking	Deductive/ Inductive	Deductive: Emphasize concepts, theories and general principles. Then, through logical reasoning, derive practical applications and solutions.
		Inductive: Start with experiences, concrete situations and cases. Then, using intuition, formulate general models and theories.
	Analytical/ Systemic	Analytical: Separate a whole into its constituent elements. Dissect a problem into smaller chunks.
		Systemic: Assemble the parts into a cohesive whole. Explore connections between elements and focus on the whole system.

polarization and division. *Dialectics* (*and*) helps us find new ways to reconcile alternatives, leverage differences, and enable unity in diversity (Rosinski, 2003, 57–58).

THE COF ASSESSMENT[7]

In 2006, I started to build an assessment tool based on the COF. The tool makes it possible to provide specific feedback to individuals and groups and identify concrete opportunities for development. I first used a paper (PDF) version of the COF assessment. Following the successful use of the instrument in that format, software experts and I developed an online assessment. The online version makes the COF assessment easily accessible to individuals, teams, and organizations around the world. You can contact me for further information; the tool is available at *www.cofassessment.com*.

The advantage of using the COF assessment to foster individual and collective development derives from the following hypotheses, which I and other coaches have verified through on-the-job use:

- When habitual solutions don't work, as is typically the case with recurrent and complex challenges, we need to review our cultural assumptions and examine our reality from alternative perspectives.
- Cultural orientations we overuse may get us into trouble (e.g., direct communication, when overdone, may bruise people and disrupt communication).
- Cultural orientations we overlook represent developmental opportunities (e.g., showing more sensitivity through appropriate indirect communication).

The COF assessment can facilitate a fruitful exploration around questions such as these:

- Referring back to your challenge, which cultural orientations may you be overdoing in this situation?
- In what ways does this get you into trouble?
- Which cultural orientations are you overlooking?
- How would this represent a growth opportunity for you?
- What would be different if you mastered that?

A project manager, specifically trained to use the COF, can administer the COF assessment to a team, division, organization, or even several corporations in the case of a merger or an alliance. Managers can review aggregate results globally and through sorting (e.g., per country, per division, per hierarchical level, per any combination of categories). Data concerning several projects in the same organization can be further aggregated to establish an organization profile. The tool allows users to

- aggregate individual results and establish *group profiles on a project basis* (e.g., team profile, organization overall profile, as well as profiles per categories/fields the project manager has predefined, such as division, nationality, management level, merging entities, et cetera)
- add *customized supplemental cultural dimensions* beyond the COF 17 standard dimensions

In truth, the cultural profile concept is somewhat of a stretch. Cultural orientations (unlike psychological preferences) depend to a large extent on the cultural context. This means that orientations frequently change (at least to some degree) depending on the situation (e.g., low context at work, high context with family and with close, longtime friends). Therefore, how can we establish a reliable cultural profile? One solution is to devise a cultural profile in each situation. The cultural profile would be accurate, but only in that situation. Another solution is to accept that an individual cultural profile is only meant to represent a default, an overall tendency.

A cultural profile does not always determine actions. For example, some people with an orientation toward competition might choose collaboration in a particular situation. Your cultural profile does not limit your potential. The opposite is true. Aware of your profile, you can discover new options outside your profile and tap into this unexpected potential. Coaches can help their coachees go through similar processes.

Methodological Considerations: Usefulness Versus Validity

Intercultural coaching assumes a "multiple realities" view of the world. Culture, from this perspective, is highly contextual, dynamic, and fluid. Capturing data through the COF assessment in a particular moment is useful for generating conversations and making sense of change processes, but not so helpful in seeking definitive truths about individuals, groups, or societies.

The questionnaire gives preference to simplicity and straightforwardness. The items are derived directly from the definition of each cultural orientation (see figure on pages 126–127). The aim is for participants to establish cultural profiles that constitute a *useful* basis for further discussion, rather than a truly *valid* measure. Paradoxically, this may sometimes yield more valid results than do properly validated psychometric instruments. The validation process often produces an illusion of absolute accuracy, which does not hold true in practice. Even the best researched and most popular assessments include assumptions and biases that might prove incorrect.

For example, many consider the Bar-On Emotional Quotient Inventory the best instrument to evaluate emotional intelligence, and it is certainly a useful coaching assessment tool (Bar-On, 2002). But I recently had the chance to review a report that showed a low score for "problem solving." One item that drove the score down had to do with a "step-by-step" approach. The assumption built into the instrument is that this method is a panacea, whereas, in my view, it reveals a Sensing (using the Myers-Briggs Type Indicator® terminology) psychological bias or/and a linear cultural bias. Intuition may be the best way to solve certain problems. Creativity—defined as the "faculty to find original ideas, different approaches, when confronted with a problem or a challenge that resists habitual solutions" (Rosinski, 2003, 187)—is essential.

Another example has to do with the apparent contradictions between separate conceptualization and research, both derived from Carl Jung's seminal work around psychological types (Jung, 1923): the popular Myers-Briggs Type Indicator® (Briggs Myers, 2000) and Dr. Katherine Benziger's Cerebral Cortex's Four Modes of Thinking (Benziger, 2006). The Judging-Perceiving (J-P) dichotomy is absent in Benziger's model. What is confusing for someone familiar with the MBTI® is that her description of the four modes *de facto* seems to assume either J or P in addition to the functions. For example, Frontal Right equates to Intuition Feeling (NF) and P. This works for me, since I have an ENFP preference, but what about someone with an NF and J preference? Benziger explains that she uses only parts of Jung's core model that have a solid physiological base, and that her work represents the synthesis of more than 30 years of neuroscience and psychology.[8] In sum, both schools can boast solid research to support their findings, and the findings are, in fact, mostly consistent. Yet the contradictions suggest that these findings are still merely hypotheses that should not be confused with an absolute truth.

The best scientific researchers employ openness and curiosity, paying close attention to what does not fit with current conceptualization. Einstein once said, "I have no special talent. I am only passionately curious." He also noted, "The important thing is not to stop questioning. Curiosity has its own reason for existing. One cannot help but be in awe when one contemplates the mysteries of eternity, of life, of the marvelous structure of reality" (Singh, 2004, 98–99).

All these qualities are also essential in global coaching; they should inspire us to exert caution when using theories, models, and psychometric instruments. When analyzing results, we should avoid either dismissing or accepting them too quickly. An open mind, together with healthy skepticism, is required to learn from any assessment. The person giving feedback needs a combination of rigor and curiosity to move beyond the illusion of absolute accuracy, to understand the instrument's biases and limitations, and to treat findings as working hypotheses.

Building a valid cultural psychometric instrument would be even trickier for several reasons:

- The notion that culture can be assessed with a questionnaire is already culturally biased.

- Language is an issue: English is widely known in international business, but it's far from universal. Translations can be problematic. For example, some concepts may not have an equivalent in a foreign language.

- Even within a given culture, built-in assumptions can distort results. When you add in cultural variables, there's a great risk that assumptions linking observable manifestations to concepts will not hold true.

Céline Rojon and Almuth McDowall of Surrey University in the United Kingdom performed a first validation study (Rojon, 2009) concerning the initial cross-validation of the Cultural Orientations Framework (COF) assessment questionnaire with the Saville Consulting Wave Focus Styles questionnaire (Saville Consulting, 2006), an existing validated measure of occupational personality. They gathered data from participants residing in the UK and Germany (total N = 222) to allow for a direct comparison. Rojon concludes, "The construct validity of the questionnaire was adequate, with convergent validity coefficients around r = .30 and divergent validity being supported by zero correlations for the majority of theoretically unrelated constructs. Concerning the comparison of the two cultures on personality, competency and cultural orientations, it was concluded that, contrary to previous findings (Ronen and Shenkar, 1985; Schwartz, 1999; House et al., 2004; Bartram et al., 2006), classifying the countries into distinct cultural clusters cannot be justified on the basis of the present results, with differences between the cultures' profiles mostly being negligible." Indeed, in this case, gender differences took precedence over nationalities. Of course, the study's authors don't imply that this will always be true. My own cultural audit of an alliance between a Dutch and a French company, which I will discuss later in this chapter, confirmed the expected national differences, which accounted for important behavioral variations (Equality versus Hierarchy and Direct versus Indirect communication). The fact that national differences come with other cultural differences is nevertheless significant. Rojon observes, "The present findings support Rosinski's (2003) inclusive and dynamic view of culture, which stands in contrast with the classical binary and static view, with its emphasis on categorizing individuals by their nationality."

This is not to suggest that the COF assessment is immune to difficulties. For example, participants in certain cultures may be reluctant to express disagreement and are therefore likely to skew measures of abilities. However, and paradoxically, the COF assessment may prove advantageous by merely striving to enable useful conversations without claiming to be absolutely valid. In intercultural coaching, it is important to give prime importance to conversations that flow *from* data rather than to the data itself or to the tools from which it is derived. With any instrument—the COF assessment included—it is critical to launch the assessment process carefully, giving clear instructions, warning against possible issues that might distort the results, and creating a safe and constructive environment that encourage candidness and growth from the outset.

In my experience, the COF assessment is well accepted by coachees. However, there are other options for addressing the cultural dimension topic. For example, coaches can use inductive approaches (Rosinski, 2003, 61–68), on their own or in combination with the COF assessment. To help coachees in this area, coaches must give attention to their own cultural orientations and how they might affect the coaching assignment. Coaches also need to understand the cultural assumptions associated with the tools and approaches they are using. The COF in coach training can help coaches gain insights about the way culture influences their own work, and awareness of how culture might affect the lives of their coachees.

CASE STUDIES

Individual executive coaching

The COF assessment is often most valuable when coaches use it systematically in the initial assessment phase and refer to it subsequently in connection with the coachee's concrete situations. The COF assessment can complement other commonly used instruments such as the Myers-Briggs Type Indicator® and the Fundamental Interpersonal Relations Orientation-Behavior™ (FIRO-B®), with the underlying common philosophy of making constructive use of differences. The FIRO-B® (Waterman and Rogers, 2007) explores three critical areas related to interpersonal relationships: Inclusion (social interactions), Control (taking the lead, making decisions, empowering), and Affection (personal relationships, openness). It distinguishes behaviors we initiate (Expressed) from behaviors we expect from others (Wanted).

In this case study, I use the example of a Belgian senior executive, a manager for a large international corporation. I have changed some details (including name) to protect confidentiality.

Tom's FIRO-B® scores in the Affection category were unusually high (8 for Expressed Affection, 7 for Wanted Affection, on a scale from 0 to 9). The COF assessment showed a clear sharing orientation (as opposed to a protective orientation) coupled with only a fair self-perceived ability to use the protective orientation when necessary. These combined results facilitated a constructive discussion around what was preventing Tom from spending sufficient time in Belgium (both at his home office and with his family) and cutting down on his tiring international travel. The results also showed Tom had a tendency to delay confrontation whenever he had to deal with difficult interpersonal situations. As his High Affection scores indicated, Tom naturally tended to show empathy and promote bonding in his team, and his team members appreciated this. However, this tendency worked as a double-edged sword. An unconscious tendency to please implied that he often overlooked his own needs and was sometimes too patient with others' subpar performance. This prevented him from confronting certain team members. The COF assessment clearly revealed that Tom needed to erect boundaries and firmly set limits (protective orientation).

As a result of the coaching dialogue, Tom started to confront one of his direct reports, whose results had been below par for over a year. He gave the worker three months to show significant improvement and reach mutually agreed-upon targets. Tom also learned from the MBTI®. He consciously moved outside his Intuition Perceiving (NP) comfort zone by devising and adhering to a detailed developmental plan in a Sensing Judging (SJ) fashion. The COF assessment helped him realize that he was not at ease with very direct communication—in a conflict or when he had to deliver a tough message and get his point across at the risk of offending or hurting others. Tom explained that his behavior was appropriate in a Belgian context but was insufficient in the Netherlands and in Denmark, where people expect more directness. Moreover, his orientation toward affective communication, coupled with a higher ability, made him realize that he sometimes overlooked the importance of precise and concise communication.

His FIRO-B® scores in the Control area were relatively high (7 for Expressed Control, 6 for Wanted Control). The COF results for control-harmony-humility shed light on these results: humility was less preferred and less mastered than harmony and control. Tom could not conceive that his direct report was simply not fulfilling his responsibilities. Tom's sense of ownership, coupled with his sensitivity, further explained why he had not confronted his poor performance more quickly: Tom had over-sympathized with his direct report's hardships. Tom realized that by playing the "rescuer" role he was keeping his direct report in a "victim" position, allowing him to use personal problems as an excuse. Such difficulties could not explain alone the poor performance. Tom had to make sure his direct report would accept and tackle his issues.

Other COF dimensions contributed insights for Tom's future career choice. His orientation for polychronic time and change confirmed his need for variety in his work. Continuing on the path of general management would allow him to honor this preference. The combined psychological and cultural awareness helped Tom identify personal tendencies that had proved counterproductive and, most important, discover new choices that helped him become more effective as a leader. In Tom's case, the following guidelines were applied to help him make sense of the data from the instruments:

- Interpretations are primarily the responsibility of the coachee.
- The coach invites the coachee to articulate what struck him: confirmations, new insights, or questions based on the results.
- The coach may propose interpretations, carefully framing remarks as hypotheses.
- The coach's observations are linked, where possible, to the coachee's concrete challenges.
- The coach facilitates a discovery process in which the coachee uses the assessment to see his reality from new perspectives, to identify strengths as well as pitfalls, and to conclude with specific new choices and actions to address challenges.

An advantage of both personality and cultural profiles is that they help reframe difficulties in terms of underused preferences rather than personal deficiencies. Awareness and conscious attention can go a long way to address difficulties. If issues were instead attributed to personal deficiencies, the coachee's self-esteem and self-confidence might suffer, thereby undermining the resolution process.

Team executive coaching

This section presents some of the COF aggregate results of an international group of 15 coaches who took part in an advanced cross-cultural coach training. Although this seminar was not a team coaching session per se, the results should nevertheless give a sense of how the COF assessment can be used with a group, and the insights that can be gained through this process. The professional coaches (12 women and three men, between ages 40 and 60) were all experienced and came from countries including the United Kingdom, Belgium, France, Turkey, Israel, and the United States.

The group might overlook underrepresented orientations; these may well include the wisdom, perspectives, and skills necessary to address challenges that resist habitual solutions. This is helpful for identifying new growth opportunities and new choices for dealing with complex challenges. In other cases, the group may systematically recognize and build upon its assets. Its cultural inclinations may be particularly suited to addressing certain challenges. Both individuals and groups can gain insights from the COF results; the results can facilitate growth both for a team as a whole and for individuals within the team.

Examining all the results is beyond the scope of this chapter; I have opted to focus on certain dimensions. Likewise, in team coaching and workshops, we concentrate on select dimensions rather than attempt to review COF results exhaustively. I have given examples of questions a coach might use with a group to raise awareness about each of the COF dimensions. The aim, as noted earlier, is to encourage coachees to generate their own interpretations rather than for the "expert" coach/facilitator to impose interpretations. The assumption is that the coachees are experts in their own professional and cultural contexts. This does not exclude sharing, when appropriate, other examples and insights, notably on how to leverage differences, and referring to the book *Coaching Across Cultures* for more information.

(1) Control-Harmony–Humility

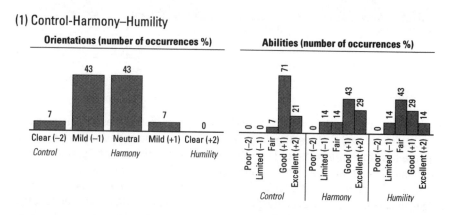

The orientation is primarily toward "control," with 92 percent declaring that they are good or excellent at taking responsibility. This is an invaluable asset for setting targets and achieving them, sometimes against all odds. On the other hand, the orientation toward the "humility" perspective is almost absent. Furthermore, only 43 percent of the group self-scores favorably on the ability to use "humility." (Generally speaking, the assumption is that responding with "slightly agree"/fair suggests hesitation and therefore is not considered favorable. In this case, 43 percent is the addition of 29 percent "agree"/good and 14 percent "strongly agree"/very good.)

A coach/facilitator might help coachees explore the data by asking questions such as these:

- What are the advantages of a control orientation?
- In what situations might a control orientation be less helpful?
- What alternatives might there be?
- Looking at individual results, do your own orientations vary from those of the group?
- What might this mean in practice?

The current results suggest that learning to accept natural limitations is a developmental opportunity. Embracing "humility" (leveraging it with "control") should help the group aim for realistic and sustainable success and resist the temptation to do whatever it takes to succeed—going to extremes, breaking down, et cetera.

(2) Scarce–Plentiful Time

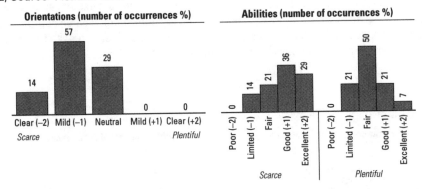

The orientation is clearly toward "scarce" versus "plentiful," reflecting the bias that "time is money" and that we should strive to use time efficiently. Furthermore, only 28 percent of the group scores favorably on the ability to use the "plentiful" time orientation. The group seems to overlook the possibility that time can be viewed as "plentiful"; this represents a developmental opportunity (the value of slowing down, of "giving time time"). However, despite the scarce time orientation and the fact that coaches are often called upon to help coachees manage their time more productively, 35 percent of the group members still admits they have trouble using time efficiently.

The coach/facilitator might observe that the group orientation reflects a mainstream Western bias and invite discussion about alternative approaches and possible advantages. The coach could highlight the paradox that by taking time (as if time was plentiful) one can better appreciate its scarcity—the eternity in one moment. It is easier to see what is really important when we step back and slow down. The coach might ask the group to give specific examples of how they could be more effective by treating time as a plentiful resource, how they could improve on their efficiency, and how they could leverage both perspectives.

(3) Being–Doing

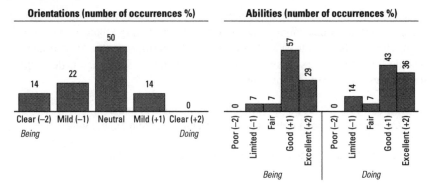

The orientation distribution is close to a normal curve (even bell shape), and abilities scores are high both for "being" and "doing." These results echo the thesis that executive coaches contribute significantly by leveraging "being" and "doing." They bring precious help into corporations where the emphasis is often on "doing" at the expense of "being." As I have argued, more "being" can paradoxically increase "doing" (achievements). The coach/facilitator might explore the group's views on the ideal distribution of a group of coaches. The coach might ask people to provide examples of where being and doing worked well together.

(4) Individualistic–Collectivistic

The distribution is close to normal, and the group looks capable of emphasizing both individual projects/attributes and affiliation with the team. This seemed apparent during the seminar, when participants showed the richness of their individuality and cultures, while constructively contributing to the group's harmonious functioning and its shared ideals.

(5) Hierarchy–Equality

The dominant orientation is "equality," as can be expected with the equality bias inherent in coaching. I argued in *Coaching Across Cultures* that coaching assumes equality but can nevertheless also benefit from a "hierarchy" orientation. Moreover, 93 percent of the group scores favorably on the ability to use equality. However, 43 percent seems to have difficulties working well in a hierarchical environment.

Questions for discussion might include:

- How prepared are you to help your coachees deal effectively with hierarchies?
- Do you run the risk of overlooking that possibility and ignore politics?
- How can you help them engage in "constructive politics"?

(6) Universalist–Particularist

The dominant orientation is "particularist," and 79 percent of the group scores favorably on adapting to particular circumstances by promoting tailored solutions. The group is likely to be flexible. With "universalism" underrepresented as an orientation, and only 35 percent favorable scores on the corresponding ability, useful developmental questions for the group might include:

- How can you take better advantage of economies of scale?
- How can you achieve better coherence when working collectively?

The challenge is to strive for both consistency and flexibility.

(7) Stability–Change

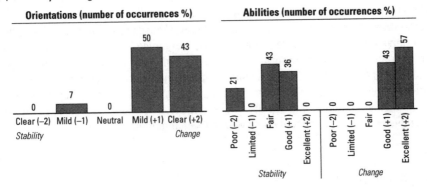

The dominant orientation is "change," with an impressive 100 percent of favorable scores on the ability to work well in a dynamic environment in which adaptability and innovation are promoted. Coaches are often referred to as change agents, but change is not the only, nor always the best, choice we have. With a limited inclination and self-evaluated ability for stability, the questions might be:

- What are the merits of stability that you might overlook?
- In your coaching, do you remember that the ideal combination often includes periods of changes alternating with periods of stability (notably for recuperation and consolidation)?
- How can you paradoxically promote change by reframing "resistance to change" into a positive "preference for stability"?

For the group, the danger would be to strive for new and radical changes at times when consolidation, disciplined maintenance, and systematic improvement of existing processes are needed. How, then, can the group find motivation in rigorous execution and disciplined practice?

(8) Direct–Indirect

More than 42 percent of the group prefers "direct" communication (although only 7 percent clearly prefers directness). Half the group, however, is either neutral or inclined toward indirect communication. This is significantly different from traditional coaching, which has assumed direct communication and disregarded indirect communication. The abilities scores suggest that group members can learn from one another and develop the capacity to be both clear and sensitive when communicating in difficult situations.

(9) Analytical–Systemic

The majority in this group prefers systemic thinking (with 86 percent of members considering themselves good or very good at it). This profile is probably unusual in Western society. This group of global coaches is culturally inclined to help others explore connections between elements, establish links, and focus on the whole system. This cultural orientation is becoming increasingly necessary in today's global and interconnected world (e.g., this book argues that we have to work in concert and across disciplines to address new global threats). We still need to use analytical thinking, however, and 35 percent of the group declares that they have only a fair or limited ability to dissect a problem into smaller chunks.

Additional comments

Beyond the data and interpretations we can offer, it is important that we, as global coaches (1) ensure participants acquire a deep awareness that goes beyond a superficial intellectual understanding of these concepts, and (2) foster development that build upon the new awareness.

Experimentation is critical. Participants learn better when they have the chance to role play challenging situations both one-to-one and in team interactions, and when these are videotaped and then debriefed. Concrete situations help participants appreciate the ways in which their cultural orientations (both individual and collective) play out, and the debrief conversations help them identify new choices that might prove more effective.

The following questions, when tailored to the particular group, have proved useful:

- What are your cultural orientations?
- How do these orientations vary in different contexts?
- How do your cultural orientations impact the way you coach/lead?

The following questions refer to the group's challenges in dealing with a different culture:

- What are their orientations, and in what key ways do they differ from yours?
- How do you reconcile the differences?

- How are you learning/growing from this (enriching your own cultures, expanding your options when coaching/leading and living)?

Coaches could ask countless questions to generate discussion and awareness around issues of culture. Additional questions might include:

- What are the dominant orientations in the team?
- How do you—as individuals—seem to be similar and different? What implications does this have?
- What cultural orientations are not represented in your team?
- How can you compensate for this absence?
- Which key people in the organization do you deal with most? What are their orientations—or what do they seem to be? How might these have affected the way your relationship has developed? How might you use this knowledge?
- To what degree are your colleagues aware of their and your orientations?
- What different orientations are operating in different parts of your organization?
- Are there dominant orientations? If so, how does your profile fit with these?
- How might you leverage differences?
- How is national culture relevant in the situation?
- Where are the potential synergies and conflicts?

The orientations in the COF are derived from very sound research across cultures. However, as I have explained throughout this chapter, culture is not so easy to capture. My experience is that individuals and groups will sometimes find a unique contextual orientation. Unlike other instruments, the COF assessment provides for additional orientations to emerge through dialogue. In fact, this is almost a preferred outcome, since it shows that participants are engaging with culture. The COF online assessment includes the option of adding supplemental cultural dimensions that can be tailored to a specific client context. I used this feature at a conference about Service with a large group of international executives. Preliminary interviews, apart from uncovering several connections with the COF dimensions, also revealed two interesting dichotomies that I captured in the form of two supplemental dimensions, including Nobility–Servitude (service viewed as a noble activity versus as servitude). Not surprisingly, a large majority (90 percent) expressed a preference for Nobility (60 percent even expressed a clear preference). However, the Servitude orientation was defined in a way that was not without merits: those who view service as servitude tend to recognize the importance of setting the necessary boundaries to avoid being exploited. Remarkably, 70 percent had unfavorable responses in their abilities to set appropriate limits when serving clients. When reviewing these results, the group's conclusion was twofold:

1. Taking better of care of oneself and of one's employees should be emphasized. (Conversely, abusing their goodwill for meeting clients' demands at all costs should be avoided.)

2. Service is, fortunately, not a zero-sum game: serving others with generosity and care is often a source of personal satisfaction, pride, and meaning. In other words, you serve yourself by serving others.

In sum, the COF assessment offers various possibilities for helping executives deal constructively with cultural diversity. Above all, it offers a language for coaches that is easy to introduce into organizational contexts and helps coachees make sense of what is going on. The COF assessment assumes a dynamic and inclusive concept of culture, which contrasts with traditional intercultural approaches. Cultural diversity, when leveraged, becomes an opportunity for personal and collective growth. However, the COF cannot be applied mechanically if we want to avoid detrimental polarization and stereotyping. By internally developing unity in diversity, we global coaches will become more credible and better equipped to promote it externally.

Organizational development: a strategic alliance between a Dutch and a French company

Beyond individual and team development, coaches can add value by facilitating organizational development (see Chapter 2). Organizations rely on three mechanisms to achieve growth: organic growth, alliances, and mergers and acquisitions (M&As).

Unfortunately, a high percentage of both alliances and M&As break down prematurely, failing to deliver the expected strategic benefits and inflicting financial damage on both partners. The main reason for failure is the human factor in general and culture in particular.[9]

The good news is that you can reverse this trend through proactive and effective management of cultural differences.

In 2009, my company was called upon to conduct a cultural audit using the COF assessment in the case of a strategic alliance between a Dutch and a French company. I will illustrate here how the Cultural Orientations Framework assessment, in combination with interviews, allowed us to gain valuable insights. (I have eliminated some details and will not describe the context to protect confidential information about this strategic alliance, which is currently under way.) Both CEOs, together with the entire top management committee, found the cultural findings illuminating and readily approved our recommendations. One committee member, who had a reputation for being particularly skeptical about these "soft" managerial aspects, commented on the precision of the cultural analysis and usefulness of the recommendations.

Two colleagues and I conducted a total of five days of interviews in France and in the Netherlands. More than 100 participants completed the Cultural Orientations Framework assessment. The high response rate confirmed people's enthusiasm about the alliance and curiosity to learn about culture. We added five supplemental dimensions to the standard dimensions based on polarities that emerged during the interviews and appeared relevant.

Looking at cultures, we noticed clear similarities and differences, as well as intermediate situations (see table below).

Key similarities and differences between the two cultures

Importance/ relevance for the alliance	**! Overusing/ Overlooking**		**Leverage!**
High	1. Scarce-plentiful time 2. Control-harmony-humility 3. Universalist-particularist 4. Monochronic-polychronic 5. Stability-change	1. Being-doing 2. Competitive-collaborative 3. Formal-informal	1. Hierarchy-equality 2. Direct-indirect 3. Active-reflective
Medium low	• Past-present-future • High-context-low-context • What-who • Generating-questioning • Proactive-reactive	• Individualistic-collectivistic • Protective-sharing • Affective-neutral • Deductive-inductive • Analytical-systemic • Planning-emergent	n/a
	Clear similarities	**Similarities with some differences**	**Clear differences**

Degree of similarity/difference

Here are some examples (among 22 dimensions) of these findings, in summary form. They should give you a sense of the type of insights that can be gained from this exercise.

Scarce–plentiful time

Orientations assessment (% of occurrences)

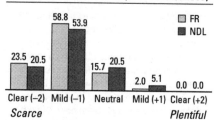

Clear (−2)	Mild (−1)	Neutral	Mild (+1)	Clear (+2)
Scarce				*Plentiful*

FR: 58.8, 23.5, 15.7, 2.0, 0.0
NDL: 53.9, 20.5, 20.5, 5.1, 0.0

Descriptions and illustrations

Asset (productivity) and potential pitfall (constant rush without necessarily devoting time to what matters the most)
- FR people seem to take more time for building relationships
- NDL to the point—tighter time frames

Key learnings from abilities assessment

Efficiency (around 80% favorable response)
Limited ability to treat time in a plentiful fashion (over 50% unfavorable responses)

Suggestions

Clarifying vision and strategy should help devote time to what is really important.
Give permission to self and other(s) to regularly slow down. Strive for effectiveness as well as efficiency.
Paradoxically, it is often by treating time in a plentiful fashion that you can appreciate its scarcity.

Control–harmony–humility

Orientations assessment (% of occurrences)

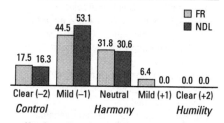

Clear (−2)	Mild (−1)	Neutral	Mild (+1)	Clear (+2)
Control		*Harmony*		*Humility*

FR: 17.5, 44.5, 31.8, 0.0, 0.0
NDL: 16.3, 53.1, 30.6, 6.4, 0.0

Descriptions and illustrations

A sense of mastery about the capacity to shape the future: "We have the power to shape the industry."
NDL: greater sense of empowerment than in FR. FR managers find ways to make things happen.
Possible anxiety when control is lacking, notably facing uncertainty

Key learnings from abilities assessment

Over 80% favorable response for "Control" (even over 90% at NDL)
Over 50% unfavorable responses for "Humility" (even over 60% at NDL)

Suggestions

Continue to capitalize on the "can do" attitude to promote progress.
Learn to take natural limitations into account to promote sustainable progress:
- Trial and error
- Accepting lack of clear-cut answers in ambiguous emergent situations
- Time to recuperate in high-working environment

Universalist–particularist

Orientations assessment (% of occurrences)

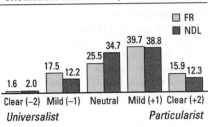

	FR	NDL
	□ FR	■ NDL

Clear (−2) 1.6 2.0 | Mild (−1) 17.5 12.2 | Neutral 25.5 34.7 | Mild (+1) 39.7 38.8 | Clear (+2) 15.9 12.3

Universalist .... *Particularist*

Descriptions and illustrations

Good news: tailored solutions help address unique clients' challenges

Issues:

- There might be some reluctance to strive for economies of scales and coherence.
- Risk of reinventing the wheel by lack of sharing/exchanges of best practices.
- Apparently not a problem now. What if more integration, synergies, and economies of scale are expected?

Key learnings from abilities assessment

Over 70% favorable responses for "Particularist"

Over 60% unfavorable responses for "Universalist"

Suggestions

Strive for flexibility combined with coherence. Articulate the overall vision for the strategic alliance to clarify the level of coherence-integration that is expected.

Being–doing

Orientations assessment (% of occurrences)

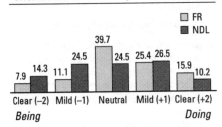

	□ FR	■ NDL

Clear (−2) 7.9 14.3 | Mild (−1) 11.1 | Neutral 39.7 24.5 | Mild (+1) 24.5 25.4 26.5 | Clear (+2) 15.9 10.2

Being .... *Doing*

Descriptions and illustrations

Results normally distributed, more on the Doing side. A recognition that it is important to invest time to build good relationships between people, to get to know each other, to "get the basic rights." Also strong motivator for many people we have interviewed.

Learning from the others, growing by broadening one's horizons is also a motivator for people.

"We need quick wins," "Define/measure success," "We need to show that this cooperation is a success."

Key learnings from abilities assessment

Ability for "Being" and "Doing" (over 70% favorable in both organizations)

Suggestions

To increase performance (Doing), building constructive relationships and engaging in personal team development is called for (Being).

Establish a culture of regular feedback exchanges around behaviors and their impact.

Do not overlook the human relationship source of motivation when planning meetings, workshops. The trust built this way facilitates subsequent collaborations.

Hierarchy–equality

Orientations assessment (% of occurrences)	Descriptions and illustrations

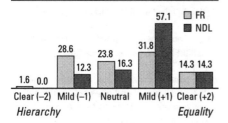

The Dutch are used to a "no nonsense" approach favoring quick decision processes and autonomy.

FR: "you need to discuss things up front/pre-sell/agree—to avoid discussions in meetings." At NDL people speak up in meetings. The FR way is regularly perceived as a barrier that reduces effectiveness in meetings.

However, in its majority, FR people declare they would prefer a more equalitarian approach.

Key learnings from abilities assessment	Suggestions

Ability for "Equality": FR: over 60% favorable; NDL over 90% favorable
"Hierarchy": FR: over 70% favorable; NDL over 60% unfavorable

As much as possible, promote more empowerment at FR (learning from the Dutch way).

For the Dutch, learn to engage in "Constructive Politics" when necessary (learning from the French way), particularly in delicate, controversial situations.

Direct–indirect

Orientations assessment (% of occurrences)	Descriptions and illustrations

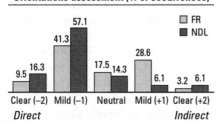

NDL: say what you mean and go to the point. Dutch may come across as much more assertive, too blunt, even aggressive at bringing their ideas or criticizing ("direct kritiek").

FR: more caution is exerted before voicing opinions in delicate situations (particularly with superiors).

No serious difficulties reported. What about after the "honeymoon period"?

Key learnings from abilities assessment	Suggestions

Ability for "Direct": FR: over 50% favorable; NDL almost 80% favorable
"Indirect": FR: over 50% favorable; NDL 60% unfavorable

Strive to leverage directness and indirectness by combining their underlying values: clarity and sensitivity

- Being clear and firm with the content while being careful and sensitive with the form
- Being direct on the substance and indirect on the process (as much as necessary to avoid loss of face)

Active–reflective

Orientations assessment (% of occurrences)

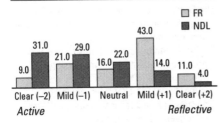

	FR	NDL

Clear (–2) — Active: 9.0 / 31.0
Mild (–1): 21.0 / 29.0
Neutral: 16.0 / 22.0
Mild (+1) — Reflective: 43.0 / 14.0
Clear (+2): 11.0 / 4.0

Clear (–2)   Mild (–1)   Neutral   Mild (+1)   Clear (+2)
Active   *Reflective*

Descriptions and illustrations

Action favored by NDL, reflection preferred by FR.
NDL: "Concrete, pragmatic"; FR: "Intellectual instinct before taking action: how is this better?"
At FR, some appreciate the NDL way: "You do it and it works or it does not. You don't ask yourself 15 questions before acting. This gives more room for creativity and spontaneity."

Key learnings from abilities assessment

"Active": FR: almost 60% favorable; NDL 80% favorable
"Reflective": FR: almost 80% favorable; NDL about 60% favorable

Suggestions

Continue to show appreciation for both action and reflection.
Venture outside one's comfort zone when appropriate:
- Do we really need to spend all this time reflecting on this subject before taking action?
- Shouldn't we reflect further on this subject before trying a concrete solution?

I insisted that our "suggestions" were meant to stimulate further dialogue, reflection, and action. I highlighted our coaching bias: as facilitators, we add the most value when we help people devise their own solutions and actions. In my experience, pertinence as well as ownership is best achieved this way, maximizing performance as well as satisfaction.

Even when acting as consultants, we displayed another bias: favoring unity in diversity rather than polarization. The descriptions and suggestions should make clear that each group has valuable lessons to teach and to learn, and that both groups will sometimes need to go outside their respective comfort zones.

The subsequent workshops with cross-organizational project teams, during which we acted as team coaches, allowed us to go one step further in the awareness building process, and then into concrete change. For example, it became apparent that some French executives were waiting for their top management to make decisions and take action (cf. hierarchy versus equality in the COF). They did not feel empowered; they believed it was up to their managers to change the situation. They did not seem to realize that they had an opportunity and a responsibility to take important actions. I challenged them to take the lead, suggesting that they ask their leaders for the authority to make certain decisions and recommending that they explain that always having to ask for permission was slowing their project. After all, the French top executives had enthusiastically embraced the cultural findings and wanted more initiative and ownership from their managers. Rather than telling my participants what to do, I asked them, "What prevents you from asking your managers to . . . ?" and, through additional questioning, helped them overcome the obstacles (mainly unconsciously self-imposed constraints). Finally, I made sure they made a specific commitment to their team with questions such as, "When can this team expect you will have had this discussion with your manager?" Some of it was done with the entire group. Some was done one-to-one to address more sensitive topics and to avoid potential loss of face.

Adhering intellectually to a cultural analysis is one thing. Modifying our own habits is another. Global coaches play an essential role in facilitating the indispensable behavioral changes, which allow the new culture to transpire. This cultural transformation has now started . . .

. . . .

ART AND COACHING ACROSS CULTURES

Breaking away from the banal and from stereotyped business language, art allows us to generate new insights and foster new behaviors. I discussed previously how an inductive approach could complement the COF deductive method (Rosinski, 2003, 61–68). The inductive approach could involve artifacts or artistic creation, even in rudimentary form: crafting a collage, drawing, et cetera.

Induction calls upon intuition, a form of immediate knowing that does not appeal to reasoning. The word *intuition* comes from the Latin *intueri*, meaning "looking carefully." This suggests that careful observation is what enables intuition to generate valuable knowledge. It implies going beyond first impressions. Intuitions often occur in the form of flashes and insights, when we relax, let go of our urge to solve the problem using logic. Incidentally, I have a pen, paper, and flashlight close to my bed: intuitions often come when I am about to fall asleep. It also happens when I am biking, reading in a comfortable chair, talking with a friend, or making the time to step back.

Art, at its best, is a powerful vehicle to raise the awareness and develop the consciousness of those who experience it. It engages our hearts and souls, not just our minds. You might recall the emotion associated with listening to beautiful music and watching a delightful movie. Beyond technical mastery, authenticity is the hallmark of true artistry. Artwork is then much more than a cultural artifact; it touches on the spiritual as well. Consider the following dialogues, which Irving Stone attributes to Vincent Van Gogh and his mother:

> "I'll have to wait until my drawing is right."
>
> "You mean you have to make your drawing right so the portraits will be good enough to sell?"

"No, I have to make my drawings right so that my drawings will be right."

"I am afraid I don't understand that, son."

"Neither do I, but anyway it's so." (Stone, 1935, 108)

Depth and refusal of superficiality, together with careful observation, also characterize the true artist. Consider Van Gogh's words, as written by Stone:

I can't draw a figure without knowing all about the bones and muscles and tendons that are inside it. And I can't draw a head without knowing what goes on in that person's brain and soul. In order to paint life one must understand not only anatomy, but what people feel and think about the world they live in. The painter who knows his craft and nothing else will turn out to be a very superficial artist. (Stone, 1935, 113)

Interestingly, it is precisely when the artist is in touch with his authentic self that he deeply touches us. The true resonance cannot be manufactured by superficial marketing ploys. Rather, it involves allowing genuine artistic expression. Incidentally, global coaches not only encourage artistic expression, but they also facilitate authentic life journeys (their own and those of their coachees).

Focusing again on the cultural perspective, art offers an important source of information about culture. Moreover, painting can, in an image worth a thousand words, convey the notion that cultural differences can be leveraged.

I ask my MBA students to illustrate lessons in global management and achieving unity in diversity by choosing and discussing works of arts (particularly painting and cinema, but possibly other forms: sculpture, architecture, poetry, et cetera) and referring to the Cultural Orientations Framework. I tell them that the artworks they select should illustrate, for each cultural dimension:

- the wisdom in each orientation
- the pitfalls for each orientation
- the synthesis of the orientations/leveraging of these alternative cultural orientations

The Great Wave by Katsushika Hokusai and *Stillness of Time* by Salvador Dali, chosen by my students,[10] illustrate this synthesis. Like them, we can choose to interpret these artworks as we wish.

The Great Wave[11] Control–Harmony–Humility

The fishermen seem small in comparison with the great wave. The enormous strength deployed by the breaking wave must be a humbling experience for these men. The wave is about to swallow these little boats.

Is this terrible fate inevitable? Somehow, the fishermen seem confident in their ability to survive, believing their destiny is still in their hands. With their experience, they muster their courage, diving straight into the wave to go through to the other end.

Strangely, despite the brutal ocean outbursts and the fierce fishermen's fight, the artwork exudes serenity rather than violence. It seems that everything will be okay. The harmony seems to emanate from the yin and yang shapes in the sea. This is mirrored by the fishermen displaying a confident combination of determination (yang) and letting go (yin).

Mount Fuji's stable presence in the background brings peace and calmness. And the shining sun provides yet another paradox.

The Great Wave shows us that we can have control, harmony, and humility all together.

Stillness of Time[12] Scarce–Plentiful Time

Clocks and watches are a constant reminder that time is passing and that it is scarce.

Apparently inspired by a Camembert dissolving under the summer sunshine, Dali painted and sculpted several melting watches.

The clock's regular ticking slows down and finally stops. Time has become plentiful. It can be savored as each moment becomes eternity. *Stillness of Time* illustrates how we can paradoxically best appreciate the scarcity of time by acting as if it is plentiful.

The following words, attributed to Nadine Stair, illustrate this notion: "I've had my moments, and if I had to do it over again, I'd have more of them. In fact, I'd try to have nothing else. Just moments, one after the other, instead of living so many years ahead of each day."

The present becomes a present when it is lived mindfully. This realization brings us into the spiritual realm, which is the subject of the next chapter. Is what is important (cultural perspective) truly important—that is, meaningful (spiritual perspective)?

NOTES

1. Rosinski, 2003, 20.
2. ICF Conference, Vancouver, 2000.
3. Let me acknowledge here Sherie Olmstead, Geoffrey Abbott, Dina Zavrski-Makaric, Eva Drazska, Nathalie De Broux, Robert Lee, Barbara Christian, and Kate Gilbert, who have contributed to the first editions in Brussels, Sydney, Prague, Rome, New York, and Oxford.
4. See *www.philrosinski.com* for more information about these seminars.
5. A more detailed bibliography can be found in Rosinski, 2003.
6. Aristotle 4th century B.C./1999, *On Interpretation*, Book 1 Part 9.
7. These sections as well as the individual and team-coaching case studies have been adapted from *www.philrosinski.com/cof* and from Rosinski, 2009.
8. E-mail correspondence with the author, 30 August 2007.
9. See notably Lee-Marks, 2005: "A virtual assembly line of studies consistently affirms that up to three-quarters of all deals either destroy value or don't meet objectives despite often benefiting from elegant strategic conceptions, optimal financing, and other textbook advantages."

    Lesowitz and Knauff, 2003: "More than three-fourths of mergers and acquisitions fail to produce anticipated results"—"The same surveys reporting the high failure rate have traced it to flawed or incomplete integration including, despite nearly two decades of coping with the problem, the botching of the part dealing with people, process, and culture."

Schoenberg, 2005: "A frequent reason put forward for these high failure rates is 'culture clashes.' Issues of cultural compatibility can be especially complex within cross-border acquisitions where the values and practices of the combining management teams reflect the influences of both their respective corporate cultures and their national cultures. For example, the DaimlerChrysler merger was seen as bringing together not only Daimler-Benz's relatively risk-averse and engineering-orientated approach with Chrysler's entrepreneurial, marketing-led style, but also as a meeting of German stakeholder values with more aggressive U.S. business practices."

Dyer, Kale, and Singh, 2004: "40 percent to 55 percent of alliances break down prematurely and inflict financial damage on both partners."

Kempner, 2005: "According to McKinsey & Co., managing the 'human side of change' is the real key to maximizing the value of the deal. The frequent failure to do so may explain why 50 percent of all deals ultimately destroy shareholder wealth."

10. The two examples are from the first course at the United Business Institute in Brussels in 2005 (given together with Dominique Ringler).

11. *Kanagawa oki nami ura (The Great Wave Off Shore of Kanagawa)* 1 print: woodcut, color, between 1826 and 1833, printed later. Katsushika Hokusai, 1760–1849. This image is a file from the Wikimedia Commons *http://en.wikipedia. org/wiki/File:Great_Wave_off_Kanagawa2.jpg*. This work is in the public domain in the United States, and those countries with a copyright term of life of the author plus 100 years or fewer.

12. *Stillness of Time* (1979) is one of Dali's works on the theme of "melting watches," which he initially painted in "The Persistence of Memory" (1931). See *www. artbrokerage.com/artist/piece/6175* and *www.salvadordalimuseum.org/education/ documents/clocking_in.pdf* (accessed on 12 May 2010).

CHAPTER 8

The Spiritual Perspective— Enabling Meaning and Unity

Spirituality is an increased awareness of a connection with oneself, others, nature, with the immanent and transcendent "divine." It is also the ability to find meaning, derive purpose, and appreciate life.

Coaching could not be global without addressing the human quest for meaning, which seems indispensible and universal.

For a long time, the average person did not have to be preoccupied with finding meaning. Indeed, on the one hand, it was readily supplied through all-encompassing religion, through mesmerizing political ideology (e.g., Communism), or the through the lifelong corporate work contract. On the other hand, people were (and still are, in many parts of the world) so busy meeting basic survival needs that they did not have the time to explore the question of meaning.

Yet, as far back as we can look, some have pondered the mystery of life: its origin, purpose, and meaning. Religious people believed God provided them with answers and guidance in the form of their particular religion. A minority of atheists thought humans themselves filled the void by inventing myths and religious practices. They turned to secular philosophy to explore the question of meaning.

The recent turbulent changes in Earth's environment, the weakening of traditional institutional providers of ideologies (churches, totalitarian political systems, employers offering stable work for the duration of one's career) and the rise of individualism (at least in developed countries) have created a relatively new and unprecedented situation: humans can no longer rely on these long-established external sources and have to find meaning for themselves, in their own lives.

The relentless pursuit of "growth" and maximization of profit, and its flip side, shallow consumerism, are increasingly insufficient avenues for meaning. Filling up is different from savoring. Quantity is not the same as quality. For the hardworking executive dedicated to increasing shareholder value, the wakeup call could be burnout or termination. For the overspending consumer, it could be illness or excessive debt.

Coaching is about helping people step back, reconnect with themselves and others, and find meaning. In the "Global Coaching Process" (2003, Part III), I showed how global coaches help people connect both with their personal desires and with the needs of others (from their families and friends to their organizational stakeholders and all the way to their communities and the world at large). There is no single static solution; all coachees will uncover their own particular and evolving answer.

MEANING AND UNITY

Meaning and unity are intimately linked: we find meaning when we become more united with ourselves and with the world. You may remember the examples of my coachees, the managing director of an investment company and the senior executive at Philips Lighting (see Chapter 2). Both were happier and more effective after they became attuned to their genuine desires and strived to make a positive difference in the world. This required exploring their personal desires (What makes you happy? What gives you positive energy? Conversely, what drains you?), as well as opportunities to serve others.

I have found that this dual and broad-based exploration of personal desires and the needs of others is an effective way to unfold a personal sense of meaning. The coaching process encourages people to act on these insights. Actions are not forced upon coachees but are associated with what they feel is truly important. Target objectives make sense and resonate with coachees. In other words, coaching enables coaches to engage wholeheartedly in and with real life. As Irvin Yalom's (1980) research (in psychotherapy) indicated, engagement is the royal avenue to combating meaninglessness and fostering instead a sense of meaning (482).

We need many technological advances and enterprises to address the formidable planetary challenges we face. We have many opportunities to facilitate the transformation toward a healthier and more sustainable world. This should be the priority.

While abusive consumerism should be combated (see Chapter 2), reasonable consumptions are still meaningful as well, when in quality rather than quantity: we can enjoy the pleasures made possible by the film industry and manufacturers of home entertainment systems among other corporations.

I would argue that we also need exciting human adventures that can bring people together. The Olympic Games and international contests offer exciting moments when people peacefully compete in concert through sports. In a different area altogether, I also envision an ambitious collective space program that would promote positive technological progress. Going to Mars, if not done at the expense of the environmental and social priorities, may be this daring journey together, a voyage in the outer universe often coming with inner spiritual journeys.

From the Moon to Mars

The desire for exploration is part of our deepest human cravings. The Explorer is one of the human archetypes (see Chapter 10). These endeavors toward new frontiers provide us with a sense of meaning.

In the twentieth century, probably no adventure struck our collective imagination better than the man setting foot on the moon. As a kid, I was fascinated by the formidable *Apollo* odyssey. Neil Armstrong, Buzz Aldrin, Michael Collins, and their followers were my heroes.

These astronauts expressed an overwhelming sense of unity, a feeling of awe watching the earth's beauty from afar, a sentiment of peace, an appreciation for being alive, and their realization that the Garden of Eden is right here on our planet (Sington, 2007).

Edgar Mitchell had these words:

> *When you see the Earth like this, and the cosmos like this, and ten times more stars, ten times as bright because of no intervening atmosphere, in the full 180-degree view, if you put your face to the windows, it's magnificent, it's overwhelming . . . . What happened was a sudden recognition of heart . . . . It made me realize that the answers to the ancient questions, "Who are we? How did we get here? Where are we going?" within science were certainly incomplete and perhaps flawed. This feeling of unity and connectedness was an ecstatic, blissful experience. When I came back, I knew my life had changed. I knew that I had to go find out what was this experience I had had. (Mack, 2008, xi)*

The rivalry between the U.S. and the U.S.S.R. prompted Americans to commit to the ambitious *Apollo* program in the 1960s; as a result, the U.S. achieved President Kennedy's incredible target of walking on the moon and safely returning back home by the end of the decade. Today, going to Mars represents a formidable opportunity for nations to work in concert—as NASA puts it, it is a "challenging, shared and peaceful activity that unites nations in pursuit of common objectives."[1]

The journey to the moon helped answer scientific questions about the moon and Earth's origins. New technologies developed during that mission have had widespread uses. The Teflon frying pan and survival blankets are two examples.[2]

The military has often given engineers the funds and opportunities to innovate and develop new technologies. Many of these advances have been applied in everyday life. The space programs would provide humanity with a peaceful and meaningful alternative. The long journey to Mars, for example, would bring considerable challenges, notably obliging voyagers to carefully preserve energy, recycle waste, and manage limited resources efficiently.

MEANINGLESSNESS AND DISCONNECTION

Meaning and unity go together. Now I would like to discuss the corollary: meaninglessness is associated with disconnection. Unfortunately, both are prevalent today.

The lack of meaning manifests itself in various ways. The most severe cases necessitate psychotherapy (or even psychiatry), but many common situations can also benefit from competent coaching. Alternatively, some people might consider spiritual practices such as shamanism, assuming the cultural gap is not an insurmountable obstacle.

Meaninglessness can arise from work that lacks intrinsic value, or whose value is not apparent. The latter case is easier to deal with; the value is there and we simply need to unfold it or reconnect with it. The mason who views his job merely as cutting stones may not feel the same enthusiasm and pride as the mason who sees himself building a cathedral. Leaders and professionals can help impart this sense of meaning. But what about work that is of questionable worth? We talked about building highly polluting cars or manufacturing unhealthy junk food. Maybe these things made sense when pollution was not a serious issue and when the consequences of junk-food consumption were unclear. But not anymore. Denial and other defense mechanisms (see Chapter 5) are ways to avoid facing the issue of doing things that lack real value. Yalom (1980) also describes the common pattern of frenetic activity that "so consumes the individual's energy that the issue of meaning is drained of its toxin" (452).

While these mechanisms may provide temporary psychological relief, they fall short of overcoming the buried meaninglessness. "When the activity has no intrinsic 'goodness' or 'rightness,' then it sooner or later will fail the individual" (452). Questions might arise: "What is the point?" "What is the purpose?" "What is the legacy I will leave behind?" Reconnecting with a sense of meaning takes a lot of courage. All of a sudden you may become, in your own eyes, the "bastard" Sartre was talking about (see Chapter 5). You know (and deep inside knew all along) that once you have uncovered the disconnection, you will have to change your ways, sometimes dramatically, to find satisfactory answers to these questions. It is not a matter of adhering to ethics or morality forced from outside. It is about responding to a call from within to achieve unity and congruence. Coaching can provide invaluable help on this journey. Coachees will find highly contextualized and nuanced answers to their questions. For example, the leaders of a company selling junk food might not be able to turn around the situation immediately, but they might drive a gradual, determined transformation. This could prove a meaningful endeavor.

A sense of meaninglessness pervades us when we realize the goals we are pursuing are not (or are no longer) authentic: they result from a social conditioning but prove ultimately unfulfilling. Such goals—great wealth, a high profile, a number one position—may appear futile to us while remaining meaningful to others.

It is easy to say we don't care about money if we have plenty of it! However, some of us may opt to live comfortably but dispense with some luxuries we now regard as vain. We may want to have an interesting job, make a contribution, and receive a reasonable compensation but do away with some trappings of success we now find pointless (e.g., getting a bigger car when we move up the corporate ladder).

Yalom warns us that meaninglessness also emerges when we step back too far from life by adopting a "galactic" (or "nebula's-eye," "cosmic") perspective (478). Such remoteness implies disconnection, which leads to pessimism and negativity. The philosopher Shopenhauer exemplifies this tendency. Although he has a reputation as a serious philosopher, it is hard to take his ideas (e.g., "happiness and goals are unattainable, because they are phantoms of the future or part of the vanished past") as seriously when one realizes how much they are tainted by his galactic perspective (479). In *Coaching Across Cultures*, I insist that we must remain grounded in reality to avoid becoming dazzled by too many possibilities (Rosinski, 2003, 30). Likewise, the spiritual perspective implies immersion in life together with a high view. Mindful presence is preferable to and quite different from abstract disconnection.

Additionally, Yalom describes clinical manifestations of meaninglessness, which therapists rather than coaches tend to encounter: existential vacuum (boredom, apathy, emptiness) and existential neurosis (overt clinical symptoms beyond the feelings of meaninglessness: alcoholism, depression, obsessiveness, et cetera) (449–450).

The disconnection that, in my experience, typically goes hand in hand with meaninglessness was starkly apparent in the following baffling experiment.

On January 12, 2007, an unusual experiment took place. Joshua Bell, one of the very best violinists worldwide, posted himself at the entrance of a metro station in Washington, D.C. He was dressed as a street musician, in jeans, T-shirt, and a baseball cap. However, for 43 minutes he played some of the most challenging and remarkable music partitions ever written, on one of very best violins ever made, a 1713 Stradivarius worth $3.5 million. He did not play familiar tunes that would have caught attention but did perform masterpieces, which had passed the test of time.

A total of 1,097 people passed by. Sadly, the vast majority paid no attention to Joshua Bell. When asked, after leaving the metro station, if they had noticed anything unusual, only one among the 40 people interviewed immediately mentioned the violinist. Bell received $32.17 in tips, not including a $20 bill from the only person who recognized him as he was ending. There was never a crowd; only one or two people at a time stopped to listen. Three days before, he had filled the house at Boston's Symphony Hall, where midrange seats went for $100.

Some people were waiting in line to buy lottery tickets. None of them turned around to watch Bell. Hoping for the jackpot, they did not seize the luck that was available right next to them.

Gene Weingarten remarks:

If we can't take time . . . to listen to one of the best musicians on Earth play some of the best music ever written; if the surge of modern life so overpowers us that we are deaf and blind to something like that—then what else are we missing? (Weingarten, 2007)

Fortunately, the experiment also brings hope. While almost everyone, regardless of ethnicity, gender, or generation, rushed through without seizing the moment, children instead consistently tried to stop to listen and watch the superb violinist. This usually meant resisting their parents' pressure to hurry and move on. Children can teach us to reignite the curiosity, sense of appreciation, artistic sensitivity, and connectivity inside us.

A shift in culture is required so that our inborn poetic sense can flourish in our lives rather than be gradually choked out and shunned. Global coaches can help people to not become trapped by a limited worldview that overemphasizes fast (scarce) time, profit (doing), and detachment (neutral). Instead, coachees can learn how to also cultivate slow (plentiful) time, relational (being), and aesthetic (affective) cultural orientations (see Chapter 7).

ADOPTING THE SUNFLOWER STRATEGY—NOTICING THE MIRACLES OF THE DAY[3]

I was touched by the Joshua Bell story and abashed when watching the video segments on the Web. I was also moved when I watched the film *August Rush* (Sheridan, 2007). I was enchanted by the magical story, inspired actors, and beautiful music.

The film is about an orphaned musical prodigy (Freddie Highmore) who uses his gift to find his birth parents (Keri Russell and Jonathan Rhys Meyers).

The film gives us a chance to feel the interconnectedness and unity that characterize our holographic universe (see Chapter 9) and the spiritual perspective. Here, music is the harmonic bond linking all humans. Music is everywhere. We just have to listen!

"Listen to the music!" is the auditory equivalent of the visual "sunflower strategy," which I will explain next.

The spiritual perspective, in my view, is that of the sunflower, resolutely turning toward the light. It is about stepping back from daily life to better discern the surrounding light and, consequently restore the sacredness in life. Barbara De Angelis (2006) writes, "Most people don't end the day feeling happy and focusing on the gifts of the day, the miracles of the day, the connections of the day. They say, 'Well, I didn't make any sales today, and didn't finish these five tasks; I didn't go to the gym . . . so it wasn't a great day . . . .' Every day can be a fulfilling day . . . if we are growing, learning, sharing, connecting, paying attention." Rather than vainly trying to get everything under control, she remarks that "we can control whether we are opening to love and joy or not."

It is easier to see the light when life looks bright. However, we all are likely to experience some form of hardship in our existence. Paradoxically, it sometimes takes a journey into the darkness to learn how to greet the light—even if that light is only a small glow.

Darkness is the experience of being deep in the hole, physically or psychologically. Away from the verdant meadows and sunny beaches, the obscure cavern sometimes comes our way. With prudence, we often avoid the fall but sometimes hardship strikes anyway. When bathed in light, we might take the brightness for granted, perhaps not even noticing the radiance around us. However and paradoxically, once caught in the somber night, in extremely challenging situations, we may regain perspective. Amazingly, the faintest glow can then appear to be more luminous than ever. This tiny ray of light becomes synonymous with hope and rejoicing. At first, this sense of gratitude helps us survive. Then, when we are out of the rut, our gratitude allows us to live life more fully. The luminous presence, once considered self-evident, now brings a deeper sense of joy every day.

The shaft of light, by its very scarcity, has exerted a stronger hold than the abundant luminosity. Back in the brightness, our challenge is to continue paying attention and to welcome these rays, abundant once again.

During my hardship experience in the mid 2000s,[4] I read Dante's epic journey down into violent hell, where hope is cruelly lost, and then up through the milder and already more serene purgatory, and finally to the gleaming paradise (Alighieri, 1321/1996). It struck my imagination.

I also read Viktor Frankl's (1959) inspirational book about his ordeal in the Nazi concentration camps. As he struggled to survive under the most atrocious circumstances, he was still able to discern a few rays of light. He decided that evil cannot extinguish us. His classic tribute to hope offers us an avenue to finding greater meaning and purpose in our own lives.

The great spiritual traditions invite us and teach us how to receive the light—meaning joy, love, life, and positive energy. Kabbalah, the Jewish mystic tradition (which has also developed in Christianity, notably with Pic de La Mirandole), literally means "reception" (Ouaknin, 2003). The Kabbalah helps people reconnect with a sense of wonder and gratitude. Even in the midst of adversity, it shows various avenues to practically engage our minds, hearts, and bodies in greeting the light that surrounds us: it may be your child playing, a colleague smiling, the sun shining, a bird singing, a stranger giving you a hand, the blessing of good health, a melodious piece of music, a breathtaking landscape . . .

This positive energy, when we let it in, allows us to shine as well, reflecting the light. As we receive the light and radiate it back in the world, we contribute to a virtuous circle of progress.

Other spiritual traditions, despite nuances, seem to compare on the essential. In Buddhism, Awakening also implies putting reality into a wide perspective, being open, listening to ourselves and to others with gentleness and compassion.

In Shamanism, the "Awakened . . . is no longer prisoner of his capriciousness, moods, beliefs, dreams, and past." What is left is "the freedom of angels, bathing in the love of what lives" (Gougaud, 1995, 280).

In my view, coaching from a spiritual perspective is not about religion in the traditional sense, and it has nothing to do with dogma. It is about inviting coachees to become more proficient at adopting the sunflower strategy in their lives: getting into a habit of letting go of negativity and mustering and sharing positive energy instead, seizing opportunities to feel compassion, gratefulness, and joyfulness. This enables coachees to become more resilient as they tackle their challenges and face hardships.

Coachees learn not to be consumed by resentment, disappointment, and frustration. They become more acceptant and tolerant of themselves and of others. They become more humble, accepting natural limitations. They regularly reflect on how to best use their energy, focusing on taking constructive actions in pursuit of their meaningful, important objectives.

Coaches can incorporate the spiritual perspective in many ways. The key is to be connected to "luminosity": letting brightness in and radiating it outward. When you are fully present in this way, you can trust your imagination and inspiration to do the rest.

Let me illustrate how I helped an executive who was feeling uneasy at work. He was treading in a complex terrain; multiple stakeholders were trying to negotiate the best possible agreements, with the goal of setting up a new business venture. Coaching from a political perspective had proved very helpful here. Still, it was not enough to increase my coachee's satisfaction and fulfillment. The spiritual perspective helped him to keep sight of his larger mission: the highly financially profitable enterprise he wanted to create was meant to serve society by making breakthrough biomedical findings available in medical treatments. He learned to connect with himself, significant others, and his mission at a deeper level.

On one occasion, sensing his stress, I proposed that we do something I had never tried before in a coaching session: walk in the forest of Soignes nearby. Uniquely, this wilderness extends into parts of Brussels: you might encounter even a deer if you walk quietly. My coachee welcomed the invitation; a few minutes later, we were in the forest. He kept talking as we walked. At one point, I asked him if he had noticed the beautiful surroundings. He admitted he hadn't paid attention. I invited him to look attentively. I also suggested touching the trunk of a huge tree, focusing on feeling and internally visualizing the tree, his body, and the contact between the two. In just a few minutes, my coachee had calmed down and felt a sense of serenity. We quickly "regained" the half hour we spent walking; my coachee had increased clarity in the last part of our coaching session and creatively addressed some of his complex challenges. He commented about the fact that nobody else was walking in the forest, despite its proximity and beauty. For him, this short detour became a metaphor for stepping back, regaining perspective, noticing, and appreciating.

ACCEPTING WHAT CANNOT BE AVOIDED—EXERTING OUR CHOICE

Coaching is about helping people discover new paths and make new choices. Viktor Frankl (1959, 75) argues that we always have a choice:

> We who lived in concentration camps can remember the men who walked through the huts comforting others, giving away their last piece of bread. They may have been few in number, but they offer sufficient proof that everything can be taken from a man but one thing: the last of the human freedoms—to choose one's attitude in any given set of circumstances, to choose one's own way.
>
> And there were always choices to make. Every day, every hour, offered the opportunity to make a decision, a decision which determined whether you would or would not submit to those powers which threatened to rob you of your very self, your inner freedom; which determined whether or not you would become the plaything of circumstance, renouncing freedom and dignity to become molded into the form of the typical inmate.

Frankl explains that life can always be meaningful, in three fundamental ways: the *active life of creation* (achievement or accomplishment), the *passive life of enjoyment* (which includes experiencing something, such as goodness, truth, and beauty, or encountering someone and loving her or him) and finally, the *courageous life of accepting suffering with dignity when suffering cannot be avoided*.

In *Coaching Across Cultures*, I discussed ways in which global coaches can help with the first two of these. With the Global Scorecard, we can help coachees find meaning by setting concrete objectives that will make a positive difference for others, including organizational stakeholders and society at large. These objectives should be intrinsically desirable for coachees, so that they will be genuinely engaged in taking the necessary actions. We can also invite coachees to take great care of themselves, and to share love and friendship. Frankl's first two ways, active and passive, correspond to Doing and Being in the Cultural Orientations Framework.

What about suffering? When faced with adversity, "when confronted with a hopeless situation, when facing a fate that cannot be changed," one still has an opportunity to "transform a personal tragedy into a triumph, to turn one's predicament into human achievement." I share Frankl's view that suffering is not necessary: "If it is avoidable, the meaningful thing to do is to remove its cause (117)." However, when it cannot be avoided, we can find meaning by changing our attitude vis-à-vis suffering. We can grow by accepting our fate with dignity and courage, thereby setting an inspiring example for others. Frankl's own story provides evidence of this—the inspirational power of dignity.

Behaving with dignity and courage in terrible circumstances is a path to spiritual growth that leads to a sense of appeasement, if not love and joy. In Greek mythology, Sisyphus was doomed to push a huge rock up a mountain. The rock then rolled down, and Sisyphus had to start all over again. In *The Myth of Sisyphus*, Albert Camus (1942) suggests that Sisyphus still had the choice to smile and make his tragic fate more bearable by accepting it with grace, instead of letting himself be mired in frustration and despair.

LESSONS FROM RELIGION AND PHILOSOPHY

Both religious traditions and philosophy propose many potential sources of meaning. I will focus on two perspectives, Judaism and Baruch Spinoza's philosophy, to illustrate the types of lessons that can inspire coaches today. I hope this will stimulate you to learn from other spiritual sources as well.

There is wisdom to be gained from all religions, even for the nonreligious. Critical thinking must complement openness of mind. We continue to witness how literal interpretations of religious texts can lead to extremism and destruction. Fortunately, there are more uniting and meaningful readings as well.

I find it most effective to refer to coachees' particular traditions. Coaches can convey their appreciation of those traditions and point out what might be relevant in the coachees' current situation. They simply need to unfold their own cultural jewels to move forward. Coaches sometimes need to do some homework to discover their coachees' worlds. Our examples will then more likely resonate with our coachees. Furthermore, the coachees will not have the impression that we are trying to convert them to a different tradition. Once this trust is established, it is easier to refer to spiritual paths we are more familiar with, not to drive coachees away from their religion but rather to broaden their perspective.

For example, many poets and spiritualists have celebrated the power of love. If you are coaching a Christian, it is appropriate to refer to Jesus Christ as an ideal role model. Jesus Christ is a source of inspiration (not just for Christians actually) when He speaks to the crowd aggressively condemning the adulterous woman: "Let the sinless man among you be the first to throw a stone at her."[5] When nobody comes forward, Jesus addresses the woman: "Neither do I condemn you. Go your way. From now on, sin no more."[6] Hesna Cailliau (2003) explains, "Jesus shows that love is a vision, a realization of what unites me to the other; thus regarding the adulterous woman: where everybody sees a fault to be condemned, he, first of all sees a woman who is suffering" (132). Beyond suspending judgment, which is critical (as all coaches already know), Jesus demonstrates how love is a splendid source of meaning and unity.

Love is also the central theme in the teaching of Rumi, one of the greatest representatives of Sufism, the mystical branch of Islam. Consider the following poem:

> Looking at my life
> I see that only Love
> has been my soul's companion.
> From deep inside
> my soul cries out:
> Do not wait, surrender
> for the sake of Love.

Reprinted with permission of HarperCollins Ltd., from *Rumi: Whispers of the Beloved* © 1999 Maryam Mafi and Azima Melita Kolin

When religion might be resisted and considered a sensitive subject, particularly in countries like France favoring secularism, philosophy offers an alternative. I am not referring to the obtuse jargon and dry abstractions that sometimes prevail and may prove of little practical use. The ancient philosophers remain a source of inspiration. For Epicurus, "philosophy is an activity, which through discourses and reasoning, bring us a happy life" (Comte-Sponville, 2000, 11–12). While the Epicurean philosophy and Stoicism shared this ultimate source of meaning, they proposed different paths to reach happiness. Pierre Hadot (1995) explains that for Zeno, founder of the latter school, happiness equated morality. The willingness to do good is the only thing that depends on us and that nobody can take away from us. Zeno stresses coherence in life, which somehow reminds me of Sartre (see Chapter 5). For Epicurus, the emphasis was different. He considered that the individual is only motivated by his own pleasure and interest. Philosophy's role is to help seek reasonable pleasure, and ultimately the only true pleasure, the pure pleasure of existing. "All the misery comes from ignorance of the veritable pleasure. Looking for pleasure, humans are incapable of reaching it, because they cannot satisfy themselves with what they have, or because they strive for what is beyond their reach, or because they spoil this pleasure by constantly fearing they will lose it" (Hadot, 1995, 180).

As Yalom had already pointed out, theological and atheist philosophical perspectives often meet when it comes to identifying practical sources of meaning. Whether humans need to discover God's meaning (theology) or invent their own (existential philosophy), they have to commit to finding and fulfilling that meaning. Helping with this pragmatic aspect, rather than with the ontological debate, which refers to "the nature of being, reality or existence," is the coach's concern (Mack, 2008, 8).

The Case of Judaism

Let me share some of the sources of meaning that Judaism (as a cultural tradition more than a religion) invites us to pursue, and which could also be considered by coaches and coachees, Jewish or not. These are drawn from an article I wrote more than ten years ago[7] and exemplify the insights that can be gleaned from delving into a particular tradition. I will illustrate the first lesson with a Hassidic story (more stories and lessons can be found in the article and the references). Incidentally, storytelling is a noteworthy way to suggest new meanings. Stories are at the heart of Milton Erickson's famous therapeutic approach.[8] Coaches can follow his example by weaving stories as metaphors into coaching. This technique is best reserved for the master coach, however; the coach's usual role is to elicit a sense of meaning from coachees themselves. Coaches should use suggestions, even as metaphors, very carefully. We should facilitate the unfolding of authentic desires and genuinely meaningful pursuits.

Joy

Ruth Westheimer and Jonathan Mark report the following story, which the Baal-Shem Tov, founder of the Hassidic movement, liked to tell. They continue with Gestom Scholem's interpretation:

> One day, prophet Elie was walking through the marketplace when the rabbi of that shtetl (village) recognized him. The rabbi asked him if someone in the little town would have a place in the World to come. Elie showed him two brothers who happened to be passing by. "These two," he said.
>
> The rabbi asked the two guys what their occupation was. "We are public entertainers. If someone is sad, we try to change their state of mind. If we see people quarrelling, we try to reconcile them."
>
> Gestom Scholem, one of the great specialists of Jewish mysticism, explains the story this way: "These entertainers were righteous, in Baal-Shem Tov's heart: they did not stay with themselves thinking of their salvation, but instead they walked across this filthy and loud market, like the Baal-Shem used to do. Their gift to transform the crudest reality to elevate it to spirituality is the sign of their strong communion with God." (Westheimer and Mark, 1995, 94)

The Judaic tradition reminds us of a wonderful purpose: creating joy for ourselves and for others. We discussed this in Chapter 5 and noticed that this message is similar to Baruch Spinoza's notion, is consistent with positive psychology, and is at the heart of coaching itself.

Hope

Hope, often accompanied by humor, enabled Jews to survive persecutions and troubled times throughout their history. Certainly the Judaic tradition has something to offer when it comes to dealing with hardship.

Judaic tradition teaches us to face reality (external and internal) as it is, in its ugliness and its beauty. We don't need to be afraid, we don't need to hide, and we should never despair! Judaic tradition, and Hassidim especially, teaches us to believe there is hope. It is an active hope, leading to a proactive attitude. It works like a self-fulfilling prophecy: by looking for solutions, we shall find them, if we let ourselves be flexible and open enough to see.

Elie Wiesel (1972) tells us, "I still hear my grand-father's voice: 'One will naturally tell you that this or that story cannot be objectively true; and so what? An objective Hassid is not a Hassid.' He was right. The call of the Baal-Shem was a call for subjectivity, for passionate commitment. The stories he told tend to demonstrate that man is more than he seems to be, and that he is capable of offering more than he seems to possess" (Wiesel, 1972, 20).

Wiesel explains, "In its universe, beggars are princes; dumb men are sages. Endowed with powers, tramps travel the earth, warm it, change it. In Hassidim, everything is possible, everything becomes possible when there is the presence of someone who can listen, love and self-disclose. That's what a Hassidic legend is: an attempt to humanize destiny" (11).

Material and spiritual beauty

In some traditions, more spirituality means less materialism. A gap—an opposition—results. The spiritually inclined see physical pleasure and wealth as futile pursuits. Likewise, materialists consider ascetic meditation bizarre. At a Jewish wedding I attended in Antwerp, the rabbi wished the married couple material and spiritual success. The Great Maguid said, "We must not separate the need of the body from the need of the soul" (Lipman, 1997). An example is that sexual pleasure is part of marriage; it is even a mitzvah (divine commandment).

Dr. Ruth explains that physical beauty is celebrated in the Judaic tradition, starting with the Torah, which says that four women were exceptionally beautiful. She points out that masculine beauty is treated with an equally open mind. Furthermore, she notes the following connection: "The Talmud asserts that a beautiful woman helps develop the man's mind" (Westheimer and Mark, 1995, 20, 49).

Rabbi Dahan notices that Judaism was most creative and productive at times of material prosperity. Materialism can and should be good, even from a spiritual viewpoint. Material success means the rich have more to give and can avoid spending time struggling to survive. Money is not a goal in itself but can be a great enabler, helping us attain joy for others and for ourselves.

Interestingly, Wiesel's book about Hassidism includes examples of poor (Rabbi Israel Baal Shem-Tov) and rich (Rabbi Israel de Rizhin) leaders, both ugly and good-looking. Poverty and ugliness are not valued as such, though. These are hardships we sometimes have to deal with, rather than conditions we should aspire to.

Spiritual beauty is crucial. "These Hassidim . . . I knew them. Touching through simplicity, fond of beauty, they knew how to love. And trust. Cheerfully, they knew how to give, to receive; they knew how to share, to participate. In their community, no beggar suffered from hunger on Sabbath. Despite their misery, despite the constant threat on their children and elderly, they did not claim or require anything from anybody; they did not think everything was due to them. Eternally surprised by any sign of goodness or compassion, they responded with gratitude" (Wiesel, 1972, 10).

Problems arise when materialism and spirituality are viewed as contradictory. Natural and legitimate needs (material or spiritual) are then repressed. Consequently, they often erupt in extreme and paradoxical ways.[9]

For example, extreme materialism can take the form of obsession: working like mad because there is never enough money, exercising and eating with extreme rigor because the body is never healthy enough (or the opposite, indulging in food all the time and becoming overweight). At some point, repressed spirituality will rise up, taking an extreme form as well: giving up a successful career altogether (to be at last with one's family), becoming critical about material pleasures and rewards.

Cultural environments and organizational systems sometimes induce painful dilemmas, as if only the body or the spirit could be nourished at any one time.

The Judaic tradition offers us a refreshing and reasonable alternative. Between extremes, there is room for moderation, for acknowledging and meeting our needs, both material *and* spiritual. We can be gentle and generous toward others and ourselves by understanding, acknowledging, and trying to meet our diverse needs and serve others.

Materialism and spirituality can—and should be—integrated if people and organizations are to thrive.

Questioning, Learning

The Talmud is a huge compilation of debates between scholars, their comments, and comments about these comments. It contains the interpretation of the Torah in areas such as legislation, ethics, ceremonies, and traditions. It includes this crucial message: "There is no one so poor as the one who is ignorant."

Wiesel writes, "Judaism never pretended to be monolithic. Its teaching is a sum, a synthesis; all currents are represented, those of the masters like those of the disciples. Given once, the Torah is received a thousand times in a thousand ways, every person contributing to enrich it" (136).

Abraham ben Samuel Aboulafia suggests seven ways to read the Torah. The fifth level, for example, invites the reader to analyze all the elements of the text itself, including the shapes of the letters: why are there 22 letters? Why is the first letter of the Torah a beith? . . .

This questioning may be surprising, sometimes shocking, for those accustomed to relying on someone else's judgment. The ability to question, however, has enabled eminent scientists like Einstein and Freud to challenge assumptions and open up radically new perspectives. This culture also implies tolerance: multiple perspectives (versus one truth) exist and are in themselves a source of richness.

Truth as Deed, Love Over Erudition, Community Over Solitude

As Martin Buber (1967) explains, "Judaism's task is not the intellectual grasping of the spiritual, nor the artistic expression of it, but its realization," and "God does not want to be believed in, to be debated and defended by us, but simply to be realized through us" (10, 94).

It is man's task to create a "true community" on Earth (Buber, 1967, 111). In the Judaic tradition, the Messiah will come when men have built such a community. The wait for the Messiah should therefore be proactive, not passive.

Early Hasidism has provided us with an example of what "true community" looks like. It is bound by brotherly love.

"The major preoccupation of Baal-Shem was to create links at all levels; what brings people together, what unifies the community was good in his opinion; what spread division was bad. Man's role, according to him, was to diminish solitude in the world" (Wiesel, 1972, 45).

Baruch Spinoza

Remarkably, the holographic model is also consistent with Baruch Spinoza's unique philosophy, which inspired the Lumières in the eighteenth century but still is not so easy to grasp (in the same way the holographic model implies a "paradigm shift" and requires an extra reflective effort on our part).

Without eliminating the possibility of "ethics" and "responsibility," Spinoza advocates for "freedom through knowing," which is quite different from the famous "free will." We can see that the latter is largely illusory: biological, psychological, social, and cultural factors can explain behaviors we attribute to people's "free will." Yet most coaches still don't realize this and wonder why coachees keep stumbling again and again over the same difficulties.

"Beatitude" is the ultimate goal Spinoza invites humans to pursue: it is the constant joy of understanding nature, of salvation in the world and through the world; it is the serenity of fully participating in life. For Spinoza, "beatitude is the normal state of the soul, from which we are separated through our illusions and lies. It is not the reward of virtue, but virtue itself." More simply, as André Comte-Sponville (2001) puts it, "it is the happiness of the wise, or wisdom itself as happiness. Its content is joy, thus love. Its object is the truth, thus everything. It is the true love of truth. Even if we are incapable of inhabiting it, it does not prevent us from discovering that sometimes it inhabits us" (83). Jérôme Grynpas explains, "It is the joy of understanding who I am and under which conditions the being I am can develop all its capacities."[10]

The various perspectives I refer to in this book are instrumental in helping coaches and coachees become more aware of the filters that condition us and determine—or at least influence—our actions beyond our awareness. For example, the Cultural Orientations Framework gives us a concrete roadmap for deciphering some of our cultural biases so we can go beyond our current cultural limitations. At the physical level, I have discussed how our nutrition impacts our health and fitness, our ability to deal with stress, et cetera. Yet many people still eat mindlessly, overlooking opportunities to go beyond their current physical limitations. Thus global coaching can facilitate the journey toward beatitude, as defined by Spinoza. It is my experience that coachees who take this journey gain serenity and wisdom. They become better able to suspend judgment, to attribute behaviors to factors beyond their collaborators' current awareness, and to open up new possibilities to help address their challenges.

The diversity element—another key theme in this book—comes into play here as well. According to Spinoza, the differences that make each of us unique allow us to think freely. The practical implication for coaches is that we need to understand, cultivate, and leverage diversity. The psychological and cultural perspectives are paving the way for the spiritual perspective.

Incidentally, Spinoza points to the "unity" of "body-mind" ("one and the same thing, but expressed in two ways"), which is also consistent with the holographic model. Moreover, he argues that nature is the totality: everything belongs to nature, and there is nothing else (i.e., no transcendence) but nature. Interestingly, when it comes to practical actions, this secular view (the term "God" that Spinoza uses should not mislead us, given his notion of *Deus sive natura*—God that is nature) can be reconciled with religious views such as Buber's, Jung's (our life purpose is to complete God's work of creation) or Teilhard de Chardin's. De Chardin's view proposes that life is a single unity; the entire living world is a "single and gigantic organism"; each individual, by playing a role in the shared enterprise, is provided with a personal sense of meaning; "although only a small fraction of those who try to scale the heights of human achievement arrive anywhere close to the summit, it is imperative that there be a multitude of climbers. Otherwise the summit may not be reached by anybody. The individually lost and forgotten multitudes have not lived in vain, provided that they, too, made the efforts to climb" (Yalom, 1980, 426).

NOTES

1. See *www.nasa.gov/exploration/home/why_moon.html*. Accessed on 13 August 2009.
2. According to Francis Rocard, astrophysicist at the CNES. JT TV5 Monde. 20 July 2009.
3. These two sections include adaptations from Rosinski, *Lessons in Global Coaching From a Journey Through Unusual Hardship*, 2007, 11–13; and Rosinski, *Coaching From Multiple Perspectives*, 2006, 8–9.
4. See Rosinski, 2007. A minor sporting injury turned into a worsening condition that could neither be explained nor cured for more than one year. The pain was such that it prevented me from sitting or standing up. Incidentally, my hardship experience reminded me how division and the absence of a global approach still permeate our society. For more than a year, the only medical or paramedical help I could find had little knowledge and apparently little curiosity for anything beyond their area of specialization. In contrast, the multidisciplinary approach I finally uncovered made all the difference and further validated the power of leveraging multiple perspectives. Professor Plaghki's multidisciplinary approach allowed him to confront viewpoints and cross-fertilize various domains of expertise. This led to the correct diagnostic. On the contrary, all lone physicians had gone down the wrong path, making costly mistakes that could have been easily avoided.
5. Bible: John 8.7 (*Weymouth New Testament*).
6. Bible: John 8.11 (*World English Bible*).
7. Rosinski, "Leading for Joy: Lessons on Leadership From the Judaic Tradition", 1998.
8. See Zeig, 1980. For example, p. xi: "Some of us wanted to get down to the 'real teaching' and would ask questions for clarification. Erickson would answer with another story. Further questions would be answered by more stories. Rather than allowing us to digest a story and ruminate upon its meaning, Erickson would start a new tale at once, sometimes using a few jokes to first catch our attention, and sometimes without using any clear transition at all."
9. More on this in Chapter 10 (concept of shadow).
10. Philosophy lesson 25 November 2008, CCLJ, Brussels.

PART III

Connecting the Six Perspectives

CHAPTER 9

Embracing the
Interconnectedness

Traditional coaching, which reflects our Western Aristotelian cultural tendencies and materialistic, scientific worldview, is often characterized by a fragmented and specialized approach. Specialization allows people to focus on their areas of expertise; the danger is that we will miss interconnections and the big picture. Referring to our six coaching perspectives, this division is tantamount to ignoring beneficial alternative viewpoints (e.g., the physically or psychologically inclined missing the cultural territory) and, most of all, missing opportunities for cross-fertilizing, leveraging diverse perspectives. We need synthesis if we are to address complex and multidimensional challenges.

Extraordinary experiences and breakthrough insights can help us shift our thinking and outlook on life. To access them, all we need is an attitude of deep openness and curiosity. We need not give up our healthy skepticism, but we do need to accept the primacy of experiences even when the findings don't fit with our current models and worldview. This is what the best coaches do when working with a coachee: they truly listen, suspend their judgment, go beyond their own preconceived ideas, and allow the coachee's potential to blossom.

In this chapter, I will present the holographic model. I will draw in particular from the astonishing *Holographic Universe*, written by Michael Talbot (1991) and building on physicist David Bohm's breakthrough ideas (*Wholeness and the Implicate Order*, 1980). Maybe synchronicity was at play when I came across Talbot's as well as Stanislav Grof's (2006) books. The holographic model provides the solid and original conceptual thread required for global coaching. Moreover, it turns out that the mathematical theory and language of the hologram are the Fourier transforms, which were at the heart of my education at Stanford University, where I obtained a Master of Science in electrical engineering.

I will also introduce the complex thinking model, which will complete our conceptual framework for global coaching. I will draw particularly from Edgar Morin's (2005) excellent work. The two models are consistent, and together they point to a new paradigm that can bring coaching to new frontiers.

HOLOGRAPHIC MODEL

A hologram is a three-dimensional image, usually made with the aid of a laser. It can be static (picture) or dynamic (movie). It looks real. However, when you reach out to touch it, all you can grab is thin air.

Hologram is derived from the Greek words *holos* (whole) and graphè (writing, drawing). Thus, "the hologram is an instrument that, as it were, 'writes the whole'" (Bohm, 1980, 183).

Holography is possible thanks to the interference phenomenon, which occurs when waves ripple through each other. For example, when waves of water emanating from pebbles dropped in a pond pass through one another, they create a complex arrangement—an interference pattern.

The coherent light from a laser is well suited for creating interference patterns that make holograms possible. Bohm explains that the laser light is passed through a half-silvered mirror. Part of the beam goes on directly to a photographic plate, while another part is reflected so that it illuminates an object. The light reflected from this object also reaches the plate, where it interferes with that arriving there by the direct path through the mirror. The resulting interference pattern is recorded on the plate. It is very complex and usually so fine that it is invisible to the naked eye. Yet, it contains, implicitly, all the information about the object.

When the photographic plate is illuminated with laser light, a wavefront similar to that coming off the original object is created. This allows us to see something that looks exactly like the object in three dimensions and from a range of possible points of view. Moreover, if we illuminate only a small region of the plate, we still see the whole structure, but in somewhat less sharply-defined detail and from a decreased range of possible points of view.

There is no one-to-one correspondence between parts of an 'illuminated object' and parts of an 'image of this object on the plate'. Rather, the interference pattern in each region of the plate is relevant to the whole object, and each region of the object is relevant to the whole of the interference pattern on the plate (183–184).

This 'undivided wholeness' property of the hologram is in such sharp contrast with the mechanistic worldview we have become so accustomed to that we often confuse it with reality itself, entertaining "the illusion that the world is actually constituted of separate fragments" (9). The optical lens illustrates this point-to-point correspondence. Lenses in microscopes and telescopes can go a long way in helping us explore the world, from tiny objects to distant stars. Yet, Bohm argues that "because of the wave properties of light, even a lens cannot produce an exact one-to-one correspondence" (184–185). Just as Newton's laws have been surpassed by Einstein's physics despite their usefulness in many situations, the "lens" mechanistic worldview needs to be transcended by the more general "hologram" conception. The hologram reveals an organic worldview, consistent with our complex and interconnected reality and necessary if we are to tackle today's difficult challenges.

A new description of the universe is emerging. This order is not to be understood solely in terms of a regular arrangement of objects in space and events in time, but "rather a *total order* is contained in some *implicit* sense, in each region of space and time." In other words, "each region contains a total structure enfolded within it" (188).

Every part of the holographic film contains all the information possessed by the whole. In other words, you can reproduce the entire original object by shining a laser beam through just a fragment of the film (although the images will be hazier when the parts become smaller). This is baffling from a mechanistic viewpoint, but not under the new complexity paradigm.

Furthermore, you can record multiple images on a single film by changing the laser beam's orientation. You can reproduce each image later by choosing the right angle for the laser beam.

Karl Pribam, professor of neuropsychology at Stanford University, looked to the holographic model in the 1960s to account for puzzling phenomena in our brain, notably:

- the vastness of our memory: our brains, much like holograms, can store a gigantic amount of memories in very little space
- our ability to recall and forget: recalling a memory is analogous to shining a laser beam to evoke a particular image. Without the right angle, though, that image will not appear.
- non-locality: memories don't seem to be localized in specific areas of the brain but are distributed throughout. Karl Lashley cut various brain

areas in rats; afterward, the rats could still perform their learned maze runs. Paul Pietsch tinkered with salamanders' brain (slicing, flipping, shuffling, subtracting, and mincing). This did not prevent the salamanders from resuming normal feeding when he replaced what was left of their brain. (See Talbot, 1991, 12–13 and 26.)

Other phenomena, such as the associative tendencies of memory and our ability to quickly recognize a familiar face in a crowd, can also be explained with additional holographic techniques.

The holographic model allows us to cast doubt on the external-internal duality, about which we usually have no second thoughts. Internally, we have feelings, thoughts, and mental representations of reality. Externally, we find the material world of objects and living beings that we can see, hear, touch, smell, and taste. Like many other coaches, I often use this dichotomy. The Cultural Orientations Framework exemplifies how we can represent salient aspects of our culture. Our orientations (internal) impact how we behave (external). By enlarging our inner territory, we gain more external choices and can become more effective. It is obvious, is it not?

Actually, reality is apparently not that simple. While useful, this separation does not explain, for example, the phantom limb phenomenon. An amputee can still experience pain, sometimes excruciating pain, in his missing limb, as if the limb were still there. I have personally experienced a similar syndrome.[1] There is more evidence that our brain can fool us into thinking that inner processes are located outside the body. Nobel Prize–winning physiologist Georg von Bekesy put vibrators *on* his blindfolded subjects' knees and then made them feel that the vibrators were *between* their knees. Talbot (1991) explains, "He demonstrated that humans have the ability to seemingly experience sensation in spatial locations where they have absolutely no sense receptor." He makes the connection with the holographic model: "Creating the illusion that things are located where they are not is the quintessential feature of a hologram" (25).

Quantum physics provides further evidence that reality is more complex than we think. If you break matter into smaller and smaller pieces, you don't just end up with tinier objects as you would expect from a mechanistic viewpoint. You discover entities such as electrons with different properties "(e.g., particle-like, wavelike, or something in between), depending on the environmental context within which they exist and are subject to observation" (Bohm, 1980, 222). Physicists believe that the entire universe is made of subatomic particles (sometimes called *quanta*) behaving in this 'chameleon-like' manner (Talbot, 1991, 33).

The holographic model gives substance to the assertion that we live in an interconnected world. It is much more interconnected than we usually think. In 1982, French physicists Alain Aspect, Jean Dalibard, and Gérard Roger proved that the Danish physicist Niels Bohr, a founding father of quantum physics, was right. They produced a series of twin photons by heating calcium with lasers and allowed each proton to travel in opposite directions. By then, they had the technology to measure faster-than-light processes. As Bohr's theory predicted, each photon maintained its angle of polarization (i.e., spatial orientation as it travels away from its point of origin) in sync with its twin photon. The pair couldn't be communicating through light between them because the light would have to travel faster than the speed of light (the absolute speed limit, according to Einstein's special theory of relativity). Aspect's experiment indicates that the connection between the twin photons is non-local (Talbot, 1991, 36, 43, 52–53). Photons remain somehow interconnected. This does not prove that the holographic model is absolutely correct, but it gives weight to a model that is consistent with experimental findings, and for now it represents the best way we have to explain this intriguing reality. The awareness of this interconnection can inspire our coaching. We can ponder the implications, asking ourselves and our coachees: how can we take fully into account the fact that everything is deeply connected?

In his research on plasmas, Bohm (once Einstein's protégé) discovered "entire oceans of particles, each behaving as if it knew what untold trillions of others were doing." He called these collective movements of electrons "plasmons" (Talbot, 1991, 38). Subatomic particles were behaving like interconnected wholes. Bohm offers a useful analogy. Imagine you film a fish swimming in an aquarium with two movie cameras, placed at different angles and hooked to two distinct TV screens. The two images will be correlated. Likewise, although particles appear to be separate from one another, they act as if they were projections of a single 'higher-dimensional' reality (analogous to the fishes seen on the two-dimensional TV screens, projections of the fish in the three-dimensional aquarium). Under certain conditions, particles may appear relatively independent. More generally, however, particles will display non-local, non-causal relationships similar to the correlation between the fishes' movements on the TV screens.

Bohm further investigated the notion of order. Order can lie beneath apparent disorder. This notion is also at the core of "chaos theory." (See notably

Gleick, 1997.) Bohm was struck by a device consisting of two concentric glass cylinders, with glycerine (a highly viscous fluid) between them: "A droplet of insoluble ink is placed in the fluid, and the outer cylinder is then turned, with the result that the droplet is drawn out into a fine thread-like form that eventually becomes invisible. When the cylinder is turned in the opposite direction the thread-form draws back and suddenly becomes visible as a droplet essentially the same as the one that was there originally" (Bohm, 1980, 227).

Bohm explains that "when the ink particles have been drawn out into a long thread, one can say that they have been *enfolded* into the glycerine." The droplet can be *unfolded* "by reversing the motion of the fluid" (228).

This phenomenon illustrates how order can be either manifest (explicit, unfolded) or hidden (implicit, enfolded). Likewise, there is order enfolded into the seemingly disorderly interference patterns recorded on a holographic film or into the apparently random movements of electrons in plasmas.

Talbot summarizes a startling and crucial assertion by Bohm: "The tangible reality of our everyday lives is really a kind of illusion, like a holographic image. Underlying it is a deeper order of existence, a vast and more primary level of reality that gives birth to objects and appearances of our physical world in much the same way that a piece of holographic film gives birth to a hologram. Bohm calls this deeper level of reality the *implicate* (which means enfolded) order, and he refers to our own level of existence as the *explicate*, or unfolded, order" (Talbot, 1991, 46). There are countless enfoldings and unfoldings between the two orders. Each subatomic particle is an ensemble, and the way an observer interacts with it determines which aspect unfolds and which remains hidden, explaining the chameleon-like property mentioned earlier.

Applying these ideas to coaching by analogy yields at least two important implications:

- People have enormous hidden potential, and through our coaching, we can help them unfold various aspects. The danger would be to quickly limit ourselves, and thereby limit our coachee's progress, by adopting the same partial viewpoints. That would be like shining laser beams within a narrow angular range, missing many other possible perspectives; it would restrict the unfolding of the coachee's potential.

- The quality of our interaction with the coachee is crucial. As you will discover in Chapter 11, this is consistent with Martin Buber's (1958) notion of "I-Thou" relationships and his notion that "all real living is meeting."

As I mentioned earlier, the Fourier transform is the mathematical language of the hologram. Dennis Gabor used it in 1947 when he conceived the idea of holography, for which he later won a Nobel Prize. (See Talbot, 1991, 27.) When I learned about the Fourier transform and its multiple applications, I was fascinated by the elegance and ingenuity of this mathematical theory and its usefulness in many domains, including electronics, optics, acoustics, and image processing.[2] One of its applications, medical imaging, helps to save thousands of human lives.[3] My professor, Ronald Bracewell (1978), explains, "We may think of functions and their transforms as occupying two domains, sometimes referred to as the upper and the lower, as if functions circulated at ground level and their transforms in the underworld" (135). What is particularly advantageous is that the detour in this underworld can often make life easier at ground level. For example, the convolution of two functions $f(x)$ and $g(x)$ (i.e., $f(x) * g(x)$) is a rather complicated, or I should say convoluted, operation (i.e., $f(x) * g(x) = \int_{-\infty}^{\infty} f(u) g(x-u) \, du$). However, the convolution in one domain is equivalent to a simple multiplication in the other domain. This means you can transform the functions, multiply these transforms $F(x) \times G(x)$ in the frequency domain, and then transform back the result to obtain the desired convolution. I don't anticipate that most global coaches will master the mathematics (I have forgotten most of this myself!), but we can keep in mind the underlying philosophy: being open and attuned to different levels of reality and creatively juggling these realms will enhance your coaching capability.

Bohm and Pribam's theories provide a radical new way to consider the world: "Our brains mathematically construct objective reality by interpreting frequencies that are ultimately projections from another dimension, a deeper order of existence that is beyond both space and time. The brain is a hologram enfolded in a holographic universe" (Talbot, 1991, 54). This does not mean that material objects don't exist. But each object has two aspects to its reality. For example, without our brain lenses, we would experience a table as an interference pattern. Which one is real, and which is illusion? As Pribam said to Talbot, "Both are real to me, or, if you want to say, neither of them are real" (Talbot, 1991, 55). To make matters even more complex, we are also part of the hologram.

Talbot's merit is in revealing daring and revolutionary implications of the holographic model, showing how it can account for a variety of amazing phenomena—phenomena that usually belong to the esoteric and paranormal domains, fascinating but apparently impossible.

I refer you to Talbot's book as well as Dr. Stanislav Grof's *When the Impossible Happens* (2006) and the late Harvard professor John Mack's *Passport to the Cosmos* (2008). Assuming you take an open-minded approach to coaching, these readings should shake your ontological conceptions.

Let me mention some of these phenomena and give some examples. I hope these will encourage you to learn more and then ponder their implications for global coaching.

- Carl Jung's synchronicity and collective unconscious

  I will elaborate on these in the next chapter. Everything is connected. It is also Bohm's opinion that "deep down the consciousness of mankind is one" (Weber, 1982, 72). However, Talbot, much like Buber (see Chapter 11), insists that individuality is not lost: "We are like the vortices in a river, unique but inseparable from the flow of nature" (1991, 81). In practice, though, we usually do not tap into the unconscious knowledge of the entire human race! The reason, according to psychologist Robert Anderson, is that a selective process of *personal resonance* is at play. (See Talbot, 1991, 61.)

- Mystical experiences

  Mystics from various traditions and times have reported a sense of unity with life—a cosmic oneness with the universe. Bohm and Pribam suggest that "perhaps mystics are somehow able to peer beyond ordinary explicate reality and glimpse its deeper, more holographic qualities" (Talbot, 1991, 63).

- Psychosis

  Montague Ullman believes psychotics share similar experiences but are unable to order these rationally. These glimpses into the holographic level of reality are tragic versions of those reported by mystics. "Schizophrenics often report oceanic feelings of oneness with the universe, but in a magic, delusional way." Manics "grandiosely identify with their infinite potential . . . . In turn, the manic becomes depressed after he returns from this surreal vacation and once again faces the hazards and chance occurrences of everyday life" (Talbot, 1991, 63–64).

- Multiple personality disorder

  In this syndrome, a person displays several distinct personalities. Moreover, the strong psychological separation between the various personalities goes together with dramatic biological changes after each switching occurs. The changes "include the abrupt appearance and disappearance of rashes, welts, scars and other tissue wounds; switches in handwriting and handedness; epilepsy, allergies and color blindness that strike only when a given personality is in control of the body" (Goleman, 1988). A woman, "admitted to a hospital for diabetes, baffled her physicians by showing no symptoms of the disorder at times when one personality, who was not diabetic, was dominant" (Goleman, 1985). By changing personalities, a "multiple" may also respond differently to drugs, may have better or worse eyesight, and will differ in "artistic talent and even in knowledge of foreign languages" (Goleman, 1988). The parts have various announced ages, genders, and backgrounds. The syndrome may represent a coping mechanism of parceling out the pain following a history of monstrous child abuse. This is an extreme example of fragmentation. A successful psychiatric treatment will allow the various personalities to blend into a single, integrated one. The disorder not only demonstrates how much our psyche can affect our body but suggests that these personalities behave like a "multiple image hologram" in people who suffer from the syndrome (Talbot, 1991, 100).

- Amazing experiences in altered states of consciousness

Stanislav Grof developed a technique using LSD to induce altered states of consciousness. Later on, he and his wife, Christina, developed Holotropic Breathwork, a non-pharmacological method of self-exploration and therapy. "With this approach, non-ordinary states of consciousness are induced by very simple and natural means—faster breathing, evocative music, and release of blocked energies by a certain form of bodywork. The experiences triggered by this approach can be very powerful, and they resemble both the states induced by psychedelics and those described in Kashmir Shaivism"[4] (Grof, 2006, 38).

In these altered states, people relive experiences that they could not possibly know or remember (that is, under the current worldview). These experiences include their own birth, intrauterine existence, and conception (Grof, 2006, 99), episodes from the lives of their ancestors (who lived long before they were conceived), from other historical periods, and from other geographic areas (without the feeling of a biological link to the protagonists of these sequences, often from other racial groups) (Grof, 2006, 117).

Grof shares mind-boggling stories of reincarnation that take individuals to emotionally charged situations in different times and places. During these episodes, they experienced a strange feeling of "déjà vu" or "déjà

vécu" ("I have been here before") and a "deep connection with the protagonists" (Grof, 2006, 135–137).

• Health and sickness; the mind-body connection

Dr. Carl Simonton and his wife Stephanie became convinced that cancer treatment, to be most effective, should deal with the total human
being as an integrated system of mind, body and emotions. They taught
their patients to use their minds and emotions to alter the course of their
malignancies, notably with visual imagery techniques. In the 1970s, they
treated 159 patients with a diagnosis of medically incurable cancer. Four
years later, 63 of the patients were still alive. Of those, 14 showed no evidence of disease, the tumors were regressing in 12, and in 17 the disease
was stable. The average survival time of the group as a whole was 24.4
months, over twice as long as the national norm of 12 months. Moreover, 51 percent of the surviving patients were able to maintain the same
level of activity they had prior to the diagnosis, and 76 percent were at
least 75 percent as active as they were. This was just extraordinary for
"medically incurable" patients. (See Simonton and al., 1992, 10–12.)

The placebo effect provides us with another provocative glimpse into the
mind-body connection. Talbot (1991) reports that in the 1950s, patients
who received sham surgery for angina pectoris "reported just as much
relief as the patients who had the full surgery." The placebo effect has
been extensively researched; various kinds of pain, asthma, peptic ulcers,
depression, rheumatoid and degenerative arthritis, diabetes, multiple
sclerosis, and cancer, among other conditions, have proved responsive to
placebo (90–92). However, we are unaware that we possess this incredible healing power, so we must be fooled into using it.

Psychologist Bruno Klopfer reports an extraordinary case that illustrates
this. A man named Wright had advanced cancer of the lymph nodes.
"His neck, armpits, chest, abdomen, and groin were filled with tumors
the size of oranges, and his spleen and liver were so enlarged that two
quarts of milky fluid had to be drained out of his chest every day." Wright
begged his doctor to let him try a new drug called Krebiozen. To the
doctor's amazement, Wright was out of bed and walking around within
a couple days. His "tumors had melted down like snowballs on a hot
stove." Ten days later, Wright left the hospital, apparently cancer-free. He
remained well for about two months. Then he read that Krebiozen had
no effect on cancer of the lymph nodes. He suffered a relapse. The physician told him a false but convincing story: he had "new super-refined,

double-strength" Krebiozen that could treat Wright's cancer. The doctor then injected Wright with plain sterile water but disguised this with an elaborate procedure. Again, Wright's recovery was dramatic. Wright remained symptom-free for another two months. However, "his improvement ended when the American Medical Association released a report stating that nationwide tests had proven Krebiozen worthless in the treatment of cancer. A few days after reading this statement, he was admitted to the hospital, and two days following admission he died" (Klopfer, 1957, 331–340).

According to the holographic model, our minds and bodies are intimately connected. In this paradigm, incredible happenings enter the realm of possibility. The case of Vittorio Micheli, duly documented and checked with X-rays (before and after), exemplifies how deep spiritual faith can lead to miraculous healing. "His hip bone had disintegrated as a result of malignant sarcoma. So little bone was left that the ball of his upper leg was free-floating in a mass of soft tissue. After a series of baths in the spring at Lourdes, his hip bone completely regenerated over the course of several months, a feat currently considered impossible by medical science."[5] Eventually, scientists may find that this natural process is possible after all. In any event, it is very rare—perhaps because it involves accessing very deep levels of the psyche. Overall, it seems that, to some extent, health goes hand in hand with a sense of unity and connection, whereas illness reveals a fracture. We have some power to create both sickness and wellness. The placebo (healing) effect has a negative counterpart in the nocebo (deteriorating) effect, as Wright's story exemplified. So it may be good news that our access to these powers is restricted. Personal growth might involve gaining, gradually, increased access to our staggering potential as we progressively strengthen our maturity, wisdom, and ability to use these capabilities constructively.

- Extrasensory perception and other paranormal abilities

  These experiences transcend the usual limitations of space and time and baffle scientists, who cannot explain such phenomena with traditional theories. Grof illustrates cases in different categories, including:

  - *Telepathy*: the direct access to another person's thought processes without using words, nonverbal clues, signs, or other conventional means of communication

  - *Out-of-body experiences*: episodes during which disembodied consciousness moves in space and accurately perceives the environment.

When such perception involves remote locations, it is called *astral projection.*

- *Precognition*: accurate anticipation of future events without any objective cues

- *Clairvoyance*: the capacity to access information about the past, present, and future without using ordinary channels

- *Psychometry*: a process of obtaining information about an object's history, or facts and impressions about a person to whom this object belonged, by extended tactile contact with that object

Grof (2006) also mentions near-death experiences (which, in their full form, typically include an out-of-body experience), encounters and communication with deceased people (who provide verifiable information that convinces Grof that this is not a hallucination), and channeling (in which a being transmits through automatic writing, speech, or action messages from a source external to his or her everyday personality) (169–173). For example, Luiz Antonio Gasparetto produced extraordinary paintings each in the style of a different famous painter—van Gogh, Picasso, Rembrandt and many others. He did this in the presence of Grof and participants in his seminar at Esalen. With just enough light for the audience to see by but too little for him to distinguish colors, he painted these works with astonishing speed, sometimes even working on two at a time—one with each hand (Grof, 2006, 184–190).

Grof refers to a session on psychometry conducted by psychic Anne Armstrong. She asked participants to "suspend any doubts about their own psychic abilities and write down everything that came to their mind, without the slightest reservation and without any censorship" after they looked at an object that "unbeknownst to other people in the group, had emotional significance" to the owner. Grof gives examples of remarkable associations the group members made. A key difference with Anne was that "she was also able to decipher her own images and associations and translate them into clear and cohesive readings" (Grof, 2006, 198–208).

- Materializations

    As Talbot (1991) explains, psychologist Erlendur Haraldsson has spent more than ten years studying Sai Baba in India, a man who can manifest specific objects on request, including rare botanical specimens, costly rings and jewels, vast quantities of food (even out-of-season fruits), and sacred ash. "Although Haraldsson admits that he cannot prove conclusively that Sai Baba's productions are not the result of deception and sleight of hand, he offers a large amount of evidence that strongly suggest something supernormal is taking place" (151–152).

Thousands of individuals have witnessed these materializations, including Grof, who personally observed at close range Sai Baba producing large quantities of candies and ashes. "All that with short sleeves that would have made any magic tricks very difficult" (Grof, 2006, 229).

- UFOs, alien encounters, and abductions

Hundreds of people in different parts of the world have independently described similar experiences with aliens. John Mack, professor of psychiatry at Harvard University, undertook a major investigation into these claims. When watching *Enlevés* ("Abducted") (Allix, 2005), which includes his testimonial and several interviews with abductees, I was struck by Mack's openness, empathy, and ingenious questioning as he tried to discover the truth. I subsequently read Mack's second book on this subject (2008). Mack concludes that those who reported encounters with and abductions by aliens were not suffering from any psychiatric condition. They were speaking sincerely. Mack (2008) explains:

I was then faced with the choice of either trying to fit these individuals' reports into a framework that fit my worldview—they were having fantasies, strange dreams, delusions, or some distortion of reality—or of modifying my worldview to include the possibility that entities, beings, energies—something—could be reaching my clients from another realm. The first choice was compatible with my worldview but did not fit the clinical data. The second was inconsistent with my philosophical grounding, and with conventional assumptions about reality, but appeared to fit better what I was finding. It seemed to be more logical, and intellectually more honest, to modify my cosmology than to continue trying to force my clients into molds that clearly did not suit them. (5)

As real as the encounters are for the "experiencers," Mack stresses, "I am not seeking to establish the material reality of the alien abduction phenomenon, that is, people's report of being taken by humanoid beings into some sort of enclosure where a variety of procedures and communications are said to take place. Rather, I am more concerned with the meaning of these experiences for the so-called abductees and for humankind more generally" (xi–xii).

In a tribute to Mack, Michael Cohen (2008) states that the "holographic universe" is the only scientific model compatible with these extraordinary experiences.

Mack (2008) notes that in many if not most indigenous cultures, the "crossover" from the unseen or "other" world into our material reality is regarded as a regular occurrence, but "in our Western or scientific/materialist society, the domains of spirit and matter have been kept separate and distinct, and the possibility of traffic between them is looked upon as doubtful if not altogether impossible" (5). He cites Madima Somé, a shaman of the Dagara people of Burkina Faso: "To a Dagara man or woman, the material is just the spiritual taking on form" (Somé, 1995, 8). Sequoyah Trueblood, a "bridging figure," son of a Native American father and a German-English mother, says that whether "the physical body is taken during an abduction is not important, for 'we are spirit'" (Mack, 2008, 7).

Mack advocates a multidisciplinary approach (since "in the case of the abduction phenomenon, it is hard even to know in what territory or territories we are working") and challenges scientists' presumption that "true objectivity—a radical separation of subject from object—may somehow be attained" (24). He further remarks, "Eastern psychology uses the idea of 'neutral mind,' neither purely objective nor subjective. It is present, mindful, and tough-minded but not attached, including both observation and feeling in the process of knowing. Perhaps it is with our neutral minds that the work with abductees should be conducted" (25).

What stands outs for the abductees and for Mack, who genuinely listened to them, is the spiritual growth that has consistently ensued from these encounters.

According to Peter, one of the "experiencers," the abduction phenomenon "reifies[6] the classic mind-body split that arguably has been responsible for so much evil in human history: a runaway intellect divorced from the heart, technology gone wild" (Cohen, 2008, 3). Cohen describes the feelings of cosmic unity and continues:

John [Mack] advocated a broader worldview than the species-centric, human-dominated view of the cosmos. John's spacious mind allowed a broader conceptualization of our place in the omni-verse, a place in which humans might co-exist with others species and, indeed, intelligently converse with them. But to do so . . . required more than radio signals and scientific intelligence—it required emotional and spiritual intelligence, including a capacity to deepen our opening to inner experience. In this way, John was a pioneering advocate of a broader view of consciousness, and of our relatedness to the entire creation. John moved us past the marriage to our own intellectual constructs, and into an awareness of our soul bond with something more unrestricted. (Cohen, 2008, 4)

Overwhelmingly, the spiritual growth arising from alien encounters and other extraordinary experiences manifests itself in a profound appreciation for life and an eagerness to help preserve our planet's fragile environment: "The abductees state that the aliens visit Earth to warn us that our cavalier tree-cutting, water-polluting, trash-dumping habits will have dire consequences if we do not change our ways. Abductees are left with not only a profound caring for the environment, but with a sense that they have encountered creatures sent by whatever power rules the universe. They particularly find that their experiences resonate with Native American religions" (*Publishers Weekly*, 2008). Several experiencers now dedicate much of their lives to protecting our ecosystems. For example, Bernardo Peixoto "seeks to stop the devastation by increasing awareness of our essential connection with the earth and sky and by mobilizing concern for the Brazilian rain forest and its life nationally and internationally" (Mack, 2008, 176).

So what does this all mean for the practice of coaching? Traditional coaching, anchored in the Western binary worldview, misses the deeply interconnected nature of reality. Consequently, listening cannot be as profound, understanding not as insightful, and presence not as authentic. Global coaches may not necessarily have to do anything differently. Their heightened awareness, their greater sense of connection with themselves, others, and the world at large, somehow shines through and is communicative. I will further describe this global coaching attitude in Chapter 11, referring to Martin Buber's "I-Thou" relationships, which are remarkably consistent with the holographic model.

Is the holographic model true? To me it seems an ingenious hypothesis and an elegant description. However, we have much more to learn. Our understanding of reality is a work in progress, and our theories are always destined to be surpassed by more accurate ones as our collective knowledge progresses. Ultimately, because we are pragmatists, what matters the most is whether our beliefs bring about effective and constructive outcomes. We are less concerned about their veracity in an absolute sense. By enriching our cultural outlook and enlarging our worldview, we can help re-enchant our lives and infuse it with meaning. The cultural and spiritual perspectives are indeed intertwined. The same applies to all perspectives. Physical exercise increases our well-being. We become more optimistic and grateful—that is, spiritually attuned. Interconnectedness, which is at the core of the holographic model, also means we take into account the links between various levels: ourselves, our teams, our companies, our families, our communities, and our nations, without forgetting the larger world (and even the multiverse!). We consider the broader impact of our decisions and daily actions. Global coaches should seize every opportunity to build bridges, leverage multiple perspectives, and foster synthesis.

We don't need to have paranormal experiences or to meet aliens to acquire a global consciousness. As I mentioned in Chapter 8, the sunflower strategy is at the heart of the spiritual perspective. We can turn to the light in its many forms. Life itself is a miracle. Love is a wonder. We can be touched by an artist's melodious music, an athlete's courageous resolve, by anonymous people's heroic actions, and of course by the planet's natural beauties. Yann Arthus-Bertrand (2009) among other photographers and filmmakers, has captured some of our earth's treasures. There are multiple paths to unfolding our humanity and sense of connection.

My thesis for the Polytechnical School in Brussels involved designing and building a device that could determine in real time when a person was in the deepest sleeping phase. The usual signal processing approach entailed a Fourier transformation to work in the frequency domain. Instead, I chose to avoid the formal detour in the "underworld" because, in this particular case, I was able to find an easier route staying at "ground level." Sometimes though, it takes a plunge in the underworld to turn an inextricable situation, a convoluted relation, into something simpler, more easily resolved. Global coaches need to be prepared to take both routes. Actually, both domains are always with us, in us.

Without renouncing coaching's goal setting,[7] we need to invite our coachees to also constantly open up and flexibly adjust to what emerges, trusting their intuition and inner wisdom. Grof (2006) comments on this "watercourse way" (it imitates indeed the way the water operates in nature):

> We try to sense which way things are moving and how to best fit into them. This is the strategy used in martial arts and in surfing. It involves focus on the process, rather than the goal or the outcome. When we are able to approach life in this way, we ultimately achieve more and with less effort. In addition,

our activities are not egocentric, exclusive, and competitive . . . but inclusive and synergistic. The outcome not only brings satisfaction to us, but serves a larger purpose of the community. . . . When we operate in this Taoistic frame-work, extraordinary beneficial coincidences and synchronicities tend to occur, which support our project and help us in our work. We come "accidentally" across the information we need, the right people appear at the right time, and the necessary funds become available. (66)

COMPLEXITY PARADIGM

Complex thinking is consistent with the holographic model. It offers insights into the simplicity paradigm and highlights what is required to shift to the new paradigm, which is more appropriate and useful in our post-modern world. I will present some of the key concepts, so we can become equipped, as global coaches, to embrace complexity. This does not mean we should give up useful simple models, but we should put these models in a broader context, being aware of their limitations and how other perspectives can complete them. Situational leadership is one example. (See Chapter 4.)

Dialectics, Recursion, Holographic Principle

Dialectics, which I brought up in my previous book (Rosinski, 2003, 57–58), is a fundamental aspect of complex thinking. Heraclitus, a pre-Socratic philosopher in the fifth and sixth centuries B.C., originated this philosophy, so it can hardly be termed a new and ephemeral management fad. This ancient way of thinking is much needed today.

Unlike his contemporaries, Heraclitus refused to follow a master and was suspicious of common knowledge. He brought the following radical views:

- Paradoxically, if we want to avoid that conflict degenerates, we need to accept that contradiction and conflict are necessary rather than pursue harmony.
- Each thing is one and contradictory with itself. It is made up of antagonistic elements, intimately interlocked. For example, high is inseparable from low; likewise day and night, male and female, et cetera.
- Harmony implies sameness, stillness, death. Conflict is inherent to diversity, to movement, to life.

- Welcoming the necessity of conflict and ensuring that it does not get out of hand has a name: justice.

My concept of a unity that embraces contradictions dates back to Heraclitus. However, many coaches and corporations still adopt a binary approach and simplistic notions of ethics, which may be counterproductive in our complex world. Think, for example, of multinational companies that sell sodas. They are proud of their commitment to "quality" and "shareholder value," and yet they are promoting an unhealthy product. Some people think these products are of very low quality, considering their poor nutritional value. Overindulging in a consumerist society, responding to mind-numbing advertising, sucking in vast quantities of junk food—all this ultimately comes with a price: obesity, diabetes, cancer, cardiovascular diseases, et cetera. This conflicting view of quality, which in now gaining momentum, is necessary to promote progress.

Physician Larry Dossey provides links with the holographic model: "We have a tendency to view illness as external to us. Disease comes from without and besieges us, upsetting our well-being. But if space and time, and all other things in the universe, are truly inseparable, then we cannot make a distinction between health and disease . . . . When we stop seeing illness as something separate and instead view it as part of a larger whole, as a milieu of behavior, diet, sleep, exercise patterns, and various other relationships with the world at large, we often get better." He notes a research study that showed most subjects who suffered from chronic headaches found themselves cured after they started to keep a diary. In this case, simply reconnecting with oneself precipitated healing. "When our focus is toward a principle of relatedness and oneness, and away from fragmentation and isolation, health ensues" (Talbot, 1991, 89).

More generally, the connection with the holographic model also becomes apparent when we consider the following inseparable polarities: wave-particle, unfolded-enfolded, part-whole, and internal-external.

As global coaches, we embrace this reality in our practice. We consider internal and external realities interlocked. For example, by opening up the internal representation of reality (e.g., using the COF as a roadmap at the cultural level, finding meaning in enduring hardship at the spiritual level, viewing politics as necessary and potentially constructive), a fresh and more effective way of engaging in the "external" world naturally follows.

That process is a *recursive* one: it works like a dance in a mutually reinforcing upward spiral. Coachees' actions in the "real" world lead to more productive outcomes, which reinforce their new outlook and beliefs, which in turn lead to greater success. Incidentally, this amplification, this generative effect, distinguishes recursion from mere reciprocity, retroaction, or regulation. Coaches celebrates the coachees' success along the way, which reinforces progress, and helps coachees overcome difficulties by treating them as learning opportunities.

Recursion is one of three principles of complex thinking according to Edgar Morin, alongside dialectics and the *holographic principle* (i.e., the whole in the part and the part in the whole).

Open System Versus Closed System

Closed systems, unlike open systems (e.g., human bodies, organizations, societies), have no source of energy/matter external to themselves.

Steven Strogatz (2003) remarks, "Scientists have often been baffled by the existence of spontaneous order in the universe. The laws of thermodynamics seem to dictate the opposite, that nature should inexorably degenerate toward a state of greater disorder, greater entropy. Yet all around us we see magnificent structures—galaxies, cells, ecosystems, human beings—that have all somehow managed to assemble themselves."

Life is a fragile victory over the universe's inexorable decay. Life is possible because it is an open system (e.g., body, organization). Negentropy[8] antagonizes entropy and equates to the open system's development—its increased complexity. Morin (2005) explains that life (biology) is characterized by a greater order than is found in physics. Yet, life also tolerates greater disorders than are found in physics. Order and disorder both increase in an organization as it becomes more complex. Our bodies live through the incessant degradation and renewal of most of our cells. Living is death and rejuvenation. But by dint of rejuvenating, we become older and eventually die (85), or in Heraclitus's words, "Live of death, die of life." Paradoxically, "life is a progress that is paid by the death of individuals" (82).

A fundamental flaw in simplistic thinking is that it tends to consider open systems as closed systems. It fails to appreciate the relations between open systems and their ecosystems, which are both "material/energetic and organizational/informational" (Morin 2005, 32). Simplistic thinking misses the fact that closed systems are doomed to crumble. Life requires openness and exchanges with its environment.

The following table summarizes the contrasts between open and closed systems.

Closed system	Open system
In a state of equilibrium	Can have apparent equilibrium—a stable yet fragile "steady state" (paradox: structure remains while components change)[9]
Static	Dynamic (stabilized disequilibrium/ apparent equilibrium)
World vision paradigm: classification, analytical, reductionist, (uni)linear causality	World vision paradigm: reality of the system lies both in the relation and the distinction of the open system and its environment
Peculiar to death	Peculiar to life
Subject to entropy (which is a measure of disorder: the higher the entropy, the greater the disorder); ultimately, entropy is greatest when the system is closed—this state of "perfect internal disorder" is synonymous with "equilibrium"	Life as a fragile victory against universe's inexorable decay/entropy (the second law of thermodynamics states that the entropy of the universe tends to a maximum). Life is possible because it is an open system.
Harmony—understood as this perfect equilibrium—equates to death. (Heraclitus argued this long before we understood thermodynamics.)	Negentropy antagonizes entropy and equates to the open system's (e.g., organizational) development—that is, its increased complexity.
Isolated but not autonomous	Autonomous but not isolated (autonomy, a crucial aim of human development according to transactional analysis (see Chapter 5) happens through openness, exchanges with others; paradoxically, we build autonomy through our dependence on others, starting with our parents).

Gödel's Incompleteness Theorem

Judy Jones and William Wilson (1995) explain:

> In 1931, the Czech-born mathematician Kurt Gödel demonstrated that within any given branch of mathematics, there would always be some propositions that couldn't be proven either true or false using the rules and axioms . . . of that mathematical branch itself. You might be able to prove every

conceivable statement about numbers within a system by going outside the system in order to come up with new rules and axioms, but by doing so you'll only create a larger system with its own unprovable statements. The implication is that all logical system of any complexity are, by definition, incomplete; each of them contains, at any given time, more true statements than it can possibly prove according to its own defining set of rules.

No system is capable of totally explaining itself nor of totally proving itself.

In other words, every system of thought is open. This has two implications.

The "bad" news is that there is a necessarily breach, a loophole. However, in coaching, many forget that models are necessarily imperfect. Coaches also sometimes entertain an illusion of absolute accuracy about psychometric tools' validity. (See Chapter 7.) The search for the ultimate model, approach, theory is a lure.

The "good" news is we have the possibility of adopting a "meta" viewpoint. By stepping back, we can allow more and more of life's complexity to weave itself into our coaching. However, we cannot totally dissociate ourselves from the system. The neutral external position is an illusion. The quality of our connection and relationship also enables the coachee to unfold fruitful qualities. Embracing multiple perspectives and paradoxes is necessary.

Progress

The interactions between the system and the eco-system can be viewed as an upward movement of the system surpassing itself into a meta-system, with increasing levels of complexity. (Morin, 2005, 32)

Global coaching facilitates this progress, enabling human growth by helping people learn from multiple perspectives. However, as coaches we must enlarge our own system before we can foster this process with coachees. For example, coaches might start by relying on psychological know-how and then broaden this system by weaving in politics, culture, et cetera. Likewise, we might initially focus on the individual and gradually consider our coachees' team, organization, and societal context. If, for instance, the coachee is an overworked executive who constantly goes beyond her personal limitations, the coach might realize that not only psychological factors but also cultural factors are at play.

This coaching evolution toward increased complexity mirrors the development of life on Earth.

Let me suggest additional implications for coaching:

- Through coaching, coachees open their system. Herein lies the opportunity to let in fresh viewpoints, new and interesting questions, and promising links. External stimuli favor creative thinking; hence, for example, the use of postcards[10] (Rosinski, 2003, 61–68).

- Coaches facilitate the unfolding of coachees' potential (holographic model). Coaches shift the angle of their laser beams to reveal facets of this potential. This notion assumes coaches interact with coachees, both as open systems.

- Coachees eventually become their own coaches. They integrate the external coach into their beings. Coachees can then conduct powerful coaching sessions with themselves. They increase their ability to adopt meta-viewpoints; they can get outside of themselves. As they continue to grow, they might eventually need new and different coaching input to address the increased complexity.

- This evolutionary process is consistent with adult development theories (see next chapter) and with spiritual development. According to the Kabbalah, sages and prophets gain a glimpse of superior worlds. The progress is in line both with secular and mystical notions of human development. For the Kabbalah, Kether (Crown) is the highest level,[11] whereas for transactional analysis, accessing the Prince[12] is the supreme echelon.

- Diversity feeds the open system. Closed systems are plagued by an absence of the diversity essential to life.

  How much diversity can an open system let in? I would argue that we need to find a dynamic equilibrium. With too little diversity, the system will implode. With too much diversity, it will explode. It is not just a question of quantity, though: when people have learned to embrace diversity, they can absorb and make constructive use of many differences. Nevertheless, coaches need to stimulate coachees without overwhelming them. Very often, I focus on the basics and gradually weave in more perspectives and more complex notions. This also applies to coaching teams and organizations.

- To play their part and help coachees in increasingly complex situations as they continue their developmental journey, coaches need to advance on their own developmental journey. This means taking in more inputs and considering new perspectives—functioning as an open system—rather than resting on their laurels. Coaches need to be truly committed to lifelong learning from multiple viewpoints.

Complexity Paradigm Versus Simplicity Paradigm

Complexity comes from the Latin word *complexus*, "what is woven together." Complexity is a fabric of inseparably associated heterogeneous constituents.

For Morin (2005), the paradigm of simplicity either separates what is linked (disjunction) or makes uniform what is diverse (reduction) (79). Either way, this is mutilation. Science is separated from humanities, business is detached from philosophy, and mind is cut off from body. By contrast, the paradigm of complexity favors distinguishing (without isolating) (Morin, 2005, 104), and combining various constituting entities. In other words, establishing links and leveraging diversity (promoting unity rather than uniformity[13]) is at the core of the complexity paradigm.

The paradigm of simplicity strives to avoid ambiguity and paradoxes. It clings to certainties. The goal is to impose order, particularly by creating separate categories, which unfortunately result in the disconnected silos many organizations struggle with. This apparent order is, paradoxically, the disorder (entropy) that characterizes closed systems. The paradigm of complexity embraces apparent disorder (ambiguity) and logical contradictions. It promotes the order that make up lively open systems.

Aimed at controlling and mastering reality, the paradigm of simplicity lacks humility. We can see this paradigm's devastating effects on Earth's ecosystems. The paradigm of complexity takes into account natural limitations. The goal is dialoguing, navigating with reality.

Interconnection is at the heart of complexity, which is in line with the holographic model.

The next table[14] summarizes the contrast between the two paradigms. Traditional coaching tends to favor the simplicity paradigm; global coaching is resolutely on the side of complexity, which transcends simplicity without excluding it.

Embracing complexity does not mean, in my view, making our lives more complicated than necessary, nor does it mean finding an excuse for indulging in muddled thinking rather than aiming for rigor and clarity. It does mean, however, striving to be accurate and observing reality with an open mind, particularly when our perceptions seem to contradict our current theories or preconceived ideas.

I agree with Morin, who believes simplification is often necessary, but with a caveat. Reduction is acceptable as long as we are aware that it is a reduction. Reduction becomes problematic when we arrogantly think we possess a simple truth beyond the apparent multiplicity and complexity of things (Morin, 2005, 134–135).

The complexity paradigm takes into account the element of chance, both in the form of unanticipated obstacles to be overcome and sudden opportunities to be seized. Therefore the coaching process cannot be treated simply as the mechanistic pursuit of rigidly predefined objectives. It needs instead to incorporate Grof's "watercourse way."

Simplicity	Complexity
Strives to put order in the universe and to dispel disorder (yet, paradoxically, disorder characterizes closed systems)	Embraces disorder and logical contradictions (yet, paradoxically, order characterizes open systems)
Sees everything as unidimensional, specialized, fragmented	Sees everything as multidimensional and interconnected; aspires to completeness (yet with the awareness that total knowledge is beyond our reach)
Sees either the One or the Multiple but cannot see that the One also can be the Multiple	Links the One and the Multiple. However, the One does not dissolve in the Multiple, and the Multiple is still part of the One.
Either separates what is linked (disjunction) or makes uniform what is diverse (reduction). This is mutilating.	Distinguishes (without isolating) and combines
Considers object distinct from subject	Conceives the inseparable link between the subject and the object
Searches for the elemental brick the universe is supposedly made of	Realizes that it is a fuzzy, complex, hazy entity. Recognizes, in particular, two breaches at the micro and the macro level.[15]
Thinking clings to certainties	Thinking is filled with uncertainties, riddled with holes, with no absolute bedrock of certitude
Programs (automatic pilot mode, predictable)	Strategies (complex responses to unexpected events)

Simplicity	Complexity
Determinism	Necessity (determinism) and chance (unanticipated obstacles to be overcome as well as sudden opportunities to be seized)
Aims at controlling, mastering reality	Aims at dealing, dialoging, negotiating, navigating with reality
Excludes complexity	Includes simplicity while transcending it

Co-Constructivism Versus Positivism

Coaches William Bergquist and Kristin Eggen (2008) advocate a complex approach and contrast "objectivism" and "constructivism." From the objectivist perspective, "there is a reality out there that we can know and articulate" (59). We can either view it directly or indirectly. In the latter case, Bergquist and Eggen refer to Plato's allegory of the cave. Plato suggests that we live with an image of reality (shadows projected on the walls of the cave) and have no basis for knowing whether we are seeing the shadow or seeing reality, given that we have always lived in the cave (60). "Not only don't we actually see reality, [but] there is something that determines which parts of objective reality get projected onto the wall" (61). In today's world, the media play a crucial role in focusing our attention on certain matters while excluding others, and in interpreting events. The media tend to shape our opinions. If we don't exercise our judgment, not only will we believe there is a simple objective reality out there but we will also confuse reality itself with the filtered view portrayed by the media.

From the constructivist perspective, "We construct our own social realities, based in large part on societal interventions—the traditions and needs of culture and the social-economic context in which we find ourselves." Initially, "these social constructions are based on deeply rooted beliefs and assumptions of specific societies and cultures" (Bergquist and Eggen, 2008, 62). We don't need to take this static view. We can construct new cultural realities that make the most of alternative cultural possibilities. I already advocated this dynamic approach (Rosinski, 2003), which had been missing in traditional static intercultural comparisons (e.g., Americans are like this, and the Japanese are like that). Incidentally, constructivism is not limited to culture; it simply refers to the notion that we generate our worldview through our experiences.

Bergquist and Eggen (2008) classify the constructivist perspectives under the static ("biased and resistant descriptions of reality") and dynamic versions ("reality created in the interplay between two of more people and /or events") (59). Morin uses the words "constructivism" and "co-constructivism" to label a similar distinction.[16]

The complexity increases as we move from objectivism (also called "positivism") to co-constructivism, and Morin contrasts these two extremes.

The positivist view has allowed us to make considerable scientific progress. However, we need the co-constructive approach, which is in line with the holographic model, to embrace our complex reality.

Freedom of choice was absent in classical economic theories, which assumed that humans behaving in a determinist fashion are undifferentiated (supposedly rational) objects. Heilbroner advocated a complex approach to move beyond this shortcoming (see Chapter 2). Co-constructivism also applies in the spiritual domain. According to the Kabbalah, God contracted His absolute presence to deliberately create a vacuum (act of "Zimzoum"). Consequently, only His reflections can be grasped. This incompleteness and imperfection gives room to human freedom of choice.[17]

Positivism (simplicity)	Co-constructivism (complexity)
Objects exist independently from the subject and can be observed and explained as such; subject is either a "noise" that is a perturbation, a deformation, a mistake to be eliminated to reach objective knowing, or a mirror, a simple reflection of an objective universe; the subject is expelled from science and at the same time	Co-constructivism: subject and object are inseparable; the world is inside our mind, which is inside the world; in this complex relationship, both need to remain open in an upward spiral of mutual enrichment
Subject mastering a world of objects	
Determinism	The regression of determinism and certainty opens the possibility of enrichment and freedom of choice

Historical Evolution of Thought (Simplified)

Let me conclude this chapter with a very simplified description of the evolution of human thought. This is adapted from Morin and Frédéric Lenoir (Lenoir, 2003). Our societies are by and large still in modernity, but they are moving toward post- (or ultra-) modernity. In this new phase, we will reconcile rationality with our longing for "re-enchanting the world," and science will become compatible with spirituality. Rationality no longer will be confused with rationalization, a pathology that consists in trapping reality in a coherent system, while dismissing anything that would contradict the coherence (Morin, 2005, 94).

As I have argued throughout this book, this shift is a necessity. It is crucial for our very survival on this planet. Coaches need to understand and embrace this new complexity paradigm. We can then raise awareness and facilitate the transformation. We must become mentally equipped to help people deal with the interconnected world we live in and play our part in fostering this movement of unification.

Pre-Modernity	Modernity	Post/Ultra-Modernity
Simplicity Subject distinct from object	Simplicity Subject distinct from object	Complexity Subject inseparable from object
Myths and gods take on a life of their own Issue: lack of reason (magical thinking)	Theories coherent but closed, partial, unilateral Issues: rationalization (in place of rationality)—what is irrational and complex is overlooked	Rationality and desire for "re-enchanting the world"

NOTES

1. The Complex Regional Pain Syndrome CRPS of type 1 (a neuro-inflammatory condition). See Rosinski, 2007, and the fascinating research findings by Vilayanur Ramachandran, 1998, 2003.
2. As Joseph Goodman states, "Just as it is convenient to describe an audio amplifier in terms of its (temporal) frequency response, so likewise it is often convenient to describe an imaging system in terms of its (spatial) frequency response" (Goodman, 1968, 1).
3. I had the chance to study this with professor Albert Macovski. See Macovski, 1983.
4. Kashmir Shaivism is a Hindu philosophy: "Matter is not separated from consciousness, but rather identical to it. There is no gap between God and the world. The world is not an illusion, rather the perception of duality is the illusion." From Wikipedia, retrieved on 22 July 2009. Based on this resemblance, Grof concludes, "They thus represent an additional proof that the phenomena

induced by LSD and other similar substances are not chemical artifacts, but genuine expressions of the human psyche" (Grof, 2006, 38).

5. See "Vittorio Micheli's Cancer Cured" (*http://avemaria.bravepages.com/articles/mar/alex.html*), retrieved on 3 May 2010, and "Les Miraculés de Lourdes—Vittorio Micheli de Scurelle—Le Chasseur Alpin et le Redoutable Cancer" (*http://fr.lourdes-france.org/approfondir/guerisons-et-miracles/liste-des-miracules*), retrieved on 4 May 2010.

6. "Reify: consider an abstract concept to be real" *www.thefreedictionary.com*. Retrieved on 23 July 2008.

7. I would not go as far as Grof when he suggests we should not focus on a predetermined fixed goal (Grof, 2006, 66), but I do believe we should not be overly attached to these goals, particularly when they lead us astray. Disconnection, which can ultimately take the form of depression, happens if we rigidly persist on the wrong path, notably ignoring our limitations or deepest cravings.

8. The negentropy concept reminds me of Spinoza's "conatus." For Spinoza, someone's conatus is its "striving to persevere in his being" (Ethics III P6) (1677/1996, 75). That is his essence and takes the form of desire (Ethics III P7) (1677/1996, 76). Comte-Sponville views conatus as the power of living or existing (2001, 122). Incidentally, the six perspectives also reveal various interrelated avenues for the conatus: physical (striving for health and fitness) all the way to spiritual (striving for unity and meaning).

9. As Morin explains, this is the case for "a whirlpool, the flame of a candle, but also our bodies, in which our molecules and cells constantly renew themselves while the ensemble remains apparently stable and stationary" (Morin, 2005, 31).

10. Likewise, I find it much easier to improvise a story for my daughter if she provides me with a starting point or characters, rather than simply expecting me to make it all up myself.

11. See notably Halevi, 1979. The notion of superior worlds that impregnate our existence is consistent with the holographic model: these worlds can indeed be considered hidden, implicit, enfolded.

12. Not to be confused with the Prince, one of the four basic political types, high on power but low on service (Chapter 6).

13. See Rosinski, 2003, 30.

14. Contains various elements adapted from Morin, 2005.

15. Earlier in this chapter, I noted that quanta (subatomic particles) don't behave as regular objects. At the macro-level, Einstein explained how time and space are not independent and transcendent realities variables but constitute an interwoven configuration. In his general relativity theory, he showed how the movement of objects can be more accurately explained by the curvature of space-time (i.e., space and time combined) rather than Newton's gravity forces.

16. See Entretien avec Edgar Morin (2): Science et Philosophie 2008.

17. See Halevi, 1979.

CHAPTER 10

Tapping into Our Multiple Heroes Within

Carl Jung (1960), the famous Swiss psychiatrist, described experiences of stunning and highly implausible coincidences: synchronicity. One participant at a recent "Coaching Across Cultures" seminar in Prague brought a pendant as her chosen artifact: a crucifix with a star of David in the middle. This jewel, custom-made for her, represented her dual culture, Christian and Jewish. She had been raised in a mixed family and learned to value both traditions. One day, this jewel was stolen from her home. A few days later she went into a jewelry store (one among many in the big city where she lived): her pendant was there on display! The thief must have sold it, and it ended up there. She bought it, feeling this symbol of dual religions was meant to be hers.

Even though the Coaching Across Cultures seminar brochure did not emphasize the religious cultural aspect, this woman hoped to learn more about her Jewish roots and leverage it with her Christian education. To her surprise, my own artifact was a rabbi puppet I had bought in Prague; I shared an article I had written linking leadership development and Judaism, for which she was grateful.

Carl Jung shares more improbable coincidences. One is the story of Monsieur Deschamps and a certain kind of plum pudding: Deschamps runs into Monsieur de Fontgibu at various stages of his life and in various locations precisely when eating this rare pudding, which de Fontgibu had first given to him when he was a boy. Another is the story of the golden scarab: one of Jung's patients had dreamed about it. Then, an unusual beetle resembling a golden scarab hit Jung's windowpane during the therapy, and served to unlock a process that had reached an impasse. As Stanislav Grof (2006) explains, "The existence of such extraordinary coincidences is difficult to reconcile with the understanding of the universe developed by materialistic science, which describes the world in terms of chains of cause and effects. And the probability that something like this would happen by chance is clearly so infinitesimal that it cannot seriously be considered as an explanation" (4).

Like Carl Jung and Stanislav Grof, I notice that if we open up to the possibility of synchronicity, these events tend to manifest in our lives. Synchronicity may represent one more glimpse into the holographic universe, unfolding (revealing) some of what was previously enfolded (hidden). Jung's "collective unconscious" may be just another way of describing this holographic veiled substrate that unites us. For Grof, the playful interaction between our psyche (e.g., dream of the golden scarab) and what appears to be the world of matter blurs the boundaries between subjective and objective reality. Grof refers to these implausible phenomena as "episodes of holotropic states of consciousness—holotropic meaning 'moving toward wholeness.'"

Grof explains that synchronicities had a profound impact on Jung's thinking and his work, particularly his understanding of archetypes, primordial governing, and organizing principles of the collective unconscious. For Jung, archetypes transcended both the psyche and the material world. They are patterns of meaning that inform both the psyche and matter and provide a bridge between inner and outer.

Building upon Jung's work, Carol Pearson (1991) mapped out the archetypes' territory. She describes a series of universal archetypes, portraying them as the multiple heroes within. All of these heroes are available to us, but we need to awaken them. It is one of our roles, as coaches, to help coachees unfold select archetypes within themselves, particularly the archetype(s) that will help them take the next step on their journey. For example, unfolding the Warrior will help coachees move from conflict avoidance to determined resolution. Similarly, the Creator can enable coachees to learn to trust their imagination and allow them to let their dreams come true.

Coincidentally (or perhaps through synchronicity!), Pearson's archetypes can be linked to the six perspectives in this book. This connection opens new avenues for coaching from multiple perspectives, by highlighting specific archetypes to unfold on the journey to sustainable and global success. We need to awaken these archetypes in our lives and learn how to seamlessly unfold and call upon them, so we can credibly and competently facilitate this process when coaching others.

The next table suggests the possible connections. It also refers to Taibi Kahler's six processes, which I will discuss later in this chapter.

Perspectives	Pearson's Archetypes	Kahler's Processes
Spiritual	Sage–Fool	Dreamer
Cultural	Explorer–Creator	Rebel
Political	Ruler–Magician	Persister
Psychological	Caregiver–Lover	Reactor
Managerial	Regular Guy/Gal–Destroyer	Workaholic
Physical	Innocent–Warrior	Promoter

GENERAL CONSIDERATIONS REGARDING THE ARCHETYPES AND SUGGESTED ACTIVITIES TO UNFOLD THEM

Life as a Journey

By considering life as a journey, coaches call upon the coachees' curiosity to embark on the adventure, their openness to seize unexpected opportunities, their courage to overcome inevitable obstacles along the way, and, perhaps most of all, their ambition to live an authentic life and make their meaningful dreams happen.

Pearson (1991) explains, "Like heroes of old, we aid in restoring life, health, and fecundity to the kingdom as a side benefit of taking our own journeys, finding our own destinies, and giving our unique gifts" (3).

Rather than merely surviving in autopilot mode, swept along by deleterious consumerism and striving for pies in the sky, we can choose to make the best of our lives, and take responsibility for making it happen. Coaches play an essential role by confronting people with their right, power, and responsibility and by facilitating their journey into uncharted territory.

Pearson invites us to "leave behind a shrunken sense of possibilities and choose to live a big life," which does not equate to "measuring up to preexisting standards" (e.g., social status, wealth) but rather to finding what is truly meaningful to us and living accordingly. "The rewards of self-discovery are great. When we find ourselves, everything seems to fall into place. We are able to see our beauty, intelligence, and goodness. We are able to use them

productively, so we are successful. We are less caught up in proving ourselves, so we can relax and love and be loved. We have everything we need
to claim our full humanity, our full heroism" (1991, 4–5).

Archetypes

Archetypes can be understood in various connected ways:

- They are guides on our journeys, each bringing "a task, a lesson and ultimately a gift." They teach us how to live. They all reside in each of us.
  In other words, we have their full potential within ourselves.
- They are holograms,[1] both within and beyond us. Pearson notes, "Carl
  Jung recognized that the archetypal images that recurred in his patients'
  dreams also could be found in the myths, legends, and art of ancient
  peoples, as well as in contemporary literature, religion, and art. We know
  they are archetypal because they leave the same or similar traces over
  time and space" (1991, 6).
- They are the heroes within, enfolded in the collective unconscious (or
  holographic substrate), ready to be unfolded.
- They are metaphors or invisible patterns that determine how we come
  forward and experience the world.

Heroes and Dragons

The more we prevent a particular archetype from manifesting itself in our
life, the more likely it is to trip us as a dragon. Consider the Caregiver. It
will teach you to care for yourself as well as for others. If you don't listen,
you may, for example, assist others to the point of fostering their dependence
(acting as a Rescuer, in TA terminology) and forget to take care of yourself.

Jung describes the life journey as an individuation process. The "Ego"
meets the "Shadow" (or "Soul," in Pearson's words), and the "Self" emerges.
Pearson describes the ego as the "container" for our life. The soul is "the
repository of all the potential of the human species, potential that lies within
each one of us, like seeds germinating and ready to sprout if external conditions are propitious (analogous to enough sun, water, and fertile soil)." The
self "signifies the achievement of a sense of genuine identity. When the self
is born, we know who we are, the disjointed parts of our psyche come together, and we experience wholeness and integrity" (1991, 28–29).

The goal is to express many archetypes without being possessed by any. By awakening our heroic potential, we turn our hidden beast into an elegant prince, as in the classic "Beauty and the Beast." We must embrace the beast to free the prince inside. Conversely, denying and repressing the shadow reinforces its power to sap us.

Not all archetypes have to be equally active in our lives. As coaches, we can help awaken the guides coachees need to address a specific challenge or move to the next stage. Contacting the Destroyer, for example, allows people to let go of anything that no longer supports their purpose.

How to Breed Our Heroes Within

As global coaches, we need to awaken our own archetypes before we can evoke them in others. If your Warrior is buried, how can you prompt others to fight rather than flee? If your Fool is locked up, how will you unfold lightness and humor when your coachee is mired in frustration?

The coach's Creator can inspire options to awaken our archetypes. Here are some tactics you can include in your coaching to evoke an archetype.

- "Shining the light of consciousness upon it" (Pearson, 1991, 19)

  Raising awareness about a particular archetype by naming it and describing its characteristics can go a long way. Your coachee may have overlooked the astuteness of the Fool, confusing gravitas with wisdom.

- Giving permission to unfold the archetype

  Once the coachee understands the merits of an archetype, you may simply need to challenge the coachee to call upon the archetype. For example, the coachee might try evoking the Fool by laughing and not taking himself too seriously. Having experienced the benefits, the coachee will be encouraged to continue.

- Referring to successes in the past and in other contexts

  If the coachee seems unable to awaken her archetype, you might ask if she was able to do so in the past, possibly in a different context. This typically boosts the coachee's confidence that she can call upon that archetype. Now she just needs to do it in a new situation. One of my coachees realized he had no difficulty contacting his Warrior in a sport contest. We then explored what was preventing him from using this competence to challenge poor business performance.

If, on the other hand, the coachee is not at ease with a particular arche-type from which she could benefit, you can propose activities likely to awaken the hero crouched in the cave. For example, an artistic activity will help evoke the Creator.

- Acting out the archetype

  You can model the archetype by playing its part and then inviting the coachee to try it out. This could be part of a role play based on a real chal-lenge the coachee is facing. The coaching session is a practice ground, a laboratory in which you have made it safe[2] to try new behaviors, show vulnerabilities, et cetera. In one seminar, we called upon professional actors to help us in this task. Acting out an unusual archetype may be awkward at first. As always, you should celebrate the attempt itself and then the first successes, as small as they may seem. This will encourage the coachee to go through the motions. Eventually, the archetype will feel like an organic expression of who he is.

- Playing the music

  Different types of music carry specific energies. For example, listening to Alan Parsons's harmonious progressive rock can evoke the Sage, while Katie Melua's crystal voice and melodious songs might awaken our Lover, and Europe's upbeat Final Countdown our Warrior.

  Invite coachees to listen to music that mirrors what they want to unfold: the Warrior before a contest, the Creator in front of a white page. They can also sing along and play a music instrument.

- Watching movies

  Similarly, movies constitute a playful way to train archetypes. Why not simply watch a comedy in order to laugh like a Fool? To boost the War-rior, turn to Sylvester Stallone's characters in *Rambo* and *Rocky*. Mov-ies can also serve as a basis for a group discussion. Participants in one of my leadership development trainings engaged in lively debate after watching *Twelve Angry Men* (Lumet, 1957). Henry Fonda as the hero exemplifies several archetypes at their best, notably the Regular Guy, who understands that everyone matters and that we should avoid giving in to first impressions and condemning someone too quickly.

- Finding and emulating role models

  Heroes often can be found in the coachee's entourage. You can ask your coachee to identify possible role models for a given archetype (or set of archetypes), inviting her to observe and question these persons, and adopt some of their outlooks and behaviors as appropriate.

- Portraying the archetypes

  Images (in a Tarot deck, for example), or costumes and artifacts (such as the Magician's hat, cape, and magic wand) can evoke a particular archetype's mood and energy. You can gather these objects for a seminar or ask your coachee to find them for select archetypes.

Beyond the determined actions the coach can inspire to hasten learning, life itself usually also offers opportunities for underused archetypes to blossom. For example, an insensitive boss may oblige an employee to assert himself to survive. Coaches can help coachees frame these challenges as learning opportunities and encourage them to muster the courage to slay the dragons.

MEETING THE ARCHETYPES

I recommend Carol Pearson's book (*Awakening the Heroes Within*, 1991) for a detailed description of the archetypes: their characteristics, the unique gifts they bring, and their various developmental levels (the shadow side, the call that might prompt awakening, and the three stages of positive development). Here I will provide a simple overview. By connecting the twelve archetypes with the six perspectives, you will discover new avenues for coaching.[3]

Physical Perspective—Stimulating Health and Fitness

Innocent

The Innocent in us believes that we can have paradise on Earth and that our lives do not have to be hard and can, in fact, be wonderful. The Innocent has the optimism to embark on the journey and move resolutely forward. The underdeveloped Innocent may be naïve and unrealistic, and prone to disillusionment and disappointment. However, an Innocent that retains faith and goodness in adversity can return from the journey as a Wise Innocent: trusting and optimistic, yet not naïve or dependent.

The Okinawa Centenarian Study (see Chapter 3) reveals that the Okinawans have extraordinarily long and healthy lives thanks to adequate nutrition, regular physical exercise, social connectedness, and an Innocent appetite for life. Compare this to some Western people half their age and yet already "old" in their minds and hearts: their pessimism (lack of contact with their Innocent within) has led them to renounce hope after a few failures, giving up the chance to claim their vitality and to embark on new ventures. Unlike the Okinawans, they take no personal responsibility for their health; instead, they ask, "What is the point?" They consume unhealthy food, settle for sedentary habits, and precipitate their own decline.

As global coaches, we need our Innocent. The best coaches exude optimism and a genuine belief that coaching can make a significant difference.

Warrior

The negative Warrior can be ruthless, coming across as a stressed-out aggressive bully. The developed Warrior, on the other hand, assertively engages in constructive conflict resolution and negotiations. The Warrior also brings us the courage and perseverance to pursue our journey and overcome obstacles along the way.

However, before psychological considerations, the Warrior needs to be strong and fit. Building physical strength, endurance, and flexibility gives us confidence and stamina. We become less vulnerable to injuries and illnesses (see Chapter 3). Being healthy means not spending time and energy to combat diseases or cope with diminished bodies. Coaches whose training is limited to psychology and traditional coaching models often tend to neglect this crucial physical aspect, at their coachees' expense.

Research suggests that when our calorie intake is low, our level of stress hormones increases, which turns out to be a very good thing: "Consuming fewer calories helps produce the consistently right amount of glucocorticoids—just enough to keep us sharp, but much less than we'd experience in a stressful situation"[4] (Willcox, Willcox, and Suzuki, 2004, 47–48). The effective Warrior needs to be alert, sharp, calm and firm at the same time.

Managerial Perspective—Fostering Productivity and Results

Regular Guy/Gal (also called Orphan)[5]

The regular Guy/Gal, or the Orphan, has experienced painful realities, and the accompanying physical and psychological wounds. The Orphan may have felt abandoned, exploited, victimized. While the negative Orphan might remain in victim mode or, in turn, hurt and manipulate others, the developed Orphan has gained humanity through this hardship. With an accepted sense of vulnerability, he[6] will allow himself to call upon others for help. The developed Orphan has acquired empathy and compassion through hardship and now wants to help others, considering that everyone matters and no one should be left alone. However, rather than promoting limiting dependence, the Orphan at its best tends to foster healthier interdependent relationships.

The Orphan also longs for security and favors realism over reckless actions. This leads to following sound management practices and avoiding unreasonable risk. When the Orphan is enfolded, inhibitions are eliminated, making room for irresponsible behavior. This can lead to disaster. Orphans warning of the dangers ahead were scoffed at in many banks and sidetracked, leading to the worst financial and economic crisis since World War II with collapses such as Fortis in Belgium (see Condijts, Gérard, and Thomas, 2009).

The Orphan knows that we can never take our safety for granted and that we have to work at maintaining it through prudent and rigorous management.

Destroyer

We can easily imagine the destructiveness and *self*-destructiveness the negative Destroyer tends to exhibit. However, the developed Destroyer brings a precious gift: cleaning up our plate so we have the space and the time we need for new ventures. This immediately improves our productivity.

My clients often fall into the trap of adding more actions and projects to a plate that is already full. I will inevitably challenge them: something has to go! What are your priorities? What is less important for you? Where should you focus, and what should you give up?

President Obama has put the Destroyer to use when reaching out to fellow country leaders (notably in South America, Iran, and Russia), attempting to build relationships with a fresh new start, striving to leave the accumulated baggage behind.

Talane Miedaner (2000) offers useful advice on how to use the Destroyer: eliminate all those petty annoyances, plug the energy drains, eliminate the "shoulds," unclutter your life, just say no and say it often, et cetera.

The Destroyer allows us to travel lightly and "weeds the garden in ways that allow for new growth" (Pearson, 2008).

Psychological Perspective—Developing Emotional and Relational Qualities

Caregiver

The shadow Caregiver may be prone to martyrdom or may provide misplaced support (helping individuals indulge in addictions or other irresponsible and damaging behaviors). The developed Caregiver displays altruism, generosity, and caring. At best, the Caregiver acts in the service of the world at large, not just a close circle of people. She empowers others (teaching how to fish) rather than promoting dependency (giving a fish).

The Caregiver's sense of service implies that this archetype is a key component in the Idealist and the Enlightened Builder we referred to in Chapter 6. However, while the Caregiver is enough to make up an Idealist, the Enlightened Builder also requires other archetypes, particularly the Ruler and the Magician.

Coaches need to genuinely care if we are to inspire coachees to care as well. I have seen many coachees transformed when they got in touch with their Caregiver. Rather than treating their employees as dispensable resources, they became concerned with workers' well-being. This new dynamic is more fulfilling *and* more effective.

Lover

Love makes us feel more alive. It helps us experience pleasure, achieve intimacy, make commitments, and follow our bliss. It allows us to bond with someone or with something.

On the shadow side, it becomes jealousy, envy, obsessive fixation on a love object or relationship, sexual violence, sexual addiction or, conversely, puritanism (Pearson, 1991, 156–157).

Love comes in different forms, particularly Eros and Agape. Eros can appear as passion: under its seduction, we sometimes give up on being reasonable and follow a riskier path. The Greek philosophers, guests at Plato's famous Banquet (Plato, 4th century B.C./1986), argued about the meaning of Eros. Socrates won the argument: love refers to something we both desire and lack. It is not completeness but incompleteness, not the happy destination but the uncertain quest.

Love stories are sometimes complicated, but love does not have to be tragic. I believe we can learn to love what we have rather than never (or only fleetingly) feel replete: our Lover would probably need some of our Sage's wisdom here, though. I like the Dutch philosopher Baruch Spinoza's definition: "Love is a joy, accompanied by the idea of an external cause" (Spinoza, 1677/1996, 105). I rejoice indeed, for example, when I think of my daughter. Eros can be parental or romantic; it can also refer to a passion for work, sports, the arts, nature, et cetera.

For the French philosopher André Comte-Sponville (1995), love is the most advanced virtue. He placed it beyond morality. Love is outside personal will. It is a grace. Coaches cannot force themselves to love their clients, but they can turn to their coachees (as we will discuss in the following chapter) with genuine empathy and full presence. In these instances, the miracle of love might happen.

Agape refers to an "inner union that allows us to develop the capacity not just to love our own loved ones, but to love the humanity and the cosmos" (Pearson, 1991, 152). Agape and Eros are complementary rather than mutually exclusive.

Cultivating a loving acceptance of ourselves[7] and a love of life reduces our dependence on others to experience joy. It also makes us more lovable.

Political Perspective—Building Power and Service

Ruler

The Ruler archetype inspires us to reclaim our power and take responsibility. As coaches, one of our essential contributions is to help coachees fully realize they have power, choice, and responsibility. In Chapter 5, I explained how I do this, notably by using transactional analysis. Coachees who tell me, "That is the way I am," or "That is the way it is," conveying a sense of powerlessness, quickly start to appreciate that they are only expressing a limited part of themselves and they are not seizing opportunities to transform situations. By the end of the first session, they begin to see new possibilities. Afterward, by engaging in new behaviors (which does require courage and discipline), they will achieve new successes, which will reinforce their enlarged worldview and will encourage them to claim more of their power.

The Ruler masters the power part of the "Constructive Politics" matrix (see Chapter 6). The shadow Ruler is merely a Prince (high on power but low on service); the developed Ruler, on the other hand, has integrated the Caregiver to become an Enlightened Builder: rather than using power solely for personal advantage, the developed Ruler is genuinely concerned about serving others (family and friends, organizational stakeholders, and the world at large—that is, the various categories in the Global Scorecard (Rosinski, 2003, 212). The Ruler knows how to build a power base and use politics to create a bountiful kingdom for everyone.

We saw earlier that coaching from a political perspective helps people systematically evaluate various possible sources of power and then proactively develop them. The Ruler archetype helps us connect with the mythical king/emperor figure, suggesting we can all be righteous kings promoting the good of society and the planet. We are in touch with our Ruler when we take complete responsibility for our lives. At the finest level, we are whole, having integrated the various archetypes to support our Ruler. The order, peace, creativity, abundance, and love that reign in our minds become outer characteristics of our kingdoms: our families, organizations, et cetera. Conversely, the deficiencies outside may reveal the internal limitations of our Rulers. For example, when not at peace with ourselves, we tend to unconsciously promote sterile conflicts. With a mindset of scarcity, we miss opportunities for collaboration and synergies, achieving lose-lose rather than win-win outcomes. Or, despite our best intentions, we cannot muster the power necessary to lead.

Interviewing managers and employees in an organization (for example, to conduct a cultural audit or to prepare for a team coaching intervention) quickly reveals the climate: trusting or suspicious, enthusiastic or blasé, service-minded or cynical, et cetera. In my experience, this kingdom's climate often mirrors the king's style.

Magician

While the Ruler (e.g., King Arthur) exerts visible leadership and is inseparable from his kingdom, the Magician uses power in a different way, acting as the advisor (e.g., Merlin), shaman, or healer. In organizations, the Ruler unfolds in the executive; the Magician is active in the consultant and probably even more so in the executive coach.

The Magician's gift is to transform reality, turning lead into gold—or, more precisely, uncovering the gold nestled in the lead. Unleashing people's potential is at the core of the Magician's mission.

At best, the Magician is a global coach, able to call upon multiple perspectives and aware of their dynamic interconnectedness. The Magician is physically, emotionally, mentally, and spiritually coupled with the great web of life and cosmos, which he perceives as a holographic universe. Consequently, for example, the Magician knows how to transform a coachee's negative stress into serene energy by recommending physical exercise and adequate nutrition, how to call upon the coachee's Destroyer to eliminate drainers, how to activate the Caregiver and Lover to harness emotional and relational support, et cetera.

Having overcome hardship, the Magician knows that losses can create room for new projects, that illnesses can help us focus on what truly matters, that failure can help prepare us for success, and that experiencing difficulties allows us to develop gratitude for what we used to take for granted.

Magicians ultimately promote joy, which is, according to Spinoza (as you might recall from Chapter 5) "a man's passage from a lesser to a greater perfection" (Spinoza, 1677/1996, 104).

The Magician is at play when we help the coachee become aware that she is repressing an emotion such as anger. When the coachee learns to externalize that buried emotion, it will stop sapping her. She can instead use the anger to assert herself, which feels much better. Anger has, in essence, been transmuted into joy. The same applies to sadness. When the coachee allows herself to grieve, she can turn the page and experience joy once again.

Conversely, the negative Magician, as a sorcerer, turns positive into negative. Even without evil intent, naming and categorization—he is a scientist versus an artist, a Sensor versus an Intuitor (cf. MBTI®), a tough versus a sensitive manager—may inadvertently shrink possibilities, turning gold into lead. I am not suggesting coaches should avoid models that involve some labeling, but we need to open up rather than close off possibilities. (The feedback shows that you often come across as tough; however, I have also noticed your sensitivity when . . . ; How could you manifest more of this caring facet of yours?) At a more conscious level, the negative Magician is the sorcerer disguised as a callous business executive or unscrupulous communication expert, a master of manipulation. The negative Magician entices children to eat junk food, and incites adults into shallow consumerism. The role of the coach here is to help the coachee become aware of the conditioning and reclaim his power by making authentic choices.

Cultural Perspective—Promoting Diversity and Creativity

Explorer (also called Seeker)

The Explorer's archetype embodies other essential attributes of the global coach, particularly curiosity. The Explorer visits unknown territories, studies within and outside her domain of expertise, and welcomes new adventures and meetings. The Explorer has the courage to brave loneliness and isolation when voyaging off the beaten tracks.

If, as a coach, you are estranged from your Explorer, you may be entrenched in one way of practicing. You may also be reluctant to leave your country to participate in international conferences or other events at which other viewpoints will be offered. As effective as your coaching methods may be, this lack of curiosity will inevitably limit your performance.

During a global leadership development seminar in Singapore, we offered a treasure hunt activity that gave participants a chance to experience firsthand the rich cultural diversity of the city and served as a metaphor both for cultivating our Explorer within and for celebrating cultural differences.

Traveling stimulates the Explorer. The travel can be far away or even close to home. You can visit your own surroundings with fresh eyes walking, biking, or kayaking to experience other facets of a region you thought you knew well. You can take the time to meet and get to know people, rather than merely rushing from one tourist site to the next. You can also activate the Explorer through study, venturing outside your own field to new frontiers.

I am surprised that few people seem to do that: as far as I can remember, none of my fellow MS engineering students at Stanford took their elective classes in the humanities. Almost none of the physicians I met made any serious effort to learn outside their area of specialization. (See Rosinski, 2007.) In contrast, the Explorer was very much alive in Leonardo da Vinci, probably the best example of a curious mind and multitalented individual. He was an artist (painter, sculptor, musician, architect, et cetera), a scientist (physician, astronomer, geologist, anatomist, et cetera), an engineer and inventor, and a humanistic philosopher (Broun et al., 2007). The diversity of his investigations and activities fed his creativity by favoring out-of-the-box thinking and cross-fertilization. His example can inspire us all. More and more, the best universities, such as Stanford University, promote interdisciplinary research to address complex, modern-day challenges.

Pearson (1991) explains, "The urge to seek the grail, to climb the mountain in search of visions, to seek wisdom, to cross new frontiers, to achieve the formerly unachievable in all areas of life seems endemic in the human race. The Seeker responds to the call of the Spirit—to ascend" (123). Ultimately, the Seeker may strive to travel internally as well as externally, experiencing the undivided wholeness of all things that is characteristic of our holographic universe.

The Explorer is very much alive in small children, whose joy in discovering the world is still unhampered by judgment about their performance. The coach's role is to help the archetype unfold again.

Creator

The Creator archetype "fosters all imaginative endeavors, from the highest art to the smallest innovation in lifestyle or work" (Pearson, 2008).

Creating starts by listening with receptive imagination. Remember that intuition comes from the Latin word *intueri*, which means "observing carefully." Beautiful and authentic creations involve some form of resonance. The artist is in tune with his deeper self and with the world at large. Creativity seems to happen when we tap into this holographic reality.

Tapping into our Creator also involves giving ourselves the permission to create. This can mean finding new ways to solve problems, infusing novelty at work, or, on a larger scale, creating our lives. While the Seeker allows us to discover new possibilities and tap into diversity, the active Creator leverages variety and pushes aside our conditioning, which has led us to live in autopilot mode with a limited sense of possibilities. As coaches, we can make those permissions explicit, substituting constraining messages for these new, liberating ones: "I don't have to go to work that early every day and can do some physical exercise instead"; "I can make the room for acting, sculpting, or whatever activity I have wanted to do for a long time"; "I can strive for effectiveness rather than perfection." Ultimately, we all can move toward creating a life we can truly call our own, making our dreams come true. This may involve minor adjustments or radical changes. "The Creator pushes us out of inauthentic roles to claim our identities. When this archetype is active, people are as consumed with the need to create a life as artists are with the need to paint, or poets with the need to write" (Pearson, 1991, 171). The calling is so great that people are willing to sacrifice money and status. A high price does not systematically need to be paid though. Authenticity can make life and work ring truer and bring more satisfaction than any commercial ersatz.

Of course, believing that we can create our own life reveals a Control cultural bias. Clearly, some circumstances are beyond our control. We can create, but we are created as well (biologically as well as socially). The goal, therefore, is to make the most of the opportunities we do have to craft our lives.

Awaking Creators who are entrepreneurs is critical for our economies (see Chapter 2). One of my coachees told me he has recently opened up to visions, hunches, and interests of various kinds, ranging from military strategy to psychology. He has started to write speeches to celebrate select people, learning about his own values in the process. This flurry of activity seems to go hand in hand with uncovering his sense of entrepreneurship.

Intercultural coaching's main aim is to help people uncover new possibilities beyond their current cultural limitations, and to unleash more human potential by tapping into the richness that lies in cultural diversity. *Coaching Across Cultures* (2003) is therefore a good resource for those willing to discover practical ways to unfold their Creator archetype.

Spiritual Perspective—Enabling Meaning and Unity

Sage

The Sage is the philosopher in us. The etymology reveals its essence: *philos* (love) and *sophia* (wisdom). As Comte-Sponville (2000) argues, the philosopher strives for happiness (much like everyone) but yearns for truth even more. The philosopher prefers a true sadness over a false joy (17).

Initially, the Sage might be searching for "the Truth" in an objective and absolute sense. Gradually, she will move away from simplicity and start to embrace complexity. She will become aware of the multiplicity and relativity of truth. The Sage in us will learn to move beyond dogma and appreciate various perspectives. She cultivates both a commitment to pursuing truth and a sense of detachment. Our relative and limited knowledge implies letting go of certainties and keeping an open attitude. The Sage ultimately strives for unity in diversity. All spiritual paths teach the love that connects us to one another.

The philosopher is completed by the spiritualist in the Sage archetype. Pearson explains that we need both our minds and our hearts to glimpse the "oneness" in the cosmos (characteristic, once again, of the holographic conception of the universe): we must develop both mind and heart to their highest levels, so we can let go and allow truth to come into our lives as gifts.

At this level, the coach's role is way beyond that of facilitating traditional goal setting and articulating of specific objectives. Measuring return on investment from the Sage viewpoint will prove elusive. The developed Sage stops fighting life and trusts its process, opening up to what emerges.

To coach as a Sage, you need to be at ease with complexity and multiple perspectives and quick to spot limiting beliefs and seize opportunities to enlarge the coachee's worldview. This involves challenging respectfully through provoking questioning, counter-examples, or metaphors. You need to be able to let yourself go, trusting what emerges, and thereby encouraging the coachee to do the same. I once coached an executive who was in an outplacement situation. After we candidly explored his desires and unique gifts, and systematically examined opportunities in the market, the executive ended up securing a better job in the company he was supposed to leave. However, he first detached himself emotionally from this organization where he had spent 20 years of his career. Had he merely tried to stay, short-circuiting the deeper exploration, he probably never would have found a renewed sense of meaning and connection with his organization.

There is a negative Sage as well: cut off rather than detached, addicted to being right and perfect, overwhelmed by relativity and unable to act, disconnected from her body (ascetic) and brain (an anti-intellectual guru who denies her own subjectivity), et cetera. This shadow version promotes disarray and alienation rather than unity.

Fool (also called Jester)

The Court Fool has a salutary role: teasing, deriding, and entertaining. By injecting humor and expressing the joy of life, the Fool takes the heat out of tense debates and helps those in power connect with their humanity by not taking themselves too earnestly.

The Sage could not really be wise without the Fool: indeed, how can we take seriously someone who is too serious? A sense of lightness and warmth, and a childlike propensity to laugh and joke, convey ease, serenity, and fulfillment. Think of the giggling Dalai Lama.

Effective coaching implies connecting with one's Fool. We smile and communicate our amusement at the human comedy. There is frequent laughter during my coaching sessions. For example, I enjoy role playing with my coachees. They have fun when I play the part of their manipulative boss or reluctant employee. Rather than staying mired in their frustration over those behaviors, they begin to accept these human traits (actually so common). The lightness makes it easier to explore more productive ways to deal with these challenging relationships and practice communicating from an OK–OK mindset.

Not only are we doing serious work, but it also feels almost effortless. The coachee leaves a three-hour coaching session in an optimistic mood, ready to tackle the challenges ahead.

In the early 1990s, I went through group psychotherapy with Janine Somers in Belgium. Most therapists I have come across unfortunately have their Fool in check; they seem to believe gravitas is required for serious work. Janine, however, frequently smiled, gently teased, and laughed. She was one of the most effective psychotherapists around. The group's energy was amazing, and people were in touch with a wide range of emotions. Similarly, Michel Chalude, with whom I learned transactional analysis (this time as a trainer), had an enjoyably deadpan sense of humor. He created a relaxed atmosphere that was conducive to learning.

Of course, the Fool (like other archetypes) should not be overused. Laughter should not prevent coachees from accessing the other important, albeit less pleasant emotions (anger, sadness, and fear), which they may have repressed; these may serve as valuable guides.

The School of Palo Alto[8] has developed a tactic some coaches (including me) typically use. A coachee might complain about an unproductive behavior associated with an unpleasant situation (e.g., micro management associated with work overload), express her inability to deal with the issue, and appear to expect some challenge. The coach might instead play "stupid": "Why would you want to change this behavior?" "You would no longer have the chance to resolve these interesting technical problems," et cetera. More often than not, the coachee herself will end up advocating for the change. To be successful, the coach needs dry humor here rather than overt laughter. Incidentally, the Palo Alto School's approach is interdisciplinary and complex (Kourilsky, 2004), very much in alignment with global coaching.

Another way to unleash the Fool inside is to focus on the comical aspect in situations and give ourselves permission to be silly. For example, I like to make faces in front of a mirror. Whatever makes you happy, don't hesitate to try it out! It is good practice for your coaching. You just need to select the appropriate context.

Pearson (1991) explains that when the Fool is alive in our lives, "we are enlivened and invigorated," even if "we may get ourselves into trouble." When there is too little of the Fool, "we may become priggish, repressed, uptight, anorexic, tired, bored, depressed, or lacking in curiosity" (222). The Fool has a zest for life, one that often erupts in the most painful moments: we may be at a funeral watching stern faces and suddenly experience a misplaced surge of hilarity. I recall when my friends and I failed to repress a belly laugh as we listened to a modern and bizarre-sounding violin piece. Fortunately, the composer was not offended: after all, his music had touched us in a joyful fashion!

When the Fool is repressed, it goes underground and incites us to unconsciously play negative games. Eric Berne (1964) revealed this dynamic. (See Chapter 5.) Pearson declares, "Better to fatten the beast a bit with good food, good company, and pleasant experiences so that it will be good-natured" (1991, 227).

The Fool, at its best, allows us to live in the moment, and for its own sake. The meaning of life resides in this celebration. The earthy enjoyment and chuckles bring us closer to others, promoting unity—whether between couples or between professional teams. These moments represent turning points.

The Fool brings us back to the beginning of the journey, albeit at a new level. We laugh, not as yet-unharmed Innocents, but as adults who have acquired the resilience to face hardship with a smile.

PROCESS COMMUNICATION

Taibi Kahler developed his process communication model from transactional analysis to help us engage in effective interactions. His typology gives insights into our various personality characteristics, psychological needs, preferred modes of management, and ways of handling stress. It is an invitation to observe how we speak and come across to others.

The holographic premise in the model makes it coherent, relevant, and practical for global coaches. For example, the way we speak and construct our sentences tends to mirror wider dynamics in our lives. The coach needs to listen to the process rather than merely focus on the content. If your coachee utters a long sentence filled with details, he may be (unconsciously) saying, "I like to build long sentences with a concern for accuracy, thereby showing I am logical, thorough, and competent." If on top of this, the coachee is neatly dressed and his office is orderly, you are likely facing someone with a strong "Workaholic process." After just a few moments, you can make predictions: the person is likely under the influence of the "be perfect" constraining message.[9] He is likely going into the OK–not OK mode under stress (attacking and over-controlling). This coachee is apt to respond well to genuine praise for his dedicated work, achievement of business objectives, and technical competence. Failure to recognize his good work will trigger the unconscious negative mechanism: the coachee will show his commitment more visibly to obtain a "stroke." By over-controlling, he will try to make you understand and acknowledge that he is serious about getting everything right.

In a few seconds, the coachee reveals one of his dynamics. The micro-level echoes the macro-level in a holographic fashion. The whole (life scenario) is indeed in the part (seconds of behavior). And the part, repeated over and over, further reinforces the whole. In this example, it should come as no surprise that this individual strives to be the best, wants to be number one, et cetera.

Taibi Kahler's theory is elegant but needs to be used with caution. As always, these predictions should serve as hypotheses and not be framed as certainties. As a coach, you may alienate others if you claim: "I have already figured you out. These are your needs, failure patterns . . . ." Prudence is required: "Did you notice how you said these words?" If the coachee is clueless, you can describe your observation and ask, "What do you make of this process?" If the coachee is still unclear, you can start to offer a hypothesis linking your remarks with other observations and feedback you have received. The more often we observe a micro-pattern, the higher the probability that it reveals an essential macro-dynamic. The coachee, actively participating in the exchange, will gradually become more aware. This does not dispense you from ensuring that you meet the coachee's needs when you communicate, but it allows the coachee to recognize warning signals: when he is not receiving the positive strokes he needs, he can either solicit them or learn to give these to himself (cultivating a self-appreciation).

The second danger is to use the tool mechanically. This will keep you from establishing the genuine type of relationship we will discuss in Chapter 11.

With practice, you will start to keep the model at the back of your mind alongside many other perspectives, which you will know how to integrate seamlessly.

Interestingly, Taibi Kahler describes six processes, which we can connect to our six fundamental perspectives.[10] Linking the two models provides us with new cross-fertilization opportunities. By treating these processes as muscles we can develop, we broaden our repertoire and enhance our ability to connect with people. We all have preferences, but all the processes are available to us, even if some may be enfolded.

In the following section, I will point out elements of each process to highlight ways in which process communication can be integrated into the global coach's toolkit, and what we should unfold to help us coach from multiple perspectives.

The Six Processes

The next table summarizes key characteristics of the various processes. I refer you to Taibi Kahler's (1988, 1982) work, from which this table is adapted, for more exhaustive information.

When I speak about, say, a Reactor (or any other process), I am referring to a person who currently displays that process. Kahler believes we all have a base process. This base process is complemented by the other processes, which appear as phases. Based on my experience, I am not convinced of that aspect of his theory. I prefer to refer to the processes at play, considering

Process	Promoter	Workaholic	Reactor	Persister	Rebel	Dreamer
Character Strengths	Persuasive, adaptable, charming	Responsible, logical, organized	Compassionate, sensitive, warm	Dedicated, observant, conscientious	Spontaneous, creative, playful	Imaginative, reflective, calm
Strongest ability	Make things happen	Take in facts and synthesize them	Nurture others and be a harmonizer	Persevere and hold fast to values and beliefs	Have fun, enjoy the present	Stay at a routine task
Favorite management style	Autocratic	Democratic	Benevolent	Democratic	Laissez faire	Autocratic (use with)
Perception	Action	Thoughts	Emotions	Opinions	Reactions	Inactions
Psychological needs	Incidence	Recognition for work and time structure	Recognition as a person and sensory appreciation	Recognition for work and convictions	Contact	Solitude
Driver	Be strong (for me)	Be perfect	Please others	Be perfect (for me)	Try hard	Be strong

(continued on next page)

Process	Promoter	Workaholic	Reactor	Persister	Rebel	Dreamer
Assertive Communication (green)	I am OK–you are OK Constructive	I am OK–you are OK Constructive	I am OK–you are OK Constructive	I am OK–you are OK Constructive	I am OK–you are OK Constructive	I am OK–you are OK Constructive
Miscommunication level 1 (orange)	I am OK–you are OK if you are strong. "You figure it out yourself."	I would be OK if I were more perfect–you are OK. "I should be perfect."	I would be OK if I were pleasing you–you are OK. Over-adapts and pleases in hopes of being accepted.	I am OK–you are OK if you are perfect. Demands that others be perfect.	I am OK if I try hard–you are OK. Tries to understand or do something. Invites others to think or act for him.	I would be OK if I were strong–you are OK. "I need to be strong to protect myself."
Miscommunication level 2 (red)	OK–not OK Blaming, manipulating	OK–not OK Over-controlling	Not OK–OK Making mistakes	OK–not OK Crusading	OK–not OK Blaming, groaning	Not OK–OK Passively waiting
Miscommunication level 3 (black)	Not OK–not OK Desperate	Not OK–not OK Desperate	Not OK–not OK Desperate	Not OK–not OK Desperate	Not OK–not OK Desperate	Not OK–not OK Desperate

that we all have our preferences: for example, some people may display their Reactor most often, their Rebel and Workaholic sometimes, and their Promoter, Persister, and Dreamer infrequently. Different blends usually emerge over time.

Some of the connections with the six perspectives should be readily apparent. The **Reactor**'s sensitivity, and ability to nurture others, means that the Caregiver is well awake. The benevolence facilitates relationship building. At the same time, the model offers new information. The Reactor's driver is a desire to please others, with the unconscious hope that she will be recognized and appreciated as a person (for what she is rather than what she does).

If a Reactor starts to speak to her manager in a low voice, with an awkward smile, chances are the Reactor is unconsciously saying: "I don't feel sufficiently recognized; I am starting to experience negative stress; I am leaving the OK–OK green zone to enter the orange zone." This is the manager's chance to express genuine appreciation, letting the Reactor know she is OK. The employee is then likely to go back to the green area. If the manager fails to grasp this signal and to understand the underlying psychological need, the Reactor will enter the red zone. She may spill her drink on the floor or make another mistake, behaving like a Victim. If the manager enters the dramatic triangle as a Persecutor or Rescuer, the Reactor will have gotten the recognition she wanted, albeit in a negative rather than a positive way. The model also suggests that a benevolent management style works best. An impersonal, autocratic style generates negative stress, resulting in low morale as well as low productivity.

How do you, as a coach, know if you are dealing with a Reactor? Compassionate, sensitive, and warm behavior (green zone) is the first clue. Then there is the Reactor's orange over-adaptation. These are all cues to pay attention to.

You need to develop all these muscles to easily communicate with your coachee on her preferred channel. Otherwise, miscommunication is likely.

You may well feel confused by now: the situational leadership model suggests, for example, a directive approach in this situation (see Chapter 4), but since you are dealing with a Reactor, the advice is to be benevolent, which is somewhat contradictory. What should you do?

As I discussed in Chapter 9, coaches need to give up the paradigm of simplicity and start embracing complexity. The art of coaching is to seamlessly integrate various approaches. In this example, you may decide clear directions take precedence, because the employee is clearly inexperienced.

But you can be benevolent in the process, by conveying warmth and appreciation for this person as a human being.

The same philosophy applies to the other processes. You may spot the **Rebel** before she utters a word. Her clothing may be particularly colorful. The Rebel wants you to notice her; she wants to provoke a reaction. She is at her best if you play with her, joking and teasing. In many ways, the Rebel could also qualify as a Fool archetype, but creativity is a larger part of her character. The Rebel is quick to offer original ideas, bring new perspectives, and challenge your theory. Don't take it personally if she attempts to break your mental construction. Don't be offended by her anticonventional outlook and habits. If you don't meet her playful need for contact, she is likely to enter the orange zone. You might notice a frown or a head-scratching gesture: she is trying to understand! If you patronize her rather than joke, she is likely to enter the red zone to get her needs met, albeit in a negative way.

You may wish to record your experiences in a learning journal. With whom are you at ease, and with whom do you struggle? You may well tend to struggle with one or two processes. For example, if you are not in touch with your own Rebel, you will be ill equipped to deal with them. If they have not developed other channels of communications to meet you in your comfort zone, miscommunication will happen. Unfortunately, you are likely to experience only the negative Rebels and build up an animosity against them. You will miss the creativity Rebels offer and the opportunity they give you to awaken your own spontaneity and playfulness.

The **Persister** often ventures into power positions where he can advocate for his opinions and fight for his convictions. Like many successful politicians, he will persevere and hold fast to his values and beliefs. If his work and convictions are not recognized, he is likely to enter the orange zone. His face will take on a sterner expression. He will stare others down with piercing eyes. If others are unaware of the underlying dynamic, they may react as Victims, either submissively (e.g., "Where have I screwed up? I feel terrible!"), or rebelliously (e.g., "You pompous idiot! Do you want my photograph?"). This will put them right into the dramatic triangle.[11] The process communication model offers more constructive possibilities. Besides attending to the task itself (in case others really did not deliver what they should have), they can simply acknowledge the Persister's opinions: "I value your opinion." If they share his convictions and ideals, they should simply express how important these are to them as well. If they disagree, they can still emphasize the legitimacy of his beliefs. By meeting his need, they will diffuse positive energy that will remove his slight negative stress, putting him back in the green OK–OK territory.

Failing to do so is likely to exacerbate the tension. In the red zone, the Persister will start crusading, using aggressive, intimidating, and bullying behaviors to make sure his opinions are heard at last. For example, he may say, very angrily, "I find it unacceptable for anyone to deliver a report of such mediocre quality!"

The **Workaholic** is responsible and organized, much like the realistic Regular Guy and the Destroyer who weeds the garden. His task focus fosters productivity and results. His logical mindset makes him a good, albeit impersonal, problem solver.

If others don't appreciate his good work or fail to respect his organized time structure, he will work harder to "be perfect." But if others miss the orange signal, the Workaholic will show his attacking face. He may shout, for example, "This report is botched!" (Notice the subtle difference between the Workaholic and the Persister: the Persister frames this as judgment, whereas the Workaholic is more factual.[12])

This outburst should make everyone understand that he is serious about producing good work! (By the way, I don't recommend making Rebel-like jokes when the Workaholic reaches this stage.)

The **Promoter**'s action orientation connects with the physical perspective. He needs excitement and favors deeds over intellectual analysis. His forte is making things happen rather than beating about the bush. He will display a charming and persuasive face to get his way.

He will thrive if a manager explains the bottom line and then lets him do his thing, meanwhile providing some healthy competition and sizeable financial rewards. If instead, a manager appears wishy-washy, the Promoter will interpret this as weakness, which he resents. His need for action unmet, he will enter the orange zone: "You figure it out, and then you tell me what you want!" If the manager still doesn't get it, the Promoter will start blaming and manipulating. He might say, with a cheeky tone, "I would have done this report in a couple of days, pal!"

I remember coaching a team of sales and marketing executives. Not surprisingly, with Promoters well represented, the team leader organized an evening of kart racing. We went through several qualifying rounds, followed by two semi-finals and a final. This was a lot of fun. I totally unleashed my Warrior, going full speed as much as possible. I ended up winning the contest and earning additional respect from my coachees. I could communicate on their channel! Had I not genuinely shared the thrill with them, something would have been missing. This is not to suggest that we should follow our clients into any activity. It is a matter of finding ventures where you can meet. It is also about sharing the Innocent's optimism: we can do this!

The **Dreamer**'s calm attitude facilitates the Sage's meditative and detached stance. Hence the connection with the spiritual perspective, in a tranquil and unruffled fashion that contrasts with the Fool's exuberance and liveliness.

The Dreamer's stillness allows her to stay imperturbably at tasks that others would not have the patience to handle. This could be a routine job in the factory or a yogi's meditation. Her imagination helps her maintain quietness. The Dreamer enjoys solitude and might thrive contemplating natural scenery.

Those who manage Dreamers need to tell them exactly what is expected and leave them alone to do it. Dreamers also need a private space and time off.

When these needs are not met, the Dreamer feels she needs to be stronger to protect herself against people and things around her. If her calmness is jeopardized by various solicitations or by confusing instructions, she will enter the red zone: passively waiting, mentally checking out. You might recall the dynamic of the negative Sage: the healthy non-attachment turns into a harmful cutting-off from reality. This behavior is unconsciously designed to obtain the necessary reflective space. Busy managers might not notice the Dreamer's inaction for a while and leave her alone. Eventually, though, this passivity is likely to backfire.

As is true for all the other processes, if needs are still unmet in the red zone (at least to comfort the OK–not OK or not OK–OK position), negative stress accumulates, leading to a level 3 of miscommunication: the whiny Dreamer and Reactor, the blaming Reactor and Promoter, and the attacking Persister and Workaholic all move into a not OK–not OK desperate mode (black). Fortunately, however, when needs are met positively, all processes share the healthy and constructive OK–OK (green).

Longing for Wholeness

All too often, trainers and coaches inadvertently promote exclusion and limitation when they label people: for example, I am a Rebel or you are a Persister (or any fancier version: you are a base Persister with a Workaholic phase).

While such labels may serve a valid role in raising your awareness, they also foster a reduced sense of identity and may even become the pretext for stagnation: since you are a Persister, you cannot possibly handle this creative task cut out for a Rebel!

The holographic model makes it clear that we have all these processes available to us. Some may be unfolded while others are enfolded. It should not come as a surprise that you may feel like a Persister on some occasions and like a Rebel on others.

In fact, while we may prefer some processes over others, we may also discover that we are longing for wholeness. When I took the test in the early 1990s, I got the Rebel sticker, which suited me fine. I still would not disown this process, but I also enjoy solitude when biking for hours in the forest, and more generally I have developed an appreciation for the unique gifts each process offers me.

This genuine appreciation for all processes, and the realization that all of them are inside us, not only makes our lives richer but also increases our ability to connect with our diverse coachees. These processes are not merely methods we learn, techniques that can sometimes feel alien to us. They become integral and claimed parts of us.

Often, life itself will provide us with unasked-for opportunities to develop our sleeping processes. If, as a Workaholic, you fancy an orderly environment, you might face unexpected circumstances and turbulences that shatter your neat and reassuring context. This is your chance to let the Promoter or the Rebel within come to the rescue. You can either accept their call, and advance on your journey toward wholeness, or refuse it and maintain a limited and limiting sense of identity.

In the next chapter, I will discuss Martin Buber's conceptualization. Models are necessary, but we need to evacuate them at times to foster genuine relationships that render us fully human.

NOTES

1. I just discovered that Pearson had already compared archetypes to holograms.
2. Notably through rules of strict confidentiality and with a benevolent, nonjudgmental attitude.
3. The particular connection I propose is not meant to exclude other possible connections. For example, one could connect the Fool's playfulness with Kahler's Rebel process and the creativity associated with the cultural perspective.

4. This diet also reduces the risk of stress-associated injury to the brain and other tissues, and protects against age-related brain disease.
5. Pearson, "Archetypes 101," 2008.
6. I refer to the archetype either as an entity (it) or as a person currently manifesting that archetype (he or she).
7. Lex Hixon talks from a progression from waiting for the Messiah to come to recognizing that the Messiah has come and is within oneself (Hixon, 1996). The Hasidic tradition is in line with the holographic model.
8. The School was known for its habit of playing with paradoxes to promote change. The humor was part of Paul Watzlawick's approach and is readily apparent in one his book's title: *The Situation Is Hopeless, but not Serious: the Pursuit of Unhappiness* (Watzlawick, 1984).
9. See Chapter 5 and Rosinski, 2003, 151.
10. I would like to acknowledge Michel Chalude, who was one of the first specialists to bring process communication to Europe. Michel suggested this connection during a lunch we had on 23 June 2008. I am building here further on the correspondence.
11. See Chapter 5 and also Appendix 1 in *Coaching Across Cultures* about transactional analysis.
12. The Workaholic typically speaks with his Adult while the Persister speaks with his Normative Parent. In the orange zone, the Workaholic is speaking from the negative Normative Parent albeit still with more factual-Adult undertones. See Appendix 1 in *Coaching Across Cultures* about transactional analysis for more information about the "ego states."

CHAPTER 11

Unity through Deep Bonding

Beyond technical mastery, the proficient juggling with models and linking of concepts, what probably matters the most in communication (and coaching in particular) is the profound desire to truly relate, to sincerely connect with others. This means genuine listening, relinquishing stereotypes and anticipations of the other, and allowing oneself to be shaped by the other's response. Despite their usefulness, models can paradoxically also prevent authentic communication!

In this chapter, I will explore Martin Buber's articulation of this crucial notion. Buber contrasts two types of interactions (or stances): "I-It" relations and "I-Thou" relationships (Buber, 1958; Kramer, 2003).

"I-It" is a functional relationship between subject and object. It involves models such as the COF to describe reality. Kramer explains: "The world of *It* is a world of things, processes, characteristics, and objects that are continuously divisible" (29)

On the other hand, *Thou* points to the quality of genuine relationships in which partners are mutually unique and whole. *I-Thou* is a "dialogue" in which a person is turning toward another with one's whole being.

Buber stressed the ambiguity of the human situation: "Without *It* a person cannot live. But one who lives with *It* alone is not a person"[1] (Buber, 32). This concerns us: without *It* we cannot coach. But with *It* alone we cannot be global coaches.

These notions may still sound somewhat mysterious but you will discover how the powerful "OK–OK" psychological attitude can be enriched from other perspectives, and ultimately deepened with Buber's notion at the spiritual level. His approach is remarkably consistent with the holographic model. Buber indicates how to overcome fragmentation and instead build unity through deep bonding. But first, let me suggest connections between adult development theory and global coaching. Not surprisingly, effective global coaching goes hand in hand with the most advanced stages of human development. This link provides us with more cross-fertilization opportunities. I will refer here to Robert Kegan's "fifth order of consciousness" and subject–object relationships, and to Jennifer Garvey Berger's adaptation of Kegan's developmental stages, particularly reaching the "Elder" stage.

ADULT DEVELOPMENT

Berger explains how coaches can benefit from Kegan's theory of adult development. This constructive-development theory is "concerned with the way each person creates her world by living it" and "the way that construction changes over time to become more complex and multifaceted" (Berger, 2006, 78).

The model sheds light on the developmental characteristics one needs to acquire to effectively engage in global coaching. Indeed, it is about gaining perspective and increasing our ability to deal with a complex and multidimensional reality.

Berger argues, "Even coaches with sophisticated understandings about their clients' differences are unlikely to fully understand the qualitatively different developmental forms of understanding adults have and the profoundly different worlds they construct as a result. An understanding of these differences allows us to be more careful listeners, to make connections we would not otherwise have made, and to suggest interventions that can lead to clients' heightened success and development" (79). She notes that "the rhythm of this movement is about increasing our ability to see more complexity in the world" (80).

Practically, we need to keep in mind that people are often looking at reality from other stages of development than ours. The coach herself must be at a higher than or at least the same developmental stage as her coachee, in order to coach in a way that is developmental for the coachee. Interestingly, Berger argues that few people ever attain the Elder stage (the fourth and last stage in her model). Yet it is at that stage that people can best reap the benefits of global coaching: "The Elder sees and understands the perspectives of others and uses those perspectives to continuously transform his own system, becoming more expansive and more inclusive. He does not use the perspectives of others to fine-tune his own argument or principles like the CEO [i.e., previous stage] does; rather, he puts the entire system at risk for change with each interaction with others" (81).

The developmental path for CEOs is to "increase their *curiosity* about other systems of understanding." This may help them "challenge their own system—not with the hope of *refining* the system, but with the hope of *transcending* it." It also involves moving "from the certainty of a CEO to the openness of the Elder," and developing "paradoxical thinking" and the Elder's "ability to see connections everywhere. She is able to look at an issue from multiple sides and see the ways the different perspectives overlap." "Elders are tuned in to all the various constituencies around them." The Balanced Scorecard needs to become a Global Scorecard (Rosinski, 2003). "Elders see multiple layers of every issue and can understand multiple perspectives" (89–90).

People with the Elder outlook are best equipped to tackle the complex global challenges we face today. As Albert Einstein noted, "The significant problems we face cannot be solved at the same level of thinking we were at when we created them" (91).

To facilitate coachees' development journey, I often start by addressing their challenges. For example, if coachees wish to increase their confidence and assertiveness, they probably don't require the Elder's outlook to be successful. On the other hand, many challenges (and increasingly so) are multifaceted: when we help coachees gradually embrace different perspectives to address these challenges, we facilitate the emergence of an Elder's viewpoint. Coaches can also point out connections between perspectives—for example, how coachees' physical fitness relates to their intellectual performance, and how their sense of meaning and purpose impacts their business performance—so they will experience themselves how the combined perspectives enable them to address specific challenges.

Robert Kegan shares troubling statistics: "among a composite sample of people from a wide range of socioeconomic backgrounds in the U.S., 79 percent have *not* reached the fourth order . . . and only a tiny percentage of people in the studies are *beyond* the fourth order." (Debold, 2008) Should we give up hope of reaching out to the majority? Is global coaching reserved for a small elite? Fortunately, Kegan says that adults typically go through a number of developmental transformations, and each transformation builds a more complex and elaborated edifice. In my experience, global coaching greatly facilitates this process. We don't want to let the lousy statistics alter our belief that people are capable of incorporating complexity and multiple perspectives. This fundamental coaching belief in the vast human potential can be self-fulfilling. But we need coachees to be open, curious, brave, and disciplined enough to engage in the process and stick with it. Juggling multiple perspectives and paradoxes takes practice. It is undoubtedly easier for some than others, but reaching the "Elder" stage should not be reserved only for a few lucky souls!

Subject–Object Relationships

Kegan describes the developmental journey, referring to the evolving nature of the *subject–object relationship* (Debold, 2008).

For Kegan, "object" refers to "those aspects of our experience that are apparent to us and can be looked at, related to, reflected upon, engaged, controlled, and connected to something else. We can be *objective* about these things, in that we don't see them as 'me.' But other aspects of our experience we are so identified with, embedded in, fused with, that we just experience them as ourselves. This is what we experience *subjectively*—the 'subject' half of the subject–object relationship." Keep in mind that for Buber, the subject–object relationship is called *I-It*, and this still leaves out the rich *I-Thou* realm.

Kegan explains that babies, in their first minutes of life, are entirely subject with no object. At the highest stage of development, exemplified by the Buddha, the "adualism" also prevails: "the self has become entirely identified with the world." Kegan points out that there is no subject at all then: "You are not looking out on the world from any vantage point apart from it."[2] I could equally argue that there is only subject and no object then. Or, more accurately perhaps, that subject and object have become inseparable. This is relational realm of the *I-Thou*. However, rather than suggesting an entire identification with the world, *I-Thou* indicates a "togetherness of close bonding," a "mutual reciprocity" (Kramer, 2003). Likewise, in Morin's complexity, "the one does not dissolve in the multiple." (See Chapter 9.) Note that the holographic model supports this "oneness of the universe" notion that Kegan depicts, and that achieving "unity" is once again viewed as the ultimate goal. Note also that Buber distanced himself from a "mysticism of absorption" ("in forms of Hindu mysticism for instance, the 'I' is seen to collapse and become one with God"). Kramer explains that for Buber, "the subject-other positions essential to genuine dialogue are annihilated in the fusion." Instead, Buber's notion of a "living bond among all separated beings" comes closer to the holographic model. For me, too, "oneness of the universe" means unity in diversity rather than bland uniformity. Otherness is indispensable for real meeting. Put in TA language, autonomy rather than symbiosis enables constructive communication.

Importantly for coaches, Kegan makes the crucial point that all the ways in which we make sense of our experience and make meaning are, each in their own way, partial. "So, [in the fifth order of consciousness] you start to build a way of constructing the world that is much more friendly to contradiction, to oppositeness, to being able to hold on to multiple systems of thinking." Kegan distinguishes negative postmodernism "that is all about trashing any ideological form, which is only deconstructive" from a more reconstructive postmodernism in which you are "building relationships among them rather than holding on to one." He says, "It is a much more positive spirit." This is precisely what we are attempting to accomplish with global coaching.

OK–OK REVISITED

As we saw in Chapter 5, the "I am OK–You are OK" injunction leads to constructive relationships fueled with a communicative sense of worthiness, respect, and trust. "OK–OK" is not limited to the **psychological** perspective but can be prolonged at other relational realms, which include politics, culture, and spirituality.

Before discussing these links, let me note that the **physical** perspective is concerned with the individual's health and fitness rather than relationships per se. The physical layer is really the foundation. One could argue that this is not a condition for establishing genuine relationships. Diseases can be painful yet potent antidotes to obstacles such as arrogance. Illness reminds us of our human limitations. Sharing suffering, which is part of the human condition, can bring people closer together. However, if, like Frankl, we want to avoid unnecessary pain, we should strive to be healthy and fit. As I discussed in Chapter 3, there is a lot we can do here. Being in shape facilitates our capacity to build joyful and fruitful relationships with others.

At the **managerial** level, a form of depersonalized relationship does exist. Much like in traditional economics theory (see Chapter 2), it can be useful to think of people as agents acting "rationally" (taking the best economical decisions such as maximizing their profit and minimizing the losses) without much—if any—consideration for psychological, political, cultural, and spiritual factors. This simplified outlook is enough, for example, to make the case for collaboration in the prisoner's dilemma.[3] "OK–OK" at this level would mean I act "rationally"—You act "rationally." As insufficient as it may seem, this stance has been the pillar of traditional economics and early management theories. It is still helpful—albeit in conjunction with other perspectives—for devising a sound business plan with precise financial calculations, and for fostering productivity and results.

Beyond the psychological perspective, "OK–OK" at the **political** level can be viewed as the combination of power and service, which characterizes "constructive politics": striving to build one's power (self) while at the same time putting this in the service of various stakeholders (others). In this sense, the "Enlightened Builder" is "OK–OK": he is able to reach his own meaningful, important objectives and enable others to achieve theirs. On the other hand, the "Idealist" is "not OK–OK" (caring for others but with limited ability to serve them), and the "Prince" is "OK–not OK" (powerful but not very concerned about serving others). The self-centered "Individual Achiever" may be doing fine working independently but will struggle in interdependent situations, where his lack of power restrains his means to achieve objectives and his poor sense of service tends to alienate others: this is "not OK–not OK."

At the **cultural** level, "OK–OK" characterizes the ethnorelative approach, which I elaborated upon in *Coaching Across Cultures*. At a minimum, we recognize the legitimacy and merits of diverse cultural preferences: our own and the other's. Hopefully, we are ready to adapt (which does not imply adoption or assimilation), integrate, and ultimately leverage differences. Here we strive for synergy, proactively look for gems in different cultures, and achieve unity in diversity. All the other combinations (involving at least one "not OK") reveal some form of ethnocentrism. (Our worldview is central to all reality.) It is obvious if we recognize differences but evaluate them negatively: when we denigrate others, we think of them as "not OK"; when we put others on a pedestal and denigrate our own culture, we treat the latter as "not OK." Ignoring differences or trivializing them often shows a lack of interest for the other culture or an absence of appreciation for its uniqueness. We are, perhaps unconsciously, viewing the other culture as "not OK."

At the **spiritual** level, "OK–OK" takes on a deeper and broader meaning still. The coach's assertiveness, mastery of constructive politics, and intercultural excellence are completed by her readiness to enter "living relationships" and her capacity to build "genuine communities." *I-It* relations are necessary and can be perfectly "OK" in a psychological sense (i.e., respect, trust, et cetera). However, *I-Thou* relationships are what makes us fully human and may represent "OK–OK" in the noblest sense. Coaching from a spiritual perspective can only occur when the quality of *I-Thou* relationships is present, albeit fleetingly.

I-THOU RELATIONSHIPS

It is beyond the scope of this book to provide a detailed account of Martin Buber's contribution. My goal here is to introduce some of Buber's notions, which, in my experience, can enrich coaches' perspectives and augment our positive impact. For those who want to learn more, I recommend Kenneth Kramer's (2003) excellent guide, which makes Buber's thoughts much more accessible. Buber warns us, though, that "*I-Thou* dialogue cannot be taught or transmitted. It can only be indicated" (Kramer, 2003, 45).

Jennifer Maione describes her experience of such dialogue: "She made me feel as though I had genuinely listened and offered something no one else had. I think that I was the one person she really opened up to" (Kramer, 2003, 20). You hopefully have had similar experiences with your coachees. This quality of relationship is fulfilling both for the coachee and the coach. It gives meaning to our enterprise.

The coach needs to master the tools and techniques (*I-It*) but cannot apply these mechanically. The art of coaching implies moving beyond technique to enter genuine relationships (*I-Thou*). It helps when we are grateful to be in this authentic relationship, in touch with our sense of lightness and humor, confident that our coaching will help make a real difference. A spontaneous willingness to learn from coachees and belief in their wisdom also enables the mutual *I-Thou* relationship. This would be trickier in psychotherapy, which does not imply the same level of equality. Just as we can be touched by musicians' grace and emotion when they play at a level beyond technical mastery, our coachees can be moved by seamless and authentic coaching. This happens when global coaches, in the flow, having mastered the art of juggling multiple perspectives to serve their coachees, exude humanity, simplicity, and lightness. We will be moved too, just like the musician will be touched by the special communion with his audience. In this happening, the coach is in contact with the full range of emotions (which allows her to readily empathize with the coachee), in touch with pragmatic considerations as well as lofty human aspirations, at ease with psychological and cultural diversity. She has achieved unity within, ephemerally yet strongly, and propagates it externally.

Buber directs us beyond the traditional subject–object dichotomy: "Rather than serving as an object of experience, *Thou* points to the quality of genuine relationship in which partners are mutually unique and whole. This living realization is neither subjective nor objective but interhuman" (Kramer, 2003, 15).[4]

I-It Relations and *I-Thou* Relationships

Buber describes two primal attitudes (*I-It* and *I-Thou*) and suggests that we live in a continuous interplay between these complementary opposites. "Each person lives in an *I-It–I-Thou* continuum, in continual alternations between the two basic life stands" (Kramer, 2003, 16). Both are necessary for coaching, but accessing *I-Thou* is required to become whole human beings. "There is no pure *I-Thou* relationship without an *I-It* point of reference. Nor can we have an *I-Thou* relationship with everyone, or in every situation. We can, however, remain open and willing to enter *I-Thou* interactions with those of similar intentions" (Kramer, 2003, 19).

Jennifer Maione mentions a disadvantage of *I-Thou* relationships: "I couldn't tell you now all the things we said" (Kramer 2003, 20). Likewise, one downside of being fully present in coaching is that it is hard for me afterward to remember exactly what was said, the links that were established, the insights that emerged. My notes are an imperfect, albeit still useful, way of capturing some of what took place in the moment. The words are helpful, but they cannot fully capture and do justice to what transpired.

Placing myself on the *I-It* side for now, let me attempt to summarize the contrasts between *I-It* relations and *I-Thou* relationships.[5]

I-It Relations	*I-Thou* Relationships
Indicate degrees of separation from others Objectifying, monological The other is objectified and reduced to the content of the observer's own experience. Benefits in practical ways	Indicate a togetherness of close bonding More immediate, mutual, and dialogical The other is invited to meet me where I stand, in open, mutual reciprocity. Required to develop personal wholeness

I-It Relations	*I-Thou* Relationships
Never spoken with the whole being Experiencing/using/knowing In space and time One-sided: singular Controlling Subject–object duality	Spoken with the whole being Event/happening Spaceless/timeless Two-sided: mutual Yielding Interhuman betweenness

Putting things in categories
In this objectified experience of the world, one does not venture outside self-reinforcing plans, schemes, and purposes
This "objective knowledge" is necessary
	Direct and open moments of mutual presence between persons
	Three characteristics[6]:
	  Directness and wholeness
	  Will and grace
	  Presence of mutuality

World of *It*. Things, processes, characteristics, and objects that are continuously divisible An individual who primarily speaks *I-It* observes things as objects, arranges them, orders them, separates them, and connects them without necessarily feeling the weight of their importance The individual perceives beings and actions as things and occurrences composed of properties and moments, as posited in spatial and temporal networks, compared and measured against other things.	World of *Thou*. Holographic universe: undivided wholeness of all things Total acceptance of the present. Glimpse at the implicate order, timeless and spaceless[7]
Relation (Ich-Es Verhältnis) Relation of physical proximity only. For example, two billiard balls can be said to be in relation to each other on a pool table. Yet they have no interpersonal relationship with each other.	Relationship (Ich-Du Beziehung)

Buber underlines the *Inborn Thou*: "In the womb the child is enfolded in a natural relationship, the bonds of which are broken at birth" (Kramer, 2003, 28). "Enfolded" is the term used in the holographic model. For Buber, then:

- The *I-Thou* relationship comes first, and the *I-It* relation emerges from it.

- The *I-Thou* continually becomes *I-It*; and only at times the *It* is capable of returning to the *Thou*.
- The *I-It* needs not become the *I-Thou*; yet to truly become a human person, one must meet the world as *Thou*.
- The *Inborn Thou* continues throughout life to seek genuine meeting (Kramer, 2003, 29).

However, this genuine meeting will no longer be the womb's fusion but rather mutual presence that affirms both persons. It is dynamic solidarity and deep bonding. "The sought-for treasure, the fulfillment of existence, can be found right here in the midst of genuine dialogue" (Kramer, 2003, 12). Buber writes, "The primary word *I-Thou* can be spoken only with the whole being . . . . I become through my relationship[8] to the *Thou*; as I become *I*, I say *Thou*. All real living is meeting" (Buber, 1958, 17). By entering the coaching relationship with our "whole being," we promote our coachee's humanity as well as our own.

This emphasis on relationships has a profound implication for coaching. In traditional coaching, dialogue and relationships—or I should say relations—are often merely a means to an end (for example, maturity, self-expression, or peace of mind). The individual's self-actualization (Maslow), autonomy (Berne), or individuation (Jung) is the goal in her developmental journey. For Buber, this self-centeredness, this individual development for its own sake, misses the mark. In remarkable alignment with the holographic model, which emphasizes our interconnectedness, Buber suggests a form of co-development or co-construction. "Real living is meeting," and we develop through this genuine connection. If dialogue is merely a mean to self-centeredness, it ceases to be true dialogue.

Practically, this does not mean that global coaches should stop helping coachees set up and reach personal goals. It does mean, however, entering the relationship attuned to the broader impact of what we do and our many connections with the world at large. It means letting go of limiting beliefs, destructive thoughts, and emotions that might prevent us from being fully present in the relationship. And it means truly appreciating the relationship itself.

We need to be "openhearted and open-minded to those whom we meet." This facilitates genuine dialogue, which "happens *between* us in a dynamic, mutual reciprocity." It is not automatic, though. *Happens* implies "it does not occur simply by my intending it to occur [but] by virtue of relational grace" (Kramer, 2003, 55–56). The best coach still needs a willing coachee.

Buber's contribution can also inform coaches about the dangers of an object-oriented consciousness (whose damaging effects have been very apparent in the 2008 world financial crisis, as I discussed in Chapter 2): "While we cannot dispense with the world of *It*, our drive to profit and be powerful needs direction from the presence of *I-Thou* relationships. It is these authentic relationships that prevent the world of *It* from overtaking us and that introduce ultimate meaning and intrinsic value into life" (Kramer, 2003, 75–76).

Genuine Community

Ferdinand Tönnies (1887/2001), who pioneered sociology in Germany, contrasted two types of social groupings, which he called *Gemeinschaft* and *Gesellschaft*.

Here is the distinction:

Gemeinschaft—often translated as community—refers to groupings based on feelings of togetherness and on mutual bonds, which are felt as a goal to be kept up, their members being means for this goal. Gesellschaft—often translated as society—on the other hand, refers to groups that are sustained by it being instrumental for their members' individual aims and goals.

Gemeinschaft may by exemplified historically by a family or a neighborhood in a pre-modern (rural) society; Gesellschaft by a joint-stock company or a state in a modern society, i.e., the society when Tönnies lived. Gesellschaft relationships arose in an urban and capitalist setting, characterized by individualism and impersonal monetary connections between people. Social ties were often instrumental and superficial, with self-interest and exploitation increasingly the norm.[9]

Buber revisited this dichotomy, advocating for Gemeinschaft. In today's individualistic organizations and societies, restoring a sense of community and solidarity seems necessary. Buber's vision implies deep bonding and genuine relationships among members: "Genuine community cannot be based on how one feels about another or about some thing. Instead, authentic community is built upon readiness in every moment to enter living relationships" (Kramer, 2003, 76).

Whereas Collectivity (Gesellschaft) is characterized by "organized union of forces" and "institutionalized social relations," Community (Gemeinschaft) is infused with "vital interaction" and with a "stream of giving and creative surrender." For Buber, "true community cannot be set forth as a goal to be obtained; rather, it arises when people learn to really listen to one another again" (77). For him, genuine community is "the inner constitution of a common life that knows and embraces differences," "the overcoming of otherness in living unity" (83, 95). It is "not only an ideal but also a direction of movement, a reality we try to build in every situation." I also share Buber's inclusive view of culture implied in his belief: "The decisive question about one's world view is whether it enables one to connect more vitally to the world or obstructs that possibility" (91).

Buber's two favorite examples of genuine community are the legendary Hasidic community and what Maurice Friedman calls the "learning community." It is striking that Buber's description could apply to the character of our international Coaching Across Cultures seminars,[10] in which multiple nationalities, languages, religions, and occupations make for diverse groups, whose participants share an open-minded, benevolent, and constructively challenging spirit. Our participants "give" as well as "get" from the seminars, and everyone "gets" more as a result: we tap into their experience and insights, and facilitate cross-learning and relationship building among us all.

> The learning community, an ever-regenerated community of people who are willing to be present to and for one another, necessarily recognizes and openly discusses multiple points of view. Diversity is not a difficulty to be overcome. A learning community's multiplicity of viewpoints provides the material for ever-recurring dialogues, because each person brings something quite concrete and unique into the communal relationship. Open-minded honesty and willingness to be changed are valued more than like-mindedness. (Kramer, 2003, 91)

Real I

Buber insists on the wholeness of the human person. For him, wholeness refers to "seamless integration of body, mind, and spirit." (Kramer, 2003, 99). Global coaches can play a decisive role in helping the "real I," the true self, to emerge when we strive to establish genuine dialogues with our coachees. For Buber, "our foremost task is to fulfill our unique, unpredictable, ever-recurring potentialities by hallowing the everyday with others" (Kramer 2003, 121).

The following table[11] distinguishes persons from individuals. Buber urges us to become persons.

Individual	Person
Lives *in* the world	Lives *with* the world
Self-referencing, me-oriented	
Necessary for basic survival	Enlarges the human enterprise
Ego-oriented	Relationship-oriented
Seeming	Unfolding

Eternal *Thou*

Through the ages, people have debated God's existence and devised various answers to the question of God's nature. Buber eludes both interrogations. Whether we believe in God or not is unimportant. Our actions and attitudes matter.[12] And, "in place of offering an interpretation of who God is, Buber posits that the *presence* of God is glimpsed through the interhuman realm" (Kramer, 2003, 129).

Buber's notion is remarkably consistent with the holographic model: God, the "eternal (or absolute) *Thou*," "forms a living bond among all separated beings" (129). "Every particular *Thou* is a glimpse through to the eternal *Thou*" (156). In our fragmented and polarized world, we can, without turning into mystics, become more attuned to this inconspicuous living bond. As global coaches, we can play our part by fostering more authentic relationships.

Furthermore, when we coach from a spiritual perspective, we help people live in a mindful, awakened fashion, and "each living moment can become sacramental" (154).

Turning

The act of turning is *from* separation *toward* deep bonding. "When we are 'possessed by a desire for possession,' we become immersed in the world of *It* regardless of what kind of idols we construct to justify this position" (Kramer, 2003, 164).

In Chapter 2, I discussed GM's regrettable decision to cancel its electric car program. Although I cannot know exactly what was in the minds of GM's top leaders, I cannot help imagining what could have ensued had they opened a reflective space and entered genuine global coaching dialogues. Coaching from a spiritual perspective could have allowed them to make more authentic decisions—meaningful decisions they perhaps were longing for but did not dare make. Perhaps their egos were still overly attached to their high-profile status, which they did not want to risk losing. Perhaps they could not imagine living a rich life on more modest incomes had they lost their jobs for making a courageous decision. Perhaps they did not see that full commitment to green technological progress could have brought positive outcomes for their companies, for themselves, and for society.

Separation keeps us away from our own authentic motives, other people's needs, and societal, planetary necessities. Buber directs us toward deep bonding instead. However, "to turn is to give up the false self-asserting self, but not to give up the 'I,' as in mysticism" (159).

Well before the rise of the coaching discipline, Buber's genuine listening was already pointing beyond active listening (which, notably and rightly, implies suspending judgment). It is characterized by:

- turning toward the other with one's whole being (body/mind/spirit)
- being fully present to the uniqueness of the situation with the other
- faithfully and attentively responding
- imagining what the other is thinking, feeling, perceiving
- asking meaning-directed questions
- attending both to what is said and to what is not said (172)

We may have missed many opportunities to enter authentic dialogues. The good news is that we can still decide to turn toward others and strive for deep bonding. We can model the way and facilitate the process. As global coaches, we can thereby play our part in fostering a worldly, genuine community.

NOTES

1. See also Kramer, 2003, 31. Kramer explains: "While a person cannot be fully human without a *Thou*, a human being cannot live without *It*. Buber himself lived much of his life in the *It*-world of gathering materials and analyzing their meanings across disciplines" (31).
2. Berger and Atkins (2009) explain subject–object relationships in Kegan's adult development theory in the following way:

   The process of transformation is moving more and more of what is unseen and unexamined in the way we understand the world—those things to which we are subject—to a place where they can be seen and examined—and become objects *for our inspection. Our unquestioned beliefs about the world are held implicitly, and those beliefs shape our experience of the world and the possibilities we perceive. As we begin to question our beliefs, ideas, theories, etc., our more explicit stance opens new possibilities and allows us to deal with greater and greater levels of complexity. This process is like taking off a pair of colored glasses so that instead of looking through them, we are able to look at them and thereby understand and gain control over their use: to select when we'd like to have the tint and when we'd rather be without. The most profound example of a move from implicit to explicit is when gradually, over time, entire meaning-making systems move from being hidden to being seen. This shift means that what was once an unselfconscious lens through which the person viewed the world now becomes something that he can see and reflect upon. (25–26)*

As elaborate and useful as Kegan's model is, it still seems to leave out the co-constructive perspective (see Chapter 9), that is the possibility for the insuparable subject–object to co-create new realities in an upward spiral of mutual enriching. This can be compared with Buber's *I-Thou* realm, also left out, and whose genuine relationships enable this deep human enriching. In other words, there is apparently more complexity still to be embraced beyond Kegan's last stage!

3. The label "prisoner's dilemma" is usually applied to "situations in which two entities could gain important benefits from cooperating or suffer from the failure to do so, but find it difficult or expensive, not necessarily impossible, to coordinate their activities to achieve cooperation" (Wikipedia).

4. Kramer (2003) explains: "By *Thou*, Buber does not mean either 'God' or 'you' as an object of my perception, or 'he,' or 'she,' or 'it,' for that matter. Rather, with the word '*Du*' Buber refers to the presence of uniqueness and wholeness emerging from genuine listening and responsible responding" (19).

5. This is adapted from Kramer, 2003, 16, 17, 18, 20–24, 26, 90, 104, 29–30, 39, 40, 44. I have added references to the holographic model (see Chapter 9).

6. They point to immediacy, presence without agendas. It includes both "choosing" to enter relationship, and "being chosen" by one who also chooses to enter relationship. It involves action and surrender. Grace is the spontaneous undetermined *presence of mutuality*, which cannot be activated by will alone. (I would simply say: "It takes two to tango.")

7. See Talbot, 1991, Part III, notably 197, 229. "The 'home' of the mind, as of all things, is the implicate order. At this level, which is the fundamental plenum for the entire manifest universe, there is no linear time. The implicate domain is atemporal; moments are not strung together serially like beads on a string" (Dossey, 1989 in Talbot, 1991, 197).

8. I have replaced Smith's translation "relation" with Kramer's choice of "relationship" to maintain consistency and respect Kramer's judicious distinction of *I-It* relations versus *I-Thou* relationships.

9. From Wikipedia. *http://en.wikipedia.org/wiki/Ferdinand_T%C3%B6nnies*. Retrieved on 30 July 2009. "Whereas the membership in a Gemeinschaft is self-fulfilling, a Gesellschaft is instrumental for its members. In pure sociology—theoretically—these two normal types of will are to be strictly separated; in applied sociology—empirically—they are always mixed."
10. See *www.philrosinski.com*.
11. Adapted from Kramer, 2003, 108–109.
12. See Chapter 8 and Kramer, 2003, 155.

APPENDIX

The Möbius Ring Model—Unity and Infinity[1]

Reflecting on my practice of coaching executives, I wondered how to graphically represent the relationship between the various perspectives. (My former engineering background may have incidentally popped up here!) The Möbius strip then stood out.

The Möbius strip, also called the twisted cylinder (Henle, 1994), is a one-sided surface obtained by cutting a closed band into a single strip, giving one of the two ends a half twist, and then reattaching the two ends (Gray, Abbena, and Salamon, 2006).

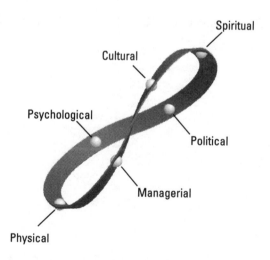

Multiple perspectives in coaching on a Möbius strip

The artist M.C. Escher created famous representations of the Möbius strip, notably one with ants crawling on the one-sided surface forming a ∞ shape (which happens to symbolize infinity). The Möbius strip represents unity and infinity at the same time: it has only one side and one edge, and ants could crawl on it forever. The mathematically inclined might enhance the model by weaving fractals into the strip, thereby producing an edge of infinite length.

The multiple perspectives could be imagined as diverse viewpoints lying on a Möbius strip (see figure). Of course, I do not think we can know the ultimate representation of a complex reality, and I doubt a single representation even exists. Multiple representations can coexist, each with their merits and limitations. This Möbius strip representation is merely an attempt at highlighting certain characteristics that seem important: unity (one side and one edge) and, at the same time, infinity. The one-side and one-edge property evokes the concept of unity we discussed earlier. Moreover, the ∞ shape visually combines dilatation and contraction, mirroring exploration and openness together with focus and closure, all necessary for creative coaching.

Finally, the duality unity-infinity inherent to the Möbius strip is a powerful reminder for global coaches that everything is interconnected. It is an invitation to leverage diversity and foster synthesis.

NOTE

1. This Appendix is adapted from Rosinski, "Coaching from Multiple Perspectives," 2006.

Bibliography

Abbott, Geoffrey. "Executive Coaching through Cross-border Mergers and Acquisitions." In *The Routledge Companion to International Business Coaching*, edited by Michel Moral and Geoffrey Abbott, 229-317. Oxon, UK and New York: Routledge, 2009.

Abbott, Geoffrey, and Philippe Rosinski. "Global Coaching and Evidence Based Coaching: Multiple Perspectives Operating in a Process of Pragmatic Humanism." *International Journal of Evidence Based Coaching and Mentoring* (Vol 5, No 1), 2007: 58–77.

Adler, Alfred. *Superiority and Social Interest* (3d rev. ed.). New York and London: W. W. Norton & Company, 1979.

Algalarrondo, Hervé. "Le Président qui ne Veut pas Vieillir." *Le Nouvel Observateur* (30 July–5 August), 2009: 30–2.

Alighieri, Dante. "Divina Commedia." *Dante, Oeuvres complètes* (French translation), translated by Christian Bec et al. Paris: Le Livre de Poche, 1321/ 1996.

Angell, Marcia. *The Truth About the Drug Companies: How They Deceive Us and What to Do About It.* New York: Random House, 2004.

Aristotle. "Organon." *Aristotle's Organon and Other Works*, edited by W.D. Ross. Open Source Books, 4th century B.C./1999. *www.archive.org/details/AristotleOrganon*.

Armstrong, Lance. *It's Not About the Bike. My Journey Back to Life.* London: Yellow Jersey Press, 2000.

Attali, Jacques. *La Voie Humaine.* Paris: Fayard, 2004.

———. "Nous Vivons l'Accouchement d'un Monde Nouveau (7–8 March)." *Le Soir*, 2009: 58.

August Rush, dir. Kristen Sheridan, 2007.

Babiak, Paul, and Robert Hare. *Snakes in Suits: When Psychopaths Go to Work.* New York: Collins, 2006.

Barbier, Edward. *A Global Green New Deal. www.unep.org/greeneconomy/docs/ggnd_Final%20Report.pdf*, 2009.

Bar-On, Reuven. *Bar-On Emotional Quotient Inventory.* Toronto: Multi-Health Systems, 2002.

Bartram, D., et al. "Personality at Work: Gender and National Differences in a Sample of 60,000 Working Adults." Paper presented at the 21st Annual Conference of the Society for Industrial and Organizational Psychology, Dallas, TX, 2006.

Bender, Charlie. "Plyometric FAQ." *WeightsNet.* 18 May 1995. *www.weightsnet.com/Docs/plyometrics.html* (accessed 7 August 2009).

Benziger, Katherine. *Thriving in Mind: The Art and Science of Using Your Whole Brain.* Carbondale, IL: KBA, LLC, 2006.

Berger, Jennifer. "Adult Development Theory and Executive Coaching Practice." In *Evidence Based Coaching Handbook*, edited by Dianne Stober and Anthony Grant, 77–102. Hoboken, NJ: John Wiley & Sons, 2006.

Berger, Jennifer, and Paul Atkins. "Mapping Complexity of Mind: Using the Subject-Object Interview in Coaching." *Coaching: An International Journal of Theory, Research and Practice* (Vol 2, Issue 1), 2009: 23–36.

Bergquist, William, and Kristin Eggen. "Ontology and Coaching: A Reflection on the Interview with Julio Olalla." *The International Journal of Coaching in Organizations* (Issue 2), 2008: 58–67.

Berne, Eric. *Games People Play.* New York: Penguin Books, 1964.

Bohm, David. *Wholeness and the Implicate Order.* London-Boston: Routledge & Kegan Paul (edition Routledge Classics 2002), 1980.

Bonini, Sheila, Lenny Mendonca, and Michelle Rosenthal. *From Risk to Opportunity: How Global Executives View Sociopolitical Issues.* McKinsey & Company, 2008.

Books. "Le Scandale de l'Industrie Pharmaceutique." *Books* (April), 2009: 14–23.

Borch-Jacobsen, Mikkel. *Making Minds and Madness: From Hysteria to Depression.* Cambridge, UK: Cambridge University Press, 2009.

Boston College Center for Corporate Citizenship. *How Virtue Creates Value for Business and Society.* Boston: Boston College-Carroll School of Management, 2009.

Bracewell, Ronald. *The Fourier Transform and its Applications.* New York: McGraw-Hill, 1978.

Brake, Terence. "Leading Virtual Teams." *Industrial and Commercial Training* (Vol 38, No 3), 2006: 116–21.

Briggs Myers, Isabel. *Introduction to Type.* Mountain View, CA: CPP (OPP for the European Edition), 2000.

Broun, Jacques, et al. *Leonardo da Vinci. The European Genius.* Brussels, Belgium: Europa 50, 2007.

Buber, Martin. *I and Thou* (2d ed.). Translated by Ronald Gregor Smith. London: Continuum, 1958.

———. *On Judaïsm.* New York: Schocken Books, 1967.

Cailliau, Hesna. *L' Esprit des Religions. Connaître les Religions pour Mieux Connaître les Hommes.* Toulouse, France: Milan, 2003.

Campbell, David. *Manual for the Campbell Leadership Index.* Minneapolis, MN: National Computer Systems, 1991.

Campbell, David, and Glenn Hallam. *Campbell-Hallam Team Development Survey Manual.* Minneapolis, MN: National Computer Systems, 1994.

Camus, Albert. *Le Mythe de Sisyphe.* Paris: Gallimard, 1942.

Cannio, Sylviane, and Viviane Launer. *Cas de Coaching Commentés.* Paris: Eyrolles, 2008.

"Capitalism at Bay." *The Economist* (18 October), 2008: 13–4.

Center for Creative Leadership. *Benchmarks Facilitators Manual.* Greensboro, NC: Center for Creative Leadership, 2000.

———. *Fitness for Leadership.* Colorado Springs, CO: Center for Creative Leadership, 2005.

Chalude, Michel. *Vous et votre Projet.* Paris: InterEditions, 2001.

"Climate Change—A Heated Debate," *The Economist*, 28 November 2009: 16.

Clutterbuck, David. *Coaching the Team at Work.* London and Boston: Nicholas Brealey Publishing, 2007.

Cohen, Michael. "John E. Mack, MD: A Tribute." In *Passport to the Cosmos* (comm. ed.), by John Mack. Largo, FL: Kunati, 2008.

Colloca, Luana, and Fabrizio Benedetti. "Placebos and Painkillers: Is Mind as Real as Matter?" *Nature Reviews Neuroscience*, 6, 2005: 545–52.

Comte-Sponville, André. *Dictionnaire Philosophique*. Paris: Presses Universitaires de France, 2001.

———. *Le Bonheur, Désespérément*. Nantes, France: Editions Pleins Feux, 2000.

———. *Petit Traité des Grandes Vertus*. Paris: Presses Universitaires de France, 1995.

———. "Seule la Loi Peut Moraliser le Capitalisme. " *Le Soir* (8–9 November), 2009: 60.

Condijts, Joan, Paul Gérard, and Pierre-Henri Thomas. *La Chute de la Maison Fortis*. Brussels, Belgium: Jean-Claude Lattès, 2009.

Cooman, Hans. "Votre Guide d'Entraînement de A à Z." *BodyTalk* (No 17), 1991: 9–16.

Crash, dir. Paul Haggis, 2004.

Curtay, Jean-Paul. *Okinawa: Un Programme Global pour Mieux Vivre*. Paris: Editions Anne Carrière, 2006.

Dans l'Ombre de la Lune, dir. David Sington, 2007.

De Angelis, Barbara. "Measure Your Life in Love." *Resource* (January), 2006: 7–9.

de Mello Meirelles, Claudia, and Paulo Sergio Chagas Gomes. "Acute Effects of Resistance Exercise on Energy Expenditure: Revisiting the Impact of the Training Variables." *Rev Bras Med Esporte* (Vol 10, No 2—English version), 2004: 131–8.

Debold, Elizabeth. "Epistemology, Fourth Order Consciousness and the Subject-Object Relationship or ...How the Self Evolves, with Robert Kegan." *What Is Enlightenment*, 2008.

De Jonghe, Pierre-Jean. *De Quelle Vie Voulez-Vous Etre le Héros?* Paris: Dunod, 2004.

Dossey, Larry. *Recovering the Soul*. New York: Bantam, 1989.

Downey, Myles. *Effective Coaching* (3d ed.). Texere Publishing, 2003.

Dyer, Jeffrey, Prashant Kale, and Harbir Singh. "When to Ally and When to Acquire."*Harvard Business Review* (June), 2004: 24–33.

Engdahl, William. "Colossal Financial Collapse: The Truth Behind the Citigroup Bank 'Nationalization.'" *Global Research.ca*. November 24, 2008. *www.globalresearch.ca* (accessed 4 August 2009).

Enlevés, dir. Stéphane Allix, 2005.

Entretien avec Édgar Morin (2): Science et Philosophie. 10 April 2008. *www.nonfiction. fr/article-960-entretien_avec_edgar_morin__2__science_et_philosophie.htm* (accessed 28 July 2009).

European Foundation for Quality Management. *EFQM Excellence Model*. 1999.

Even, Philippe, and Bernard Debré. *Savoirs et Pouvoirs. Pour une Nouvelle Politique de la Recherche et du Médicament*. Paris: Le Cherche Midi, 2004.

A Fish Called Wanda, dir. Charles Crichton and John Cleese, 1988.

Fisher, Roger, and William Ury. *Getting to Yes*. New York: Penguin, 1981.

Frankl, Viktor. *Man's Search for Meaning*. London: Rider, 1959.

Genesis, dir. Claude Nuridsany and Marie Pérennou, 2004.

Gilbert, Kate, and Philippe Rosinski. "Accessing Cultural Orientations: the Online Cultural Orientations Framework Assessment as a Tool for Coaching." *Coaching: An International Journal of Theory, Research and Practice* (Vol 1, No 1), 2008: 81–92.

Gleick, James. *Chaos: Making of a New Science* (new ed.). London: Vintage, 1997.

Godard, Alain, and Vincent Lenhardt. *Transformational Leadership*. New York: Palgrave Macmillan, 2000.

Goleman, Daniel. "Probing the Enigma of Multiple Personality." *The New York Times* (June 28), 1988.

———. "New Focus on Multiple Personality." *The New York Times* (May 21), 1985.

Goodman, Joseph. *Introduction to Fourier Optics*. San Francisco: McGraw-Hill, 1968.

Goudsmet, Alain. *L'Athlète d'Entreprise*. Brussels, Belgium: Editions Kluwer, 2002.

Gougaud, Henri. *Les Sept Plumes de l'Aigle*. Paris: Seuil, 1995.

Grabbe, Dieter. *Souple et en Pleine Forme Grâce au Stretching*. Aartselaar, Belgium: Chantecler, 2002.

Grau, Norbert. *Le Stretching Global Actif au Service du Geste Sportif.* Guilherand-Granges, France: Impressions Modernes, 2002.

Gray, Alfred, Elsa Abbena, and Simon Salamon. *Modern Differential Geometry of Curves and Surfaces with Mathematica* (3d ed.). London: Chapman & Hall, 2006.

Greene, Robert, and Joost Elfers. *The 48 Laws of Power.* New York: Viking, 1998.

"A Green Revolution—Saving the World Will Not Be Cheap (in "A Special Report on Business in America")," *The Economist,* 30 May 2009.

Grof, Stanislav. *When the Impossible Happens.* Boulder, CO: Sounds True, 2006.

Guillebaud, Jean-Claude. "L'Injonction Paradoxale. " *Le Nouvel Observateur* (TéléObs 12 February), 2009: 66.

Guissard, Nathalie, and Dominique Dejaeger. "Le Stretching Musculaire: Mise au Point." *Clés pour la Forme* (#8, 4), 2004: 2–5.

Hadot, Pierre. *Qu'est-ce que la Philosophie Antique?* Paris: Gallimard, 1995.

Halevi, Z'ev Ben Shimon. *Kabbalah, Tradition of Hidden Knowledge.* London: Thames & Hudson, 1979.

Hall, Edward. *Beyond Culture.* New York: Anchor Books, 1976.

Hall, Stephen. "'The Truth About the Drug Companies' and 'Powerful Medicines': The Drug Lords." *The New York Times* (14 November), 2004.

Hartman, Michael, et al. "Resistance Training Improves Metabolic Economy During Functional Tasks in Older Adults." *Journal of Strength and Conditioning Research,* 21(1), 2007: 91–5.

Haskell, William, et al. "Physical Activity and Public Health: Updated Recommendation for Adults from the American College of Sports Medicine and the American Heart Association." *Medicine & Science in Sports & Exercise,* 2007: 1423–34.

Heilbroner, Robert. *The Wordly Philosophers—The Lives, Times and Ideas of the Great Economic Thinkers* (rev. 7th ed.). London and New York: Penguin Books, 2000.

Henle, Michael. *A Combinatorial Introduction to Topology.* Mineola, NY: Dover, 1994.

Hersey, Paul. *Situational Leadership.* Escondido, CA: Center for Leadership Studies, 1979–1993.

Hixon, Lex. *Coming Home: The Experience of Enlightenment in Sacred Traditions.* Larson Publications, 1996.

Hofstede, Geert. *Culture's Consequences* (2d ed.). Thousand Oaks, CA: Sage, 2001.

Home, dir. Yann Arthus-Bertrand, 2009.

Horton, Peter. "Peter Buys an Electric Car," *Los Angeles Times,* 8 June 2003.

House, Robert, et al., eds. *Culture, Leadership, and Organizations. The GLOBE Study of 62 Societies.* Thousand Oaks, CA: Sage, 2004.

Hulot, Nicolas. *Le Syndrome du Titanic.* Paris: Calmann-Lévy, 2004.

Janssen, Thierry. *La Solution Intérieure. Vers une Nouvelle Médicine du Corps et de l'Esprit.* Paris: Fayard, 2006.

Jones, Judy, and William Wilson. "An Incomplete Education." 1995. *www.miskatonic. org/godel.html* (accessed December 2008).

Jung, Carl. *Psychological Types* (rev. of original English translation). Princeton, NJ: Princeton University Press, 1923/1971.

———. *Synchronicity: An Acausal Connecting Principle.* (Edition translated by R.F.C. Hull, Princeton/Bollingen Paperback, 1992). Princeton, NJ: Princteon University Press, 1960.

Kahler, Taibi. *Process Communication.* Little Rock, AR: Taibi Kahler Associates, 1982.

———. *The Mastery of Management.* Little Rock, AR: Kahler Communications, 1988.

Kaplan, Robert, and David Norton. *The Balanced Scorecard.* Boston: Harvard Business School Press, 1996.

Kassirer, Jerome. *On the Take. How Medicine's Complicity with Big Business Can Endanger Your Health.* Oxford, UK: Oxford University Press, 2004.

Kauffman, Carol. "Positive Psychology: The Science at the Heart of Coaching." In *Evidence Based Coaching Handbook*, edited by Dianne Stober and Anthony Grant, 219-253. Hoboken, NJ: John Wiley & Sons, 2006.

Kempner, M. "When Rumors Thrive, Your Deal's in Trouble." *Mergers and Acquisitions*, 40(4), 2005: 42–50.

Keynes, John Maynard. *The General Theory of Employment, Interest and Money*. Cambridge: Macmillan Cambridge University Press, 1936.

Ki-moon, Ban, and Al Gore. "Investir Pour une Croissance Verte" (28 February-1st March). *Le Soir*, 2009: 52.

Klopfer, Bruno. "Psychological Variables in Human Cancer," *Journal of Prospective Techniques*, 31, 1957: 331-340.

Kluckhohn, Florence, and Frederick Strodtbeck. *Variations in Value Orientations*. Evanston, IL and Elmsford, NY: Row, Peterson and Company, 1961.

Knuttgen, Howard. "What is Exercise?" *The Physician and Sportsmedicine* (Vol 31, No 3), 2003.

Kourilsky, Françoise. *Du Désir au Plaisir de Changer*. Paris: Dunod, 2004.

Kraemer, William, and Nicholas Ratamess. "Fundamentals of Resistance Training: Progresion and Exercise Prescription." *Medicine & Science in Sports & Exercise*, 2004: 674–88.

Kramer, Kenneth Paul. *Martin Buber's I and Thou*. Mahwah, NJ: Paulist Press, 2003.

Lambert, Andrew. *What's New in Coaching and Mentoring? An Update*. London: Corporate Research Forum, 2008.

Lee-Marks, M. "The Destructive Force of Aquisition Denial." *Mergers and Acquisitions*, 40(4) , 2005: 47–53.

Lenhardt, Vincent. *Au Coeur de la Relation d'Aide*. Paris: InterEditions-Dunod, 2008.

Lenhardt, Vincent, and Philippe Bernard. *L'Intelligence Collective en Action*. Paris: Village Mondial, 2005.

Lenoir, Frédéric. *Les Métamorphoses de Dieu: la Nouvelle Spiritualité Occidentale*. Paris: Plon, 2003.

"Les Economistes Surpris par la Crise." *Le Soir* (4–5 April), 2009: 16–7.

Lesowitz, T., and T. Knauff. "The Human Factor in the Post-Merger Mix." *Mergers and Acquisitions*, 38(12), 2003: 30.

Levitt, Theodore. "Marketing Myopia." *Harvard Business Review*, 1960.

Lipman, Doug. *The Soul of Hope. An Epic Tale of the Baal Shem Tov*. (Cassettes) West Somerville, MA: Doug Lipman, 1997.

Mack, John. *Passport to the Cosmos* (comm. ed.). Largo, FL: Kunati, 2008.

Macovski, Albert. *Medical Imaging Systems*. Englewood Cliffs, NJ: Prentice-Hall, 1983.

"The Madoff Affair—Dumb Money and Dull Diligence." *The Economist*, 20 December 2008: 17–8.

Mailhes, Laetitia." Californie—Le Rail Siffle la Fin du Tout-Voiture. " *Enjeux* (February), 2009: 66–8.

Maslin, Janet. "The Case for Another Drug War, Against Pharmaceutical Marketers' Dirty Tactics." *The New York Times*, 17 March 2008.

Megginson, David, and David Clutterbuck. *Techniques for Coaching and Mentoring*. Oxford, UK: Elsevier, 2005.

Miedaner, Talane. *Coach Yourself to Success*. Chicago, IL: Contemporary Books, 2000.

Moeller, Scott. "Almost Every Significant Research Study Argues that Acquiring Companies Lose Value for Their Shareholders When They Attempt Takeovers." *Financial Times* (October 6), 2006: 2.

Moral, Michel, and Geoffrey Abbott. *The Routledge Companion to International Business Coaching*. Abingdon, UK and New York: Routledge, 2009.

Morin, Edgar. *Introduction à la Pensée Complexe*. Paris: Editions du Seuil, 2005.

The New Oxford Dictionary of English. Oxford, UK and New York: Oxford University Press, 1998.

Nollet, Jean-Marc. *Le "Green Deal"—Proposition pour une Sortie de Crise*. Brussels, Belgium: Le Cri édition, 2008.

Okinawa Centenarian Study. "Investigating the World's Longest-Lived People." *Okinawa Centenarian Study*. 2008. *www.okicent.org* (accessed 20 November 2008).

Ouaknin, Marc-Alain. *Mystères de la Kabbale*. Paris: Assouline, 2003.

Page, Linda. "Thinking Outside our Brains: Interpersonal Neurobiology and Organizational Change." *International Journal of Coaching in Organizations*, 4(2), 2006: 22–31.

Palmer, Stephen, and Almuth McDowall, eds. *The Coaching Relationship*. London and New York: Routledge, 2010.

Passmore, Jonathan, ed. *Excellence in Coaching: The Industry Guide*. London: Kogan Page Limited, 2006.

Pearson, Carol. "Archetypes 101." 2008. *www.herowithin.com/arch101.html* (accessed 16 October 2008).

———. *Awakening the Heroes Within*. New York: HarperCollins, 1991.

Perrin Towers. "Current M&A Cycle Creates Shareholder Value." 2006.

Petersen, Melody. *Our Daily Meds. How the Pharmaceutical Companies Transformed Themselves into Slick Marketing Machines and Hooked the Nation on Prescription Drugs*. New York: Farrar Straus Giroux, 2008.

Philips. *Illuminating Ideas: Welcome to Lighting*. Eindhoven, The Netherlands: Koninklijke Philips Electronics, 2008.

Pierard, Pascale. "Le Sport Contre la Nicotine." *Play Sport*, 3, 2006: 30.

Plato. "The Banquet." *Plato's Symposium*, translated by Seth Benardete. Open Source Books, 4th century B.C./1986. *www.archive.org/details/PlatosSymposium*.

Pratt, William. *Digital Image Processing*. New York: John Wiley & Sons, 1978.

Publishers Weekly. "Review: 'Passport to the Cosmos.'" In *Passport to the Cosmos*, by John Mack. Largo, FL: Kunati, 2008.

Quenk, Naomi. *Beside Ourselves*. Palo Alto, CA: Davies Black, 1993.

Ramachandran, Vilayanur. *Phantoms in the Brain* (2005 ed.). London: Harper Perennial, 1998.

———. *The Emerging Mind*. London: Profile Books, 2003.

Ratamess, Nicholas, et al. "Progression Models in Resistance Training for Healthy Adults." *Medicine & Science in Sports & Exercise*, 2009: 687–708.

Reymond, William. *Toxic. Obésité, Malbouffe, Maladies, . . . Enquête sur les Vrais Coupables*. Paris: Editions J'ai lu Flammarion, 2007.

Robbins, Stephen. *Organizational Behavior* (4th ed.). Englewood Cliffs, NJ: Prentice-Hall, 1989.

Rogers, Diane. "Strong Medicine." *Stanford* (September/October), 2006: 48–57.

Rojon, Céline. "Cultural Orientations Framework (COF) Assessment Questionnaire in Cross-Cultural Coaching: Initial Recommendations from a Cross-Validation with Wave ® Focus Styles." *International Coaching Psychology Review*, 2009.

Ronen, Simcha, and Oded Shenkar. "Clustering Countries on Attitudinal Dimensions: A Review and Synthesis." *The Academy of Management Review*, 10(3), 1985: 435–54.

Rosinski, Philippe. *Coaching Across Cultures*. London and Yarmouth, ME: Nicholas Brealey Publishing, 2003.

———. "Coaching From Multiple Perspectives." *International Journal of Coaching in Organizations* 4(4), 2006: 16–23.

———. "Constructive Politics: Essential to Leadership." *Leadership In Action* (Vol 18, No 3), 1998: 1–5.

———. "Fostering Individual and Collective Development Using the Cultural Orientations Framework Assessment." In *The Routledge Companion to International Business Coaching*, by Michel Moral and Geoffrey Abbott (Eds.), 145–62. Oxon, UK and New York: Routledge, 2009.

———. "Le Coaching Comme Humanisme Pragmatique. Séance Académique d'Ouverture du Diplôme Spécial en Coaching ICHEC, 5 Février 2004." Brussels, Belgium, 2004.

———. "Leading for Joy: Lessons on Leadership from the Judaic Tradition." *European Forum for Management Development* (No 3), 1998: 61–7.

———. "Lessons in Global Coaching from a Journey Through Unusual Hardship." *International Journal of Coaching in Organizations* (Issue 4), 2007: 6–20.

———. "The Applications of Coaching Across Cultures ." *International Journal of Coaching in Organizations* (Vol 1, No 4), 2003.

Rumi. *Rumi: Whispers of the Beloved.* Translated by Azima Melita Kolin and Maryam Mafi. London: Thorsons, 1999.

Sartre, Jean-Paul. *L'Existentialisme est un Humanisme.* Paris: Editions Nagel, 1946.

Saville Consulting. *Saville Consulting Wave Focus. Focus Styles.* Jersey, UK: Saville Consulting Group, 2006.

Schoenberg, Richard. "Dealing With a Culture Clash: Richard Schoenberg Explains How Risk Orientation Can Determine the Success of M&As." *Financial Times* (23 September), 2005: 3.

Schwartz, Shalom. "A Theory of Cultural Values and Some Implications for Work." *Applied Psychology: An International Review,* 48(1), 1999: 23–47.

"See How Easily You Can Calculate Your One Rep Max." *www.build-muscle-and-burnfat.com.* Retrieved on 20 June 2009.

Seligman, Martin. *Authentic Happiness: Using the New Positive Psychology to Realize Your Potential for Lasting Fulfillment.* New York: Free Press, 2002.

Seligman, Martin, and Mihalyi Csikszentmihalyi. "Positive Psychology: An Introduction." *American Psychologist,* 55(1), 2000: 5–14.

Servan-Schreiber, David. *Anticancer.* Paris: Editions Robert Laffont, 2007.

———. *Guérir.* Paris: Editions Robert Laffont, 2003.

Simonton, O. Carl, Stephanie Matthews-Simonton, and James Creighton, *Getting Well Again* (reissue). New York: Bantam Books, 1992.

Singh, Simon. *Big Bang.* London: Fourth Estate, 2004.

Smith, Adam. *An Inquiry into the Nature and Causes of the Wealth of Nations.* New York: Modern Library, 1776/1937.

Smith, David. *Free Lunch. Easily Digestible Economics.* London: Profile Books, 2008.

Somé, Malidoma. *Of Water and the Spirit.* New York: Arkana, 1995.

Souchard, Philippe. *Le Stretching Global Actif.* Méolans-Revel, France: DésIris, 1996.

Spennewyn, Keith. "Strength Outcomes in Fixed Versus Free-form Resistance Equipment." *Journal of Strength and Conditioning Research* (Vol 22, No 1), 2008: 75–81.

Spinoza, Baruch. *Ethics.* London: Penguin Books, 1677/1996.

Steffny, Herbert, and Ulrich Pramann. *S'Entraîner pour un Marathon.* Aartselaar: Chantecler, 2005.

Stewart, Edward, and Milton Bennett. *American Cultural Patterns.* Yarmouth, ME: Intercultural Press, 1991.

Stober, Dianne, and Anthony Grant (Eds.). *Evidence Based Coaching Handbook.* Hoboken, NJ: John Wiley & Sons, 2006.

Stone, Irving. *Lust for Life* (2001 reprint). London: Arrow Books, 1935.

Strogatz, Steven. *SYNC—The Emerging Science of Spontaneous Order.* New York: Theia, 2003.

Talbot, Michael. *The Holographic Universe.* London: HarperCollins Publishers, 1991.

Toffler, Alvin. *Powershift*. New York: Bantam Books, 1990.

Tönnies, Ferdinand. *Tönnies: Community and Civil Society* (original German title: *Gemeinschaft und Gesellschaft*). Edited by Jose Harris. Translated by Margaret Hollis. Cambridge, UK: Cambridge University Press, 1677/2001.

Trompenaars, Fons. *Riding the Waves of Culture* (2d ed.). London: Nicholas Brealey Publishing, 1997.

Tsai, Jeanne. "Joy to the World—A Stanford Psychologist Examines How Culture Influences Our Emotions." *Stanford* (September/October), 2006.

Twelve Angry Men, dir. Sidney Lumet, 1957.

Vaillant, George. *Adaptation to Life*. Boston: Little Brown, 1977.

Van Den Bosch, Paul. *Manuel d'Entraînement du Cycliste*. Aartselaar, Belgium: Chantecler, 2007.

Van Rensbergen, Walter. "L'Entraînement du Marathonien." *BodyTalk* (No 131), 1996: 9–12.

"Wall Street Excess—Looting Stars." *The Economist*, 31 January 2009: 72–3.

Waterman, Judith, and Jenny Rogers. *Introduction to the FIRO-B® Instrument*. Mountain View, CA: CPP, 2007.

Watzlawick, Paul. *The Situation Is Hopeless, but Not Serious: The Pursuit of Unhappiness*. New York: W.W. Norton & Co., 1984.

Weber, Renee. *The Enfolding-Unfolding Universe: A Conversation with David Bohm* (in *The Holographic Paradigm*, ed. Ken Wilber). Boulder, CO: New Science Library, 1982.

Weil, Andrew. *Health and Healing: The Philosophy of Integrative Medicine and Optimum Health* (rev. ed.). New York: Mariner Books, 2004.

———. *Spontaneous Healing: How to Discover and Enhance Your Body's Natural Ability to Maintain and Heal Itself*. New York: Alfred Knopf Inc., 1995.

Weingarten, Gene. "Pearls before Breakfast." *Washingtonpost.com*. 8 April 2007. *www.washingtonpost.com/wp-dyn/content/article/2007/04/04/AR2007040401721.html* (accessed 26 January 2009).

Westheimer, Ruth, and Jonathan Mark. *Le Septième Ciel ou la Sexualité dans la Tradition Juive* (French translation). Translated by Jean-Pierre Quijano. Geneva, Switzerland: MJR, 1995.

Whitmore, John. *Coaching for Performance* (3d ed.). London and Yarmouth, ME: Nicholas Brealey Publishing, 2002.

Wiesel, Elie. *Célébration Hassidique*. Paris: Editions du Seuil, 1972.

———. *Rashi*. Translated from French by Catherine Temerson. New York: Shocken Books, 2009

Willcox, Bradley, Craig Willcox, and Makoto Suzuki. *The Okinawa Diet Plan—Get Leaner, Live Longer and Never Feel Hungry*. New York: Three Rivers Press, 2004.

———. *The Okinawa Program: Learn the Secrets to Healthy Longevity*. New York: Three Rivers Press, 2001.

Wilmore, Jack, David Costill, and Larry Kenney. *Physiology of Sport and Exercise* (4th ed.). Champaign, IL: Human Kinetics, 2008.

Wilson, Carol. *Best Practice in Performance Coaching*. London and Philadelphia: Kogan Page, 2007.

Wilson, Duff. "Harvard Medical School in Ethics Quandry." *The New York Times*, 2 March 2009.

Yalom, Irwin. *Existential Psychotherapy*. New York: Basic Books, 1980.

Zeig, Jeffrey. *A Teaching Seminar with Milton H. Erickson*. New York: Brunner/Mazel, 1980.

Index

About the Author

Philippe Rosinski is a world authority in executive coaching, team coaching, and global leadership development, sought by premier international organizations. He is the first European to have been designated Master Certified Coach by the International Coach Federation.

He has pioneered a global approach to coaching that leverages multiple perspectives for greater creativity, impact, and meaning. The Harvard Business School chose his ground-breaking book *Coaching Across Cultures* (2003) as its featured book recommendation in the category of business leadership. His innovative approach of bringing the crucial intercultural dimension into the practice of coaching has won him worldwide acclaim.

Since 1999, he is principal of *Rosinski & Company*, an international network organization that helps leaders, teams, and organizations unleash their human potential to achieve sustainable high performance. Previously, he was the Director of Custom Programs at the Center for Creative Leadership Europe.

Since 2008, Rosinski is a professor in the MBA program for global managers at the Kenichi Ohmae Graduate School of Business in Tokyo, Japan.

His goal is to help people honor their true desires and live happier and more productive lives. His approach fosters genuine commitment, essential for sustainable high performance. It enables people to make the most of differences, to build thriving teams and organizations, and to bring a constructive contribution to society.

Rosinski has written several articles, including "Coaching from Multiple Perspectives" (2007), "Leading for Joy" (1998), and "Constructive Politics" (1998), which show how alternative and multiple perspectives can enrich traditional coaching and leadership development for maximum impact. He has also contributed chapters to several books: *Evidence Based Coaching Handbook* (2006), *Excellence in Coaching* (2006), *Best Practice in Performance Coaching* (2007), *The Routledge Companion to International Business Coaching* (2009), and *The Coaching Relationship* (2010).

Prior to his career in coaching and leadership development, he spent six years in the engineering field as a software engineer in the Silicon Valley, California, and as a project manager in Brussels.

Rosinski received an Electrical and Mechanical Engineering degree from the *Ecole Polytechnique* in Brussels. He holds a Master of Science degree in Electrical Engineering from *Stanford University* and the Executive Master in Management degree from the *Solvay Brussels School of Economics and Management*. He is also certified to use a variety of psychometric instruments and is the author of the *Cultural Orientations Framework (COF) online assessment* available at *www.cofassessment.com*.

Rosinski has spoken at numerous international conferences. He participated in the first International Executive Coaching Summit (1999), and initiated and led the first European Executive Coaching Summit (2003). He currently serves on the Editorial Board of *Coaching: An International Journal of Theory, Research and Practice*. He also serves on the Global Advisory Panel of the Association for Coaching.

Philippe Rosinski lives near Brussels with his family.

For more information and to contact the author, please visit:

www.philrosinski.com — Rosinski & Company's website

www.globalcoaching.pro and — Philippe Rosinski's books
www.coachingacrosscultures.com